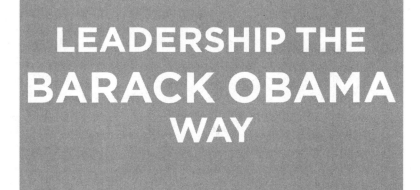

LEADERSHIP THE
BARACK OBAMA
WAY

ABOUT THE AUTHOR

Dr. Shel Leanne is President of Regent Crest, a leadership development firm whose clients hail from Fortune 100 companies located across the world. Dr. Leanne gives talks and conducts workshops focusing on leadership best practices at companies, conferences, and nonprofit organizations. Prior to launching her company, Dr. Leanne worked for McKinsey & Company and for Morgan Stanley in New York and London. She then served as a full faculty member at Harvard University from 1997-2001. Educated at Harvard (B.A.) and Oxford (master's and doctoral degrees), Dr. Leanne's work has been cited or published in *Newsweek*, *The Wall Street Journal*, and Businessweek.com. She is the author of *Say It Like Obama and Win!*, and *How to Interview Like a Top MBA*. Dr. Leanne can be contacted at www.drshelworkshop.com.

LEADERSHIP THE BARACK OBAMA WAY

LESSONS ON TEAMBUILDING AND CREATING A WINNING CULTURE IN CHALLENGING TIMES

SHELLY LEANNE

New York   Chicago   San Francisco   Lisbon   London   Madrid   Mexico City
Milan   New Delhi   San Juan   Seoul   Singapore   Sydney   Toronto

Library of Congress Cataloging-in-Publication Data

Leanne, Shelly.
    Leadership the Barack Obama Way : lessons on teambuilding and creating
a winning culture in challenging times / by Shel Leanne.
        p.   cm.
    ISBN 978-0-07-166402-8 (alk. paper)
        1. Leadership.   2. Success.   3. Obama, Barack.   I.   Title.
HD57.7.L4358   2010
658.4'092—dc22   2009046354

1 2 3 4 5 6 7 8 9 WFR/WFR   0 9

ISBN   978-0-07-166402-8
MHID   0-07-166402-5

McGraw-Hill books are available at special quantity discounts to use as premiums
and sales promotions or for use in corporate training programs. To contact
a representative, please e-mail us at bulksales@mcgraw-hill.com.

CONTENTS

CHAPTER 10

FACE AND OVERCOME CONTROVERSIES

227

CONCLUSION

251

NOTES

255

ACKNOWLEDGMENTS

I have greatly enjoyed teaching about leadership, focusing on leadership best practices and topics such as building high-performing teams, leading high-performing teams, emerging as a strong leader, motivating workers, and building a strong "personal brand." As I have taught or spoken on such topics in a wide variety of environments—conferences, companies, and nonprofit organizations—a trend has emerged over the past two years. Countless leaders of all backgrounds and levels of achievement—from seasoned corporate CEOs to young emerging managers and from the heads of corporations to the directors of nonprofits—have inquired about Barack Obama, the young dynamic leader who rose on such a fast trajectory to unprecedented levels of success. Regardless of whether particular leaders supported Obama's stances, they universally viewed Obama as a highly accomplished leader who wields formidable leadership skills. "What is Barack Obama doing?" they would ask. They wished to understand how Obama had managed to capture the imagination of so many people and to motivate so many people to action. How does he build such high-performing teams? How does he develop team cultures that seem so unified and energized? What leadership best practices and principles enable his success, and what can we learn from them? This book is intended to address these questions, providing a valuable glimpse into one of the most unique and accomplished leaders in recent years.

It is a particular pleasure to write this book, because some of my former college mates or professional colleagues now work with the Obama administration. They are "titans"—people who represent the best and the brightest, who are committed to excellence and innovation, and who have sterling track records.

I have enjoyed delving into what about Obama inspires them and has compelled them to work with Obama during this historic period.

Just as I benefited from outstanding coaching and leadership development training as I began my professional career, I hope this work will aid you. Just as I enjoyed teaching about business concepts and leadership in my courses while serving on the faculty at Harvard University, I also enjoyed writing this book immensely, and I owe a special thank you to the many people who supported me throughout the writing process.

I would like to thank my precious son Joshua, who lights my life each day. A special thank you to my parents, Barbara Geiger and the late Dr. David Geiger, Sr. Thank you to Christine Baker, Mildred Geiger, Ted Small, Audrey Gross-Stratford, Toby and Aukje Brouwer, Yvonne Chang, Ruby Lue Holloway, and Jane Tanner, who have provided such support. A hearty thank you to my wonderful cousins, and to my aunts and uncles, including William Geiger, Ann Lewis, Edward Geiger, Sr., Joyce and Joe Montgomery, Thomas and Eunice Holloway, Thelma Geiger and family, Sandra and Sam Cook, Andrew Geiger and family, Johnnie Scott and family, and the late Geraldine Roby. Thank you to my siblings and their spouses: Stacia Geiger-Alston and Thomas Alston; David Geiger, Jr. and Kim Geiger; and Sandra Geiger Richardson and Bruce Richardson. Thank you to David White, Susan Watanabe, Kweku Ampiah, Lorelee Dodge, Bonnie St. John, Derek Geiger, Carolyn Holloway, Marty Geiger, Reginald Brown, Paul Rudatsikira, Blaise Bryant, Eleanor Kim, Averill Pritchett, Lesley Szabo, Helen Dorini, Andy Varcoe, Emily Kao, Greg Jessner, Patricia Phillips, Kristin Kellet, Alice Peck, Cynthia Haines, Sheryl Doering, Margarita Rodriguez, and Jennifer Gonzales. Thank you to Reverend

Dr. H. Beecher Hicks, Jr., the ministers and members of Irvine Presbyterian Church, Reverend Ray Webb, Janet Webb, and the absolutely wonderful faculty and staff of St. Jeanne de Lestonnac School.

Very importantly, a huge thank you goes to McGraw-Hill's Mary Glenn for her wonderful guidance, to Peter McCurdy and Tania Loghmani for their dedication, and to Vasundhara Sawhney.

Barack Obama's leadership practices and principles have made him one of the most distinguished leaders of recent years. Over the course of his exceptional career, Obama has developed and refined outstanding leadership practices and skills that have helped pave his path to success. A master of the craft of leadership, Obama has transcended traditional divisions of ethnicity, socioeconomics, region, party affiliation, and race to attain one notable achievement after the next: becoming president of the century-old *Harvard Law Review*, an Illinois state senator, a U.S. senator, and president of the United States. En route to the U.S. presidency, Obama's excellent leadership abilities allowed him to defeat the "Clinton machine," energize millennials, expand the American electorate in an unprecedented manner, secure a 2 million-strong donor base, and inspire the largest crossover of Republican voters in recent history, winning 53 percent of the popular vote—more than any nonincumbent candidate for the presidency since Dwight Eisenhower in 1952. The magnitude of Obama's success reflects the effectiveness of his leadership skills.

What is Barack Obama doing? What leadership practices have enabled him to gain the confidence of so many people? How does he convey vision so effectively, securing such high levels of support? How has he built such a strong reputation and gained friends in so many nontraditional places? What enables him to build unified, high-performing teams? What practices enable him to motivate and mobilize key target groups? What lessons can we learn from his success in leveraging technology? What leadership techniques have allowed him to face and overcome controversies? This book explores these issues.

Leadership the Barack Obama Way focuses on the art of leadership, the building and exercise of influence, and the practices and principles that have enabled Obama to attain outstanding levels of success. Leaders in all fields—business, law, nonprofit, academia, policy making, politics—can benefit from the lessons we glean about how Obama gains the confidence of others, communicates vision excellently, builds winning teams, and enables his teams to pursue paths to success. For readers new to leadership, *Leadership the Barack Obama Way* will introduce you to important leadership practices and principles. For well-seasoned leaders, this book provides a highly valuable look at how Barack Obama has employed key leadership principles and practices to become one of the most distinguished leaders in recent years. Chapters are organized to delve into the practices and principles Obama's employs to lay a foundation for leadership, build effective teams, and pave his teams' paths to success. Importantly, each chapter highlights ideas and provides questions for thought to help you apply the best practices we distill, allowing you to further develop and refine your own leadership skills. The insights can help bring you greater effectiveness as you make early impressions, establish and sustain a strong reputation, build teams, motivate and mobilize people, employ technology in pursuit of designated goals, draw on diversity, face controversy, and steer a path to success.

Regardless of what you think of his politics, Obama's achievements are remarkable. His ability to win confidence, connect with listeners, and exercise outstanding leadership skills has from the earliest days of his career generated great excitement. With his ascension to the presidency of the *Harvard Law Review*, the media frenzy began in earnest, as observers deemed Obama a "rising star." The attention increased exponentially with Obama's widely praised 2004 Democratic National Convention Keynote Address. Press coverage in newspapers such as *The New York Times* and *The Wall Street Journal* pinpointed Obama as a dynamic leader to watch. The words used to describe him—*magnetic, electrifying, charismatic, exceptional*, a future *titan* of the Democratic Party—spoke of his great potential.

On the world stage, too, Obama captured the imagination of countless people. The media abroad referred to him as a *transformational* figure. The 200,000-strong audience he attracted in Germany in 2008, unprecedented for an American speaking in Europe, signaled his soaring international popularity. As Nobel Laureate Archbishop Desmond Tutu commented, "When John F. Kennedy was elected in 1960, there was a thrill around the world, but not anything quite like this. This is unique."[1] Similarly, former South African president Nelson Mandela commented, "Your election to this high office has inspired people as few other events in recent times have done. Amidst all of the human progress made over the last century, the world in which we live remains one of great divisions, inequality, poverty and injustice... You, Mister President, have brought a new voice of hope that these problems can be addressed and that we can in fact change the world and make of it a better place."[2]

Obama's achievements are equally noteworthy in terms of organization and business execution—Team Obama, neighborhood team leaders, precinct captains, No Drama Obama. Karen Tumulty observed that Obama's presidential campaign was that "rare, frictionless machine that [ran] with the energy of an insurgency and the efficiency of a corporation."[3] Barack Obama's campaign benefited from outstanding team leadership, an all-hands high-performance culture, excellent organization, and exemplary execution. Obama took the strategic use of technology to new heights, establishing a new gold standard for leveraging technology in support of an organization's goals. He blended leading-edge technology seamlessly with bricks-and-mortar, on-the-ground organizing, reinventing how mobilization occurs and paving his way to victory. With these successful efforts, Obama earned the adoration of the most accomplished business leaders. We have much to learn from the leadership practices that enabled Obama to leverage technology so effectively in support of his designated goals.

One key to Obama's success: he has embraced important leadership best practices and principles, tailoring and blending them to create his own unique style. Obama exemplifies the answer to the age-old question, 'Are people born to be leaders or can leadership be learned?' He shows resoundingly that leadership can be learned, developed, refined. He serves as a case in point, having transformed himself from a teen in search of identity, to a young man who during college studied avidly the speeches of Martin Luther King, Jr. and the civil rights movement, and sharpened his leadership abilities through hands-on experience as a community organizer in Chicago. Obama's early experiences provided him with leadership lessons and skills that facilitated his rise to the pinnacle of the *Harvard Law Review*. On his trajectory to the U.S. presidency, Obama developed and refined his leadership skills further, even amid his losses. Through his successes, and sometimes through his setbacks, Obama has demonstrated the truth of timeless leadership principles and the great value of many leadership best practices. He has refined his skills to become the able leader we see today.

Indeed, by the time Obama reached the U.S. Senate, he demonstrated such impressive leadership skills that he inspired the Lion of the Senate, Democrat Edward Kennedy, to endorse his presidential bid over that of Kennedy's long-time friend Hillary Clinton. Obama also impressed so greatly one of the most influential women in the world, billionaire Oprah Winfrey, that she cast aside her longstanding policy of remaining outside of the presidential political fray, not only endorsing Obama, but stumping for him on the campaign trail. She did this, as she told CNN talk show host Larry King, "Because I know him personally... what he stands for... was worth me going out on a limb for."[4] Caroline Kennedy, the daughter of American icon John F. Kennedy, endorsed Obama both in *The New York Times* and on the campaign trail, likening Obama to her father in the way he inspired others. Even Maria Shriver, wife of California Republican governor Arnold Schwarzenegger, took the "audacious" step of endorsing Obama in California before the crucial 2008 Super Tuesday primary.

By the time of the 2008 presidential campaign, Obama wielded such strong leadership abilities and conveyed his vision for the future so effectively that he stirred the hopes of the young. "Support Obama" campaigns proliferated quickly on college campuses around the United States. Young Americans responded with excitement not just in college towns, but throughout the country, with dynamic young leaders such as Chris Hughes, the cofounder of Facebook, lending their talents to Obama's campaign. With outstanding business instincts, Obama marshaled this excitement so effectively that his campaign became referred to as a *phenomenon* and a *movement*. Obama succeeded in yielding an enthusiastic young voter turnout of a size not seen since 1972, when the U.S. voting age was first lowered to 18. As momentum continued to build, Obama's leadership met and exceeded expectations, and other titans of the Democratic party, such as John Edwards, offered their support. Governor Bill Richardson called Obama a "once in a lifetime leader" and helped Obama make inroads with the Hispanic vote, once considered off limits to the African American presidential candidate.

Given his strong leadership abilities and success, Obama has made gains throughout his career in securing support from a wide variety of people. In 2008, he benefited from the largest crossover of Republican support for a Democratic presidential candidate in history. Organizations such as republicansforobama.org emerged, prompting *The Economist* to report on the rise of *Obamacans*—the new term coined for Obama's Republican supporters. Colin Powell backed Obama's presidential run on October 19, 2008, calling him a "transformational figure." Obama gained support among not only moderate Republicans, but fiscal and social conservatives too. Prominent leaders provided their endorsements, including William Donaldson, the chairman of the U.S. Security and Exchange Commission under President George W. Bush; Paul O'Neill, U.S. secretary of the treasury under President George W. Bush; and Ben Bernanke, chairman of the Federal Reserve. Religious conservative Pastor Rick Warren referred to Obama as a "friend" and Obama won 32 percent of the white evangelical vote between 18 and 29 years old, an astonishing figure for a Democratic presidential candidate. Even conservative evangelical leader Pat Robertson offered glowing words in the aftermath of the November 2008 election, stating:

> [T]his is the most amazing campaign that I think we've seen in our lifetime or maybe in this century. Obama is absolutely brilliant and I'd like to make a prediction. He can be one of the great presidents of the United States if he

doesn't get pulled too far off the center... If he governs the way he said he's going to... he has the smarts and the charisma to pull this nation together and be a simply outstanding president.[5]

What leadership practices have enabled Obama to inspire people from such widely divergent backgrounds throughout his career, from his time as a community organizer to his current role as U.S. president? What leadership practices and principles have enabled him to pave paths to such notable achievements? As *Leadership the Barack Obama Way* explores these questions, the book benefits from a broad look at Obama's life and career, and the leadership practices, philosophies, and skills Obama has developed over time. The story of Obama's life has, after all, become legendary. Obama was born the son of a Kenyan man who was raised in a mud hut; his grandfather hailed from the small village of Alego, served as a cook, and carried a passbook to travel in his own country.[6] Raised in Hawaii and Indonesia, the diversity of Obama's upbringing lay in place important elements of his worldview, helping him develop an ability to thrive amid diversity and to connect with others across cultures.

This background served him well during his work with the Developing Communities Project in Chicago, described by some as a "church-based social action group."[7] There, Obama led a coalition of ministers to improve living conditions in impoverished neighborhoods suffering from crime, drugs, and unemployment.[8] As Michelle Obama noted, during those years Obama began to refine skills in selling himself to others in spite of his differences from them.[9] He became adept at shining a light on common ground and empowering people to bring change into their own lives—now hallmarks of his leadership.

As Obama continued on his leadership journey, he earned a highly coveted spot as one of 80 student editors of the *Harvard Law Review*, the most prestigious student-run law review in the United States—a crowning jewel for law school students. With great skill, he became the first African American president of the century-old journal. As his law school colleague Bradford Berenson observed, "I have worked in the Supreme Court and the White House and I never saw politics as bitter as at *Harvard Law Review* in the early '90s." Among the skills Obama honed as law review president were his abilities to articulate a compelling vision, forge consensus among "warring factions," build a sense of camaraderie among diverse team members, and lead by example. As Obama moved on to a political career, his effective leadership skills enabled him to overcome what could have been notable challenges—his youthful age, his race, his "funny name." In a country still beset with racial tensions, he won during his senatorial and presidential campaigns the support of voters in regions with negligible minority populations. He soon took his place in history, forty-five years after Martin Luther King, Jr. delivered his powerful "I Have a Dream" speech, as the first African American presidential nominee of a major political party—one of many watershed moments.

Leadership the Barack Obama Way presents and distills the highly effective leadership practices and principles Obama has employed and embraced over the years. Chapter 1, "First, Win Trust and Confidence," examines the best practices that have enabled Obama to build trust and confidence among so many supporters. We explore how Barack Obama makes strong first impressions with his assuredness and charisma. We examine how Obama has mastered the art of strong second impressions: his skillful use of voice and intonation, gestures, and "props" help to reinforce the strong first impressions he creates. We delve into "third impressions" and consider how first, second, and third impressions work together to lay a foundation for wielding effective leadership.

Chapter 2, "Communicate Your Vision Effectively," explores Obama's exceptional skill in conveying his vision in ways that allow others to understand, "see," and ultimately embrace his vision. Obama understands that for successful leadership, forming a strong vision is not enough: leaders must be able to convey their visions in both understandable and compelling ways. He recognizes people must be able to "see" the vision in order to believe in it. Time and again, Obama's skill in articulating a vision has allowed him to "elicit nods" from supporters. We explore the practices that allow Obama to convey vision so effectively. In particular, we delve into how Obama employs words that resonate with his listeners and uses vivid language that helps listeners to conceptualize his vision. We review the way in which he acknowledges the challenges he will face in pursuing visions he puts forth, and presents his vision and goals in ways that underscore their viability. We look at elements of persuasion he draws on to get to "yes," inspiring people to embrace and support his vision.

Chapter 3, "Leverage a Strong Reputation," examines Barack Obama's success in building and leveraging a strong reputation. The sterling reputation Obama has built has provided a solid foundation for his leadership. He has established thick "Teflon," which helps him to persuade millions of people to support his vision, to form diverse coalitions, and to withstand controversy. We consider specific elements of his reputation, including his reputation as a leader who offers an open ear, wields a fair hand, remains true to his word, and stays above the fray. We also explore the way Obama exudes strength and remains cool under fire, which reinforces his effectiveness as a leader.

Chapter 4, "Make Friends in Unusual Places," delves into one of Obama's most distinct leadership traits: his remarkable ability to build fruitful alliances with people of widely diverse perspectives, to reach across aisles, to address longstanding grievances effectively, and to move dialogue beyond traditional boundaries. His ability to make friends in unusual places helped accelerate his trajectory to the White House, as others quickly recognized his ability to transcend traditional boundaries and perceived him as a unifier. We explore the practices that facilitate Obama's ability to make friends in unusual places, including his practices of "going where potential friends are," refusing to limit himself to expected allies, adopting a win-win mind-set, meeting others on common ground, showing respect to potential friends, and leveraging friends to continually expand his network of support. Also key: Obama refuses to hold grudges, a practice that has broadened his network of supporters. Obama's keen ability to make friends in unusual places has fueled his progress in challenging areas such as health care reform and Middle East peace, and played a role in inspiring his 2009 Nobel Peace Prize. Through multiple leadership roles, Barack Obama has demonstrated the value of making friends in unusual places, and his practices have helped him forge multiple roads to success.

Chapter 5, "Build and Lead a Winning Team," presents the best practices that have allowed Obama to build very unified, high-performing teams. We explore how Obama pays attention to style and culture, identifies his priorities, determines the ideal team skills mix, staffs to match skills with key responsibilities, and ensures team members embrace team culture and values. We review the way Obama benefits from a "mighty brainstorm," increases the number of leaders who support his mission, empowers leaders, and makes roles and responsibilities clear. Together, these practices enable Obama to form teams that produce excellent results.

Chapter 6, "Move Beyond 'High Performance' to 'All Hands,'" provides a valuable look at the "all-hands" culture that characterized Obama's 2008 presidential campaign. More than "high-performance" in character, all-hands cultures are distinguished by the deep loyalty and commitment of team members and a strong sense that team member contributions are valued highly. We examine the leadership practices Obama employs to promote an all-hands culture, including his practices of providing affirmation, matching skills and interests, rewarding excellence, training participants well, and focusing on a sense of community. We consider his efforts to "usher abrasive personalities out" in order to preserve a united culture and strong morale. We explore how Obama manages expectations and "rallies the troops" in an effort to sustain an all-hands culture.

Chapter 7, "Use Diversity as a Source of Strength," delves into the ways in which Obama draws on diversity as a source of advantages in his endeavors. Obama rejects any notion that excellence and diversity are mutually exclusive. He has successfully built teams composed of the "best and the brightest" that are also highly diverse. Importantly, Obama recognizes that diversity can be more than just ethnic, and he benefits from the broad array of diversity, including variety in socioeconomic, national, regional, political, and religious backgrounds, among others. Obama draws on diversity as a source for insights, networks, and coalition building. His skill in identifying multiple sources of diversity, forming diverse teams, building a strong sense of camaraderie among disparate parties, and leveraging the networks of diverse team members has served as a significant source of his leadership strength.

Chapter 8, "Make Technology Your Friend," explores Obama's effectiveness in leveraging cutting-edge technology in support of his mission and goals. Obama has shown considerable skill in choosing his technology partners, in identifying the technological habits of his target groups and capitalizing on them, and in using technology to build relations with members of his target groups. His practice of keeping an eye on the end goal has helped ensure that as he deploys technology, it facilitates progress toward his designated goals. Obama has also demonstrated many best practices in using technology to enhance internal team capabilities, strengthening morale, team culture, and management processes.

Chapter 9, "Motivate Your Target Groups, Organize to Succeed," presents the leadership practices that have helped Obama to gain and leverage excellently the enthusiastic support of one of his target groups, young people. A key to Barack Obama's success as a 2008 presidential candidate was his ability to energize and motivate young people to register and vote. We examine how Obama recognized the potential of his key target group and avoided the follies of ignoring this key target group. We delve into his best practices of empowering appealing leaders, paying attention to points of contact, identifying special interests, and pinpointing primary tasks that facilitated his work in mobilizing this key target group. We examine how Obama amplified his efforts through use of fruitful channels and networks, how he motivated his target group with the power of *you*, how he built momentum with low-lying fruit, and how he used training and an "enabling" organizational structure to channel the enthusiasm of young people effectively. Notably, the lessons we learn can be employed to motivate and mobilize other key groups.

Chapter 10, "Face and Overcome Controversies," explores the practices and techniques that have allowed Obama to emerge from controversial situations largely unscathed, with his strong ethical reputation intact. Obama embraces the philosophy that *how* a leader responds to controversy makes all the difference between success and failure. Not only has he survived large controversies, but he has also thrived in their aftermath. Obama's success in addressing and overcoming controversies flows from several key leadership practices, such as identifying his goals and keeping them central in his mind, leveraging props excellently, exuding humility, acknowledging error head on, and restating his strong ethics. We explore these important leadership practices and consider how to apply them.

Let's explore the practices and principles that have helped to make Barack Obama one of the most distinct leaders of recent years.

PART I

LAY A FOUNDATION FOR OUTSTANDING LEADERSHIP

FIRST, WIN TRUST AND CONFIDENCE

"Now that's a leader."

Such was the reaction of millions of viewers in the United States and around the world on the second night of the 2004 Democratic National Convention, when Barack Obama stepped onto the stage and delivered an electrifying Keynote Address. The occasion marked, for most observers, a first glimpse of this young leader. It marked Obama's defining moment, when he formed a first impression so positive and so strong that it catapulted his career to new heights, greatly accelerating his trajectory from a first-time candidate to the U.S. Senate to President of the United States and "leader of the free world"—a journey he made in only four short years.

On that pivotal night in 2004, Obama's outstanding use of body language and image enabled him to reach out to TV viewers around the globe and open a positive dialogue even before he uttered a first word. With his confident gait, squared shoulders, assured smile, confident wave to the audience, and commanding stance, Obama evoked a sit-up-and-listen response. In him, people saw a confident, charismatic leader.

While body language and image allowed Obama to grab people's attention quickly through a strong first impression, his exceptional use of voice and intonation enabled him to sustain that attention through an excellent second impression. The deep timbre of his voice—his natural asset—reinforced the initial view. Obama skillfully controlled his voice to convey excitement, disapproval, urgency, and passion. He amplified his voice when appropriate, glided it up a half-octave when needed, and allowed it to diminish or fall flat at key times. He also varied the emotional texture of his tone—making it wistful at times, affectionate at others, indignant when appropriate—giving greater depth and impact to his words. Through masterful use of voice and intonation, Obama drew attention to key points, evoked an emotional response from the audience, rallied viewers to his words, and made his speech much more memorable.

Obama's gestures were equally effective, enhancing his delivery: knocking on an imaginary door; pinching his fingers at key times; writing words on air with an imaginary pen; raising his hand like a bar in a sweeping upward motion; holding his palm out like a stop sign. Obama combined these and many other gestures to drive home key points. Other well-timed gestures, such as placing his hand over his heart during a deeply felt testimony, allowed Obama to convey great emotion and sincerity. Obama reinforced these impressions with a strong third impression as he uttered words that resonated with the audience, conveying his commitment to American values and his embrace of laudable ethics. He came across as authentic, passionate, capable, and worthy both of trust and of leadership.

Public and media reaction to Obama's Keynote Address was immediate. Many viewers were moved to tears; others spoke of how the speech had swayed them. The media described Obama and his speech as magnetic, electrifying, energizing, and inspiring. The exceptional response testifies to Obama's success—within the span of a short, 20-minute address—in creating excellent first, second, and third impressions. In short, Obama won trust and confidence.

In the days that followed, the press continued to praise what many considered to be Obama's masterpiece of oration. "One of the best [addresses] we've heard in many, many years," CNN's Wolf Blitzer declared. "That's as good as they come…This is a fellow who is talking beyond the Democratic base to the whole country.…It was terrific," political analyst Jeff Greenfield commented. The media deemed Obama a rising star.

The notable impact of Obama's defining moment in 2004 and the enduring impressions it created testify to the power of early impressions. Let's delve into what has enabled Obama to form such strong early impressions both during his 2004 Democratic National Convention Keynote Address and on many other occasions throughout his career.

⇥ RECOGNIZE THE POWER OF EARLY IMPRESSIONS ⇤

Obama understands that if you aspire to be a highly effective leader, you must win the trust and confidence of the people you hope to lead. People must trust your capabilities and judgment and believe that authority is well vested in you. In the absence of trust and confidence, little else follows. An important early task of all

> In the absence of trust and confidence, little else follows. An important early task of all effective leaders, therefore, is to earn the trust and confidence of those they seek to lead.

effective leaders, therefore, is to earn the trust and confidence of those they seek to lead.

To this end, Obama has demonstrated he understands the power of early impressions. The moment one person first moves into the presence of another, an opinion is formed. It is as if this initial image is etched in stone, becoming a lasting impression that, once formed, is hard to dislodge. Observers make up their minds quickly and tend to refer to that first impression long after it has been made. If it is negative, the ramifications can be significant. If positive, the first impression can help form a strong foundation for exercising effective leadership. Whether the impression is positive or negative, it takes a great deal of concerted effort to wear down the first impression enough to clear the slate and sketch anew. A first impression thus represents an important opportunity to create a positive lasting image that can be leveraged in support of effective leadership. It is best to get off to a strong start and avoid situations in which you must work hard to reverse the damage of a poor first impression. Skilled leaders make the most of this initial opportunity.

Indeed, Barack Obama has made an art of building strong early impressions. The deliberateness with which he walks, his careful choice of attire and setting, his demeanor and the tone with which he addresses people, calibrated by occasion, work together to serve his positive purposes. Like other notable leaders such as John F. Kennedy, Martin Luther King, Jr., Bill Clinton, and Ronald Reagan, people have seen and responded to the highly positive impressions they have formed of Obama and his passion, confidence, and command. The wide array of people who have supported Obama is striking, and includes politicians, large donors, small donors, policymakers, homemakers, white-collar workers, blue-collar workers, college students, and people from all ethnic and socioeconomic backgrounds. This testifies to the strength of the early impressions he makes. Obama even garners praise from opponents across the political aisle, including Louisiana governor Bobby Jindal and conservative Christian evangelical leader Pat Buchanan.

Obama's success in creating such strong early impressions is not new. As with many aspects of his distinguished leadership, he has developed, practiced, and refined over the years his skill in creating such strong early impressions. A review of Obama's career, as far back as his college days, reveals high consistency in how much he has impressed others early on. Michael J. Wolf, for instance, who took an eight-student senior seminar on international politics and American policy with Obama at Columbia University in the 1980s, recalls Obama "stood out" and engaged in rigorous debate.[1] Gerald Kellman, who interviewed Obama for a community organizing job in Chicago after college, hired him on the spot. He recounts how a confident, energetic young Obama impressed him exceedingly with his articulated desire to "make fundamental change," to drive change "from the grass roots," and to learn.

Adhering to the idea that practice helps drive toward perfection, Obama studied the speeches and oration of Martin Luther King, Jr. during college. By the time he reached law school, his contemporaries noted he sometimes spoke with a distinguished ministerial delivery, reminiscent of a southern African American minister. With study and practice, Obama delivered speeches that inspired and greatly moved others. This strengthened his reputation and aided his ascension to the presidency of the *Harvard Law Review*.

During his third year of Harvard Law School in 1991, Obama met with Judson H. Miner, the head of the Chicago law firm Miner, Barnhill, & Galland. Miner joined the long list of people immediately impressed by the young Obama. He hired

Obama and readily served as his mentor, introducing Obama to the power players of Chicago.

During his run for the U.S. Senate, Obama's strong early impressions helped him inspire so much trust and confidence that he broke through traditional barriers to win the Democratic nomination for the U.S. Senate. Obama acknowledged the early impressions he was able to establish and sustain, and he recalled, "We defied conventional wisdom about where votes come from because the assumption is, whites won't vote for blacks, or suburban folks won't vote for city people, or downstate won't vote for upstate.... We were able to put together a coalition that said, you know, people are willing to give anybody a shot if they're speaking to them in a way that makes sense."[2]

This Illinois victory was followed by more historic firsts—Obama's victory in the Iowa Democratic presidential caucus in January 2008, a win that surprised a nation, making millions of Americans realize his presidential bid, once considered improbable, was indeed viable. On the evening of the Iowa victory, Obama delivered a speech that inspired more Americans, viewing him for the first time, to take a good look and consider his candidacy. On that occasion, his ability to create a strong first impression served him excellently.

Even in defeat, Obama came before the viewing audience confident and determined to continue forward to victory in the 2008 Democratic presidential nominating process. He spoke with assuredness and determination, thereby inspiring trust and confidence. Following his loss on April 22, 2008, in the Pennsylvania Democratic primary, for instance, Obama delivered one of the more powerful speeches of his presidential campaign, culminating in the oft-repeated refrain, "Yes we can!" He succeeded in projecting himself as a winner even in the aftermath of that short-term defeat. In doing so, he kept supporters' morale high and momentum moving forward even amid a setback. At that time—as throughout his career spanning community organizing work, teaching as a law professor, work as a firm lawyer, and politics—the strong early impressions Obama formed helped establish his credibility as a leader.

What accounts for his long, consistent record of success in creating such positive first impressions? What is Obama doing? What practices have enabled him to earn such high levels of trust and confidence throughout his career? Let's delve into some of his best practices—his skillful use of image and body language, voice and intonation, and props; and his ability to form strong third impressions through strong starts, successful efforts to convey his solid ethics, and preparedness.

⇥ CREATE A STRONG FIRST IMPRESSION ⇤
THROUGH IMAGE AND BODY LANGUAGE

Is the adage true that first impressions matter? Aspiring leaders ask me this question more consistently than most other questions as I teach about leadership in seminars, conferences, and corporate retreats. Can first impressions really be that important? Through years of work with Fortune 50 executives, leaders of highly successful entrepreneurship companies, and the heads of leading nonprofit organizations, I have seen what inspires people to follow such leaders. I can say with certainty the answer is a resounding yes. First impressions matter. First impressions last. Leaders should think of a first impression as a critical, one-time opportunity—a crucial, defining moment.

> First impressions matter. First impressions last. Leaders should think of a first impression as a critical, one-time opportunity—a crucial, defining moment.

Through image and body language, even before you utter a word, you open a dialogue that speaks volumes.

Through image and body language, even before you utter a word, you open a dialogue that speaks volumes. Obama understands this and provides an outstanding example of how to maximize positive early impressions. He is excellent at establishing first impressions—truly, from the first moment. Note his purposeful walk; the visual contact he makes with audiences early on, stretching his hand to them in a friendly wave that narrows the physical distance between them; the confidence he exudes through his posture. From the moment Barack Obama steps in front of an audience, he conveys charisma through many nonverbal attributes such as his bright smile and the confident sparkle in his eyes. This marks the beginning of a conversation of sorts. His success with first impressions reminds us that body movement and image speak a language to the audience as potent as anything said aloud.

Good eye contact has also been valuable to Obama. Like Bill Clinton, Obama rarely hesitates to establish strong eye contact. He thrives on connecting with his audiences and is energized by this. As he talks to audiences, he draws the room in as he looks to one side of the room, sometimes with a slight nod of acknowledgment, then to the other side. As Obama varies his gaze throughout his discussion, naturally and smoothly, he engages onlookers more fully. Audience members perceive this as respectful, welcoming them; they deem Obama trustworthy—a leader who will look them in the eyes. That good early impression lasts.

The confidence displayed by Obama's pat-on-the-back greetings with some people who introduce him is also an early action that communicates his comfort and assuredness. He is at ease. Standing before lecterns, feet placed firmly, back straight and shoulders squared, he sends a message of confidence and authority. Where there is a lectern, he often places hands on each side of it, taking control. The lectern, for him, never serves as a crutch or an obstacle between him and his audiences.

In rising as fast as he has, from obscurity to clinching the Democratic presidential nomination, Barack Obama has shown how full of impact a strong first impression can be. From his confident gait as he enters a room, to his exiting wave, Obama captivates with highly effective body language. Imagine if, instead of exuding such confidence, Obama walked on stage with his chin lowered and shoulders slouched. What a vastly different image, with all the lack of confidence that would convey. Imagine if he were to offer only a sheepish wave, or fidget often with his hands on the podium. We have all encountered leaders for whom body language served as a hindrance to effective leadership rather than as an aid. If a leader enters a room with a slow, despondent gait and speaks to her or his team with an unenthusiastic expression and slumped shoulders, that body language conveys a lack of confidence even if she or he speaks words intended for an opposite effect. When choosing between words uttered and body language, consciously or unconsciously, most observers assume body language speaks the truth. If leaders cannot convince themselves to believe in a message, as indicated through their body language, others will not believe their message either.

In contrast to this, Obama's body language works to project him as a capable leader. He demonstrates that persons seeking to present themselves as leaders—worthy of authority and fit to be followed— should "walk the part" and "act the part." Through first impressions, these actions can lay an important foundation for commanding authority.

Obama shows that leaders should also "dress the part." Like his body language, Obama uses his image to his advantage. The variation of the old cliché "You are what you wear" holds abundant truth. For Obama, his style of dress and his clean-shaven appearance convey an image of a straight shooter, a man with good moral values, a hard worker. There are, of course, successful leaders who adopt very different appearances. It is possible to imagine the successful businessman who wears shoulder-length hair swooped back in a ponytail, or a successful businesswoman who breaks with advice to dress conservatively and wears ornate jewelry and bright makeup. But images convey messages also, and those who choose to break from tradition sometimes find they must work a little harder to gain the confidence of others, because their image does not fit neatly with expectations. There is no right or wrong, but Obama's choice is to present an image that is highly consistent with the values he has sought to represent in himself—as an everyday man with solid down-home values.

Moreover, Obama skillfully tailors how he presents himself by occasion. If seeking to convey respect for a solemn, important occasion, he might wear a dark suit and tie. If seeking to connect with a youth group, he might don more casual attire. If addressing an audience during a more informal occasion, he might appear in a casual shirt with his sleeves rolled up. His success in presenting a positive image evokes comments from people such as "He looks like a hard worker" or "He looks like someone you can trust." Obama shows that excellent use of image can serve as another factor in creating strong early impressions.

⤳ GATHER THE RIGHT PROPS AROUND YOU ⤶

Buttressing this, Obama takes care to gather the right props around him. The use of props serves as an important way to create impressions and to reinforce key messages conveyed through effective body language and image. I use the term *props* broadly to denote accessories, objects, settings, and even people whom you might gather around you for an occasion. Props, chosen carefully, can serve as important sources of nonverbal messaging. For example, a carefully chosen setting for delivering remarks or leading groups can be very important. If a politician seeks to project herself as having strong religious values, she might choose to deliver remarks from a place of worship, for instance. A leader seeking to show connectedness to youth might deliver a talk on a college campus.

Similarly, carefully chosen accessories can convey subtle but important messages. A Democrat wearing a red tie can convey openness to Republicans. A leader wearing an American flag pin on his lapel can convey patriotism. Other types of objects and people can serve similar ends. Consider, for a moment, if a leader seeks to look presidential. What props might she use? She might flank herself with large national flags on each side of a lectern to convey authority as she delivers remarks. If a speaker strives to appear strong on foreign policy, what props might he use? He might choose to invite military leaders to stand behind him when he makes public remarks.

Barack Obama has shown considerable skill in using props and "staging" to reinforce his messages. When he first announced his bid for the White House, he delivered his remarks in Springfield, Illinois, a location that evokes memories of President Abraham Lincoln. The setting functioned as a prop. In choosing Springfield, Obama underscored the historic significance of his candidacy, his commitment to core American values, his adoration for American history, and his commitment to the strong values associated with Lincoln, such as courage and integrity.

When addressing the Reverend Jeremiah Wright controversy during his 2008 presidential campaign, Obama carefully considered the nonverbal messages he would send through the props around him. He needed to address the incendiary words of Reverend Wright, given his association with the controversial minister—an association many Americans believed contradicted Obama's claims that he believed in unity. The controversy surrounding his relation-ship with Wright posed one of the greatest threats to the future and foundation of Obama's presidential run. Understanding the grave importance of addressing public concerns about his relationship with Wright, Obama chose with care the location where he deliv-ered his remarks. The setting and his other props reinforced the message he sought to convey. Dressed in a suit with an American flag pin adorning his lapel, Obama delivered his remarks in a serious tone, with a serious demeanor. His body language and voice con-veyed important nonverbal messages—humility, respect, sincerity. While he was denouncing the divisive words of Reverend Wright from the lectern, the other props— large American flags flanking each side of the lectern—conveyed the message that Obama is patriotic and loyal to core American principles. The backdrop helped frame his remarks and sent a positive message.

As you seek to present yourself as a leader, remember the potential role props can play, asking yourself relevant questions. What props are ideal? Are there accessories, objects, settings, or even people who can help you send nonverbal messages that reinforce a strong positive early impression? The answer depends in part upon the circumstances—your designated audience, the prevailing mood, the goals of your remarks, and the subject mat-ter, for instance. Use props well and with great effect.

⇥ FORM OUTSTANDING SECOND IMPRESSIONS ⇤
THROUGH VOICE AND INTONATION

After a leader comes out with a commanding, confident air, exuding the charisma of a leader, what then? Follow through with strong second and third impressions. It's the fall-or-flight idea: after a strong first impression, either you fall down, failing to sustain that impression, or you take flight, building upon the strong initial impression you have created. Obama has demonstrated a keen ability to create strong second and third impressions. Let's take a deeper look.

It's the fall-or-flight idea: after a strong first impression, either you fall down, failing to sustain that impression, or you take flight, building upon the strong initial impression you have created.

While many leaders have learned to pay attention to first impressions, they often neglect another significant opportunity: the chance to establish outstanding second impressions. Voice and intonation play a role here: both are important tools for creating a strong second impression. Consider the example of a 6-foot 1-inch, 180-pound man who begins to speak with a high-pitched squeak of a voice. We would immediately reassess our initial impression of this man, which might have naturally attributed to him qualities of strength given his large physical stature. The opposite also holds true. Imagine meeting a very little woman who immediately transforms our perceptions of her strength as she speaks with a deep, commanding voice. Voice and intonation can indeed strengthen first impressions and sometimes override them, for better or for worse.

One dimension of voice that creates an immediate impression is the quality of the voice—its natural pitch and resonance. For Barack Obama, his commanding baritone is a natural asset. It sounds pleasing to the ears and very authoritative. For leaders whose vocal pitch and tone are not such natural assets, however, tone quality can be improved and enhanced with practice and voice techniques. Leaders should view their voice tone and quality as another tool they can improve and hone for making positive impressions.

Beyond natural tone quality, Obama shows that how a leader uses her or his voice remains important to impressions that are formed. There are multiple dimensions to verbal communication beyond the words actually spoken, and *how* words are said—the volume, emotional texture, pitch, pace, and inflection—can sometimes be as important as what is being said. Effective voice and intonation can move people, make words more memorable, and make communication more effective overall. When using elements such as volume and pace skillfully, leaders can deliver powerful remarks, eliciting such responses as "Something tugged inside of me." Barack Obama achieves this sort of impact through skillful use of his voice and intonation, which helps him form strong early impressions.

Obama developed his outstanding oratory skills over time, refining his speaking abilities and techniques as he taught at the University of Chicago Law School and as he served in the Illinois Senate, for example. Those experiences provided him with ample opportunities and valuable experience in debating issues and guiding rigorous discussion. As we see in *Say It Like Obama and Win!*, Obama has turned oration and an ability to form strong second impressions into some of his greatest strengths. *Say It Like Obama and Win* provides an in-depth assessment of the techniques and practices Obama employs so successfully. Let's review some of his techniques here.

Obama has mastered the art of varying his pitch, volume, vocal color, and inflection. This is one important aspect of what makes his use of voice and diction so highly effective. Obama avoids a monotone delivery. He varies how he vocalizes key words: his voice crests and falls when needed. The versatility of his inflection—changes in the pitch of his voice—adds depth to what he says, in a manner that cannot be achieved through the written word alone. For example, Obama knows how to lower his pitch while also slowing his cadence, drawing attention to a point as if he were underlining key words on a chalkboard.

Obama also adds dimension to his communication with vocal color. He can turn his voice wistful, hopeful, dismissive, and a host of other emotional textures, as circumstances require. His ability to alter the emotional content of his voice helps him come across as a highly capable speaker and leader. Obama has shown the power of altering the volume of his voice, amplifying and diminishing his voice at key moments. He knows how to punch important words at ideal times. He often increases his volume to a crescendo during his speeches, thereby focusing attention on the main points of his talks. Just as he puts power in his volume when rousing a crowd, Obama knows how to allow his voice to trail off when speaking of something of which he disapproves. Amplifying and washing away: Barack Obama uses volume to enhance the efficacy of his delivery and to project himself as a skilled leader.

Obama's outstanding use of pacing—quickening or slowing his cadence—also helps him come across as a skilled speaker and leader. With well-chosen pacing, he slows when enunciating important ideas. He adopts clipped sentences, short and punchy, at key moments, driving points home. Obama adeptly leverages the power of silence, using dramatic pauses to focus attention on important ideas. He knows how to let silence endure a bit—very dramatic pauses that often heighten the reaction from listeners. Taken together, voice and intonation—punching words at the right time, quickening or slowing the cadence, varying the tonal color, varying the rhythm of words—can help establish outstanding second impressions.

Obama's effective use of gestures adds to his ability to make strong second impressions. Unlike some other speakers, Obama gestures quite frequently when he speaks. His gestures work in tandem with modulations of his voice and tone, animating his words and giving greater depth to his remarks. They serve as fluid extensions of his words. Obama's success in creating strong second impressions shows us that gestures, employed effectively, can promote a positive image of a leader by creating a sense that a speaker is at ease and connected to the audience. Obama, in particular, employs gestures in ways that create the feel of a one-to-one conversation, as if he were standing next to you conversing, rather than on a podium addressing an audience. Whether he is stretching out his hand to an audience, pinching his fingers to underscore points, motioning a finger to his ear, or waving an index finger as a sign of admonition, his gestures transform his speeches into dialogues. Listeners feel more directly engaged and view Obama as a leader at ease and in command.

Well-chosen gestures also help Obama convey that he is deeply wedded to the issues about which he speaks, adding to the passion many people view as a key part of his charisma. When Obama places his palm over his heart gently, he conveys deeply held emotion, for example. Obama uses a wide range of gestures to animate his speech: a motion of his fingers toward himself, beckoning someone near; a quick flick of his hand, shooing someone away; his knotted fist pounding on an imaginary door; his pinched fingers scrolling letters in midair; his palm held out to the audience, conveying sincerity. These and many other gestures help Obama breathe greater life into his words, increasing the descriptive nature of his speech and underscoring key ideas. Obama shows us that when we are seeking to form strong second impressions, gestures can work together with voice and intonation to serve the purpose well.

⇥ BENEFIT FROM THIRD IMPRESSIONS: ⇤ STRONG STARTS, ETHICS, AND PREPAREDNESS

> Third impressions can also help earn trust and confidence. Third impressions can include strong starts, successful efforts to convey strong ethics, and preparedness.

Third impressions can also help earn trust and confidence. Third impressions can include strong starts, successful efforts to convey strong ethics, and preparedness. Obama shows how it is possible to use each to strengthen positive early impressions and make strides in projecting oneself as a capable leader.

Begin Strong

Part of Obama's ability to forge such a strong connection with listeners and to form strong third impressions, thereby earning greater trust and confidence, can be reduced to two words: strong starts. By "start strong," I mean Obama makes concerted efforts to begin his remarks or speeches in a way that grasps attention, resonates with listeners, taps into the prevailing mood, or helps lighten any existing tensions. There are no hard-and-fast rules about how this is done. What constitutes a successful start is determined by the specifics of time, place, and persons. At times, it is most important to focus on key issues from the get-go, getting straight to the point. At other times, an emotive statement sets a more appropriate mood. There are thus many ways to start strong—a moving quotation, a vivid anecdote, a light-hearted joke, a direct statement about the topic of discussion, to name a few.

Obama is consistently strong with his starts, catching attention early and steering that attention well. He remains keenly aware that if leaders begin their remarks in a weak manner, they will need to spend too much time recovering, trying to persuade people to give them another look. Whether drawing on a cherished quotation or recounting a memorable anecdote, Obama captures attention early and steers it well. In practice, his motto is, "Get off on the right foot the first time."[3] It is a practice that we see through his successes as far back as the 1980s, when he served as a community organizer in Chicago. Reverend Alvin Love, pastor of the Lilydale First Baptist Church who has served as the Developing Communities Project president, recalled how Obama impressed him immediately with a strong start. With his first comments, Obama demonstrated that he had open ears. Love remembers, "He was interested in finding out what I thought could be done in the community about issues like public safety and employment, rather than giving me some long-winded spiel." Obama successfully identified how to connect with the pastor, and the positive early impression inspired Love to support Obama's work.

When delivering his historic "A More Perfect Union" speech on race relations during the presidential campaign on March 18, 2008, Obama used the notable event to present a "strong start" to the viewing public. He began the speech with patriotic words that connected well with listeners: "We, the people, in order to form a more perfect union."

When addressing the Muslim world with a seminal speech delivered in Egypt on June 4, 2009, entitled "A New Beginning," Obama's strong start included two words that spoke volumes and set a positive tone: *assalaamu alaykum*. In those two words of a common Arabic spoken greeting meaning "peace be upon you," listeners in Egypt heard respect, a willingness to greet them in familiar terms, a desire to reach out and beyond past grievances, and a willingness to forge a better relationship. This made for a strong start.

When introducing his nominee for the U.S. Supreme Court, Judge Sonia Sotomayor, on May 26, 2009, Obama delivered a strong start with a highly appropriate tone of reverence. He explained,

> Of the many responsibilities granted to a President by our Constitution, few are more serious or more consequential than selecting a Supreme Court justice. The members of our highest court are granted life tenure, often serving long after the Presidents who appointed them. And they are charged with the vital task of applying principles put to paper more than 20 [sic] centuries ago to some of the most difficult questions of our time.

With such a reverent start, Obama enhanced his chances of making a positive impression among his observers.

Even in the light of defeat, Obama skillfully chooses his opening words. Following his loss of the Pennsylvania primary in 2008, for example, Obama projected the loss as a "win-because-we-narrowed-the-margin" situation. He stated:

I want to start by congratulating Senator Clinton on her victory tonight, and I want to thank the hundreds of thousands of Pennsylvanians who stood with our campaign today.

There were a lot of folks who didn't think we could make this a close race when it started. But we worked hard, and we traveled across the state to big cities and small towns, to factory floors and VFW halls. And now, six weeks later, we closed the gap. We rallied people of every age and race and background to our cause. And whether they were inspired for the first time or for the first time in a long time, we registered a record number of voters who will lead our party to victory in November.

Obama remains so acutely cognizant of the importance of beginning strong that if placed in an awkward position publicly, he takes steps immediately to reset the tone of the conversation before he proceeds with his remarks. A notable example of this occurred in December 2006, when Barack Obama appeared before a group of 2000 evangelical Christians at a conference on HIV/AIDS at Saddleback Church in southern California. Another politician speaking at the same event, Senator Sam Brownback, spoke minutes before Obama. Standing on the church podium, Brownback addressed the primarily white Christian audience. As he began his speech, Brownback turned to Obama seated behind him and joked, "Welcome to *my* house."

Shock registered in the audience with those words. Barack Obama is a Christian, and we were sitting in a church! Brownback's words seemed, rightly or wrongly, racially charged because they suggested that even though Obama was Christian, the church was not his house simply because white Americans comprised the majority of audience members. It is possible to argue that Brownback did not, in fact, intend this meaning. But the words were highly insulting and placed Senator Obama in a very awkward position, particularly since some isolated conservative evangelical groups had sought to have Obama disinvited from the conference, given his views on issues such as abortion.

In response, when Obama moved to the lectern minutes later to begin his own speech, he offered greetings from his church, deliberately underscoring that he was Christian. He then proceeded to offer Brownback compliments, expressing admiration and respect for Brownback's work on issues such as HIV and poverty, a truly gracious beginning in light of the insult he had just suffered. But before Obama proceeded with the heart of his comments, he took the opportunity—having placed himself on the moral high ground by refusing to come out swinging—to turn to Senator Brownback, seated behind him, and say, "There is one thing I've got to say, Sam. This is my house, too! This is *God's* house."

The crowd erupted in applause. With his words, Obama reset the tone. Had he not done so, he would have started "weak" and proceeded forward in a compromised position, which could have undercut his message to the audience. Instead, Obama kept his eye on the importance of strong starts and successfully recast the dialogue, proceeding with a well-received talk.

Convey Strong Ethics

Another technique that has helped Obama create strong early impressions, winning trust and confidence, is his deliberate practice of conveying his high ethical standards. When a leader succeeds in conveying strong ethics early on, it often brings rewards down the road. Conveying strong ethics early on helps to create a reservoir of goodwill, particularly when backed by subsequent deeds that reinforce the positive impression. It helps to "develop Teflon"—such a strong ethical reputation that a leader can withstand accusations, mudslinging, and controversy. When controversy arises, there is a greater likelihood that people will respond by thinking, "No, that does not fit the impression I have of this leader." People are much more willing to keep an open mind and to refrain from making quick, harsh judgments. They are more prone to await an explanation and give a leader a chance.

> Conveying strong ethics early on helps to create a reservoir of goodwill, particularly when backed by subsequent deeds that reinforce the positive impression.

Obama takes the opportunity to convey his strong ethics early on. During his pivotal 2004 Democratic National Convention Keynote Address, for example, Obama expressed his commitment to American values and laudable ideals. He commented:

> I stand here knowing that my story is part of the larger American story, that I owe a debt to all of those who came before me, and that, in no other country on earth, is my story even possible. Tonight, we gather to affirm the greatness of our nation, not because of the height of our skyscrapers, or the power of our military, or the size of our economy. Our pride is based on a very simple premise, summed up in a declaration made over two hundred years ago, "We hold these truths to be self-evident, that all men are created equal. That they are endowed by their Creator with certain inalienable rights. That among these are life, liberty, and the pursuit of happiness."

With these words, Obama began to form positive early impressions among millions of observers. Similarly, when he announced his presidential bid in Springfield, Illinois, on February 10, 2007, he took the chance to convey his ethics before the media. He spoke about what he had learned as a community organizer among impoverished neighborhoods in Chicago:

> It was in these neighborhoods that I received the best education I ever had, and where I learned the true meaning of my Christian faith....
>
> It was here we learned to disagree without being disagreeable—that it's possible to compromise so long as you know those principles that can never be compromised; and that so long as we're willing to listen to each other, we can assume the best in people instead of the worst.

Notably, when controversy arose in 2008 about Republican vice presidential nominee Sarah Palin's daughter Bristol, a teenager pregnant out of wedlock, Obama took the opportunity to quell what could have become a larger media frenzy over the story. He refused to try to capitalize on the controversy. Quite the opposite, he implored the media to let the story rest. "Let me be as clear as possible," Obama said before the media. "I think people's families are off-limits, and people's children are especially off-limits. This shouldn't be part of our politics. It has no relevance to Governor Palin's performance as governor or her potential performance as a vice president." Obama said further that the media should "back off these kinds of stories" and helped douse the fire beneath the story by observing that his own mother was only 18 when he was born. "How a family deals with issues and teenage children, that shouldn't be the topic of our politics, and I hope that anybody who is supporting me understands that's off-limits." For many taking a first look, they observed Obama adhering to ethics of the highest standard because "it was the right thing to do." The ethics he displayed resonated well.

For those observing Obama for the first time, Obama also established a strong early impression with the care he exercised when criticizing the policy positions of his opponents during the 2008 presidential campaign. Before criticizing presidential candidate John McCain, for instance, Obama would usually first affirm and praise McCain's laudable service to the country and underscore that though they disagreed on policies, he believed McCain to be an honorable man. He would often do the same when commenting about his then-political rival Senator Hillary Clinton.

Overall, Obama's care in conveying strong ethics has aided him throughout his career in forming strong early impressions. This has helped him win the trust and confidence he has needed to achieve such high levels of success.

Convey Preparedness

Demonstrating preparedness and a keen mastery of relevant issues is another key way in which Obama establishes a highly positive early impression. Throughout his career, Obama has created and maintained a reputation as someone who prepares thoroughly and works hard to address issues at hand knowledgably. He demonstrates a strong mastery of relevant subjects and a command of issues under consideration, reinforcing the idea that he is a capable, trustworthy leader.

During law school, for example, his classmates referred to him as having a "first-rate legal mind." He demonstrated this through outstanding performance in class discussions and consistent preparedness that together fueled his success in becoming the first

African American president of the prestigious *Harvard Law Review.*

As a community leader in Chicago during the mid-1980s, Obama demonstrated his commitment to thorough preparation as he organized community members for meetings with policy leaders and decision makers—people who could help them gain resources and programs to address their needs. Obama was known to prepare talking points for residents to help guide them as they spoke before powerful decision makers and to conduct debriefings after such meetings.[4] As he sought to bring new leaders and community residents onboard with his program, he impressed many of his new recruits quickly with his preparedness, inspiring them to ultimately support his cause.

Decades later, people continue to rave about Obama's preparedness. During the early phase of his presidential run, for example, civil rights leader Jesse Jackson commented that, though he unsure whether Obama had sufficient experience to become U.S. president, he remained overwhelmingly impressed by Obama's "mental preparedness" and the tremendous mastery of relevant policy issues that Obama had already demonstrated. Similarly, Obama's hallmark preparedness has swayed some detractors, prompting them to offer praise. After giving his third press conference around his 100th day in office, for example, Obama showed a strong mastery of the key issues affecting America and Americans, inspiring Tavis Smiley—once one of Obama's harshest public critics—to offer beaming approval on national TV, praising both Obama's formidable knowledge of relevant issues and his success in conveying his preparedness to the viewing public. Obama's preparedness helped him to appear as a highly competent and talented leader.

EMPLOYING THE LESSONS

We have seen how Barack Obama uses body language to engage listeners, convey confidence, and impart important messages. We have seen also how he uses voice, intonation, and props to reinforce the positive first impressions he creates. Through his consistent practices, Obama has been able to build outstanding first, second, and third impressions, winning the trust and confidence of others. The strong early impressions Obama creates lay the foundation for the notable influence he wields.

As you think about the practices that have allowed Obama to create and benefit from strong early impressions, consider how these practices can enhance your own leadership. Keep these questions in mind:

- What are the first impressions I create?
- What are the second impressions I create?
- Have my first and second impressions helped me to build trust and confidence among those I seek to lead?
- Bearing in mind the key ways Obama wins confidence— exuding charisma, effective use of body language, excellent use of voice and diction, gathering the right props, etc.—what are my strengths in creating strong early impressions?
- In which ways can I most improve the first and second impressions I make?
- Have I adequately considered the third impressions I make and how they can potentially strengthen my leadership?
- Do I "begin strong"? In what ways can I improve?
- Do I convey strong ethics? In what ways can I improve?
- Do I demonstrate preparedness? In what ways can I improve?

CHAPTER 2

COMMUNICATE YOUR VISION EFFECTIVELY

A key part of outstanding leadership is an ability to communicate vision excellently. Indeed, some scholars define leadership itself as the process of forming a vision for others and wielding effective power and influence to bring that vision to fruition. For Barack Obama, the ability to communicate vision has served as an important part of his success in building highly effective teams and securing buy-in as he moves his teams toward designated goals.

The importance of a clear vision, articulated excellently, should not be underestimated. Teams are, after all, more than just groups. A key facet that distinguishes a team from just any group is a shared vision. High-performing teams are usually distinguished by team members who are working diligently and effectively toward a clear vision.

The importance of a clear vision, articulated excellently, should not be underestimated. Teams are, after all, more than just groups. A key facet that distinguishes a team from just any group is a shared vision.

A vision reflects the overarching goal of a team, toward which the work of that team is directed. It expresses the long-term goal, "the big picture"—the reason the group exists, what efforts are seeking to achieve. Articulated well, a vision helps to direct action and can resonate so strongly as to become a motivating force, inspiring support. Thus, one of the most important early tasks of a leader is to communicate a clear vision in order to lay the very foundation for "all else that follows." This provides a base for successful leadership.

Consider the success of a leader such as John F. Kennedy. His leadership brings to mind his vision of the world he sought to bring to fruition—marked by prosperity, dedicated citizens making contributions to America's well-being, and American success in winning hearts and minds abroad. Similarly, Ronald Reagan's vision of America brings to mind ideas of strength at home and abroad, defense of the "American way of life," and strong family values. Business leaders have also forged roads to success beginning with the articulation of strong visions. Lee Iacocca, as chairman of Chrysler Corporation, set forth a lucid vision: "Quality, hard work, and commitment—the stuff America is made of. Our goal is to be the best. What else is there? If you can find a better car, buy it."[1] He aligned his company excellently with this vision and transformed a challenged organization into a success.

> [Obama] knows it is not enough to form a vision and to believe in it profoundly. To achieve a vision, successful leaders must communicate their vision to others in effective, understandable and compelling ways, enabling others first to grasp the vision and ultimately inspiring them to embrace it.

Obama has demonstrated considerable success in his ability to communicate a vision. Like other successful leaders, he knows it is not enough to form a vision and to believe in it profoundly. To achieve a vision, successful leaders must communicate their vision to others in effective, understandable, and compelling ways, enabling others first to grasp the vision and ultimately inspiring them to embrace it.

How does Barack Obama communicate his vision in ways that resonate so profoundly? Obama understands that the art of conveying vision involves knowledge sharing, skillfully done, so that others understand the "big picture," view it as desirable and achievable, and are motivated to support it. For Obama, articulating vision successfully is a five-part process, through which he creates fruitful conditions; uses words that resonate; paints a desirable picture; shows his vision is viable; and inspires people to embrace his vision. More specifically, Obama focuses on creating fruitful conditions for others to receive his ideas, steering attention to common ground and establishing a sense of "we-ness." He takes steps to ensure his vision might be well received, employing words that resonate with target audiences. Recognizing that people must "see" to believe, he employs well-chosen details to paint vivid pictures and present his vision in understandable terms. He ensures his vision is perceived as viable, acknowledging the challenges ahead and demonstrating the logic of his ideas. As demonstrated in *Say It Like Obama and Win!*, Obama persuades people to embrace his vision by employing a wide array of rhetorical tools to help "elicit a nod." Let's take a closer look at the practices that have brought him such success.

⇥ STEER ATTENTION TO COMMON GROUND ⇤

As Obama seeks to convey vision successfully, he adheres to a mantra that *common* ground is *fertile* ground for conveying and receiving ideas. If you win hearts and minds, he believes, it becomes easier for others to embrace your ideas, partner in

As Obama seeks to convey vision successfully, he adheres to a mantra that *common* ground is *fertile* ground for conveying and receiving ideas. ...[He] takes steps to establish a sense of we-ness....

your efforts, and ultimately participate in change. Obama therefore takes steps to establish a sense of we-ness, and the common ground he establishes provides the space for "acceptance" and "embrace" to take place.

As in most areas of his leadership, Obama developed the skill of establishing or shedding light on common ground over time. He has learned that to establish a sense of we-ness, leaders must first know their audience, understand their purpose, and craft messages ideally in light of these understandings. He remains acutely aware of the importance of this and places great value on it. As Obama told *60 Minutes*, "One of the things I'm good at is getting people in a room with a bunch of different ideas—who sometimes violently disagree with each other—and finding common ground, and a sense of common direction."[2]

Obama was spurred to become "good at this" in part because of his extraordinarily diverse ethnic and cultural background. In Hawaii and Indonesia, where he was raised, Obama was challenged from a young age to break through traditional definitions of identity and culture in order to form friendships with people very different from himself. His family life itself, with a mixture of relatives from Kenya, Kansas, and Indonesia, provided Obama exposure to varied religions as well as perspectives of life outside of the continental United States. Even once he moved to the continental United States to attend college, Obama continued to meet and befriend people very different from himself, living off-campus in New York for a time with a Pakistani housemate and enjoying long chats with Puerto Rican neighbors.[3] Interacting with people of differing backgrounds and perspectives, Obama gained experience viewing issues from different vantage points, while identifying areas of commonality sometimes less apparent to others.

While no doubt challenging during his youth, Obama's need to tear down barriers and build up bridges to people very different from himself laid a foundation for many of his future successes. He became adept at identifying commonalities and using them as a means for articulating his ideas in ways that resonate with others. For example, Obama's tenure as a community organizer in Chicago during the 1980s marked his first time working so extensively in an impoverished African American community. Charged with unifying community church leaders and mobilizing residents to press for needed resources, the 24-year-old Obama needed to earn the trust and confidence of community leaders and residents who universally viewed him as an outsider. Obama has spoken widely about how important these early years were in his leadership formation. As he acknowledged, "It was in these neighborhoods that I received the best education I ever had.... [it] taught me a lot about listening to people as opposed to coming in with a predetermined agenda."[4]

Determined to be effective on the inside, Obama spoke with residents one-to-one about their fears and dreams. Meeting them in sitting rooms, barbershops, and churches, Obama sought out residents where they were, met them in their spaces of comfort. Among the skills he deepened during those years was his ability to listen, something that has become one of his most powerful leadership tools. In listening, he also became adept at discerning areas of commonality. He became skilled at shining a light on those areas of common ground. This helped him become more effective at communicating his vision. This then fueled his success in reaching across divides with a distinctly personal touch, employing his words wisely to persuade, inspire, and motivate others to action.

Michelle Obama has noted that his years as a community organizer helped Barack Obama discern "how he would impact the world."[5] He began to refine skills in communicating his vision to others successfully, in spite of his differences from them. Within the organization he helped lead in the mid-1980s in Chicago, the Developing Communities Project, Obama put his skill to use, selling his vision of grassroots-driven change that inspired a diverse set of church leaders to work together across Catholic/Protestant divisions. Obama built bridges among these leaders that led to consensus and a sense of camaraderie. Obama also communicated his vision effectively, persuading leaders and residents of the Altgeld Gardens public housing project that if they organized together, they could secure needed resources. He conveyed his vision effectively, motivating them to try. The net effect: Obama helped to secure employment training services, playgrounds, and after-school programs; he also helped bring about efforts to remove asbestos from apartments in the highly impoverished community.

In law school, Obama continued to hone his ability to highlight areas of common ground, as a part of the key steps to articulating a vision. He created and maintained peace among titan personalities on the *Harvard Law Review*. "I have worked in the Supreme Court and the White House and I never saw politics as bitter as at *Harvard Law Review* in the early '90s," Mr. Berenson, a Harvard Law School contemporary, observed. "The law school was populated by a bunch of would-be Daniel Websters harnessed to extreme political ideologies."[6] During his days as president of the *Harvard Law Review*, Obama sold his vision of the future of the *Review* to conservative and liberal-minded students alike, gaining widespread support for his bid to become president of the *Review*. As a result of his ability to articulate his vision effectively, Obama became the first African American president of the century-old *Harvard Law Review*.

The trail of successes continued to the Illinois Senate, where Obama's skill in highlighting common ground among Republicans and Democrats helped him to communicate a vision excellently and to secure landmark legislation. There are, of course, few more vivid examples of Obama's skill in steering attention to common ground in order to create conditions that allowed his vision to be well received than the success of his 2008 presidential campaign. Obama attracted supporters from all walks of life—investment bankers, homemakers, working class laborers—and from all ethnic backgrounds—whites, blacks, Latinos, Asians, Indians. The numbers of his supporters quickly swelled into the millions and helped yield the largest expansion of the American electorate in U.S. history.

Obama's success is more than just good fortune. It reflects what can be summed up in a three-phrase mantra: Tear down barriers, build up bridges, shed light on common ground. Obama's efforts drive toward the establishing a sense of we-ness, which helps create the space for an embrace of

> Obama's success is more than just good fortune. It reflects what can be summed up in a three-phrase mantra: Tear down barriers, build up bridges, shed light on common ground.

vision to take place. How, specifically, does Obama build a sense of "we" where before often others perceived only an "us" and "them"? Let's explore the practices and techniques Obama uses to tear down barriers and forge fruitful ties.

Elephants in the Room

One practice that Obama employs to make people more receptive to his vision and ideas is to identify and address head-on any "elephants in the room." Obama acknowledges sources of potential discomfort and takes steps to address those matters early on. Many leaders know that when they are seeking to influence and guide others, some issues present obstacles from the outset and can undercut their leadership efforts, pursuit of goals, and team unity. In those instances, some leaders make an often damaging error: they attempt to ignore the issues, as if holding their breaths and hoping the matters might fade away. Obama takes quite the opposite tact. He addresses such issues head-on, sometimes with touches of humor, directly acknowledging such matters in order to nullify them, rendering them relatively harmless as he moves forward in pursuit of his designated goals. This approach often works.

When Obama was a 24-year-old community organizer in Chicago's roughest neighborhoods seeking to unify and lead church leaders, for instance, one elephant in the room was his sheer inexperience. He was a recent graduate of an Ivy League school, having received his bachelor's degree from Columbia University. Imagine this young Obama—clean-cut, lanky, dressed a bit like a preppie—walking into a sparse meeting room with seasoned church leaders from one of Chicago's roughest neighborhoods and trying to persuade them that he could lead them and help them organize neighborhood residents to press for change and attain greater resources. It is not hard to conceive of the skepticism he received. He was horribly young. He was not from Chicago. He had not been raised in the continental United States. He had never done such extensive work in such an impoverished African American community. He was not even a member of a church at the time! Above all, Obama lacked direct experience as a community organizer. Yet, in how he addressed this situation, we see vintage Obama leadership style.

Rather than pretending his lack of experience was not a point of notable concern for the pastors and other community leaders, Obama acknowledged the issue directly. According to Dan Lee, a deacon at a Catholic church who eventually served as president of Obama's Developing Communities Project, Obama told the community leaders, "I know you all think I'm a young whipper-snapper...." But he continued with confidence, "Let me set your fears to rest. We're going to learn together."[7] In his tone and words, the leaders heard frank acknowledgment, uttered with a confident air. This encouraged the leaders to give Obama a chance. They lay aside the issue of his experience and allowed him to present his vision, explaining what he sought to achieve and how he intended to achieve it. Obama succeeded in persuading many of the leaders to band together, supporting the efforts.

In more recent years, as Obama has run for elected public office, the elephants in the room have included his race, his "funny name," and the fact that his father came from a developing part of the world and was raised in a hut. Given the history of race in the United States, for leaders less skilled than Obama, this background might have presented obstacles too challenging to surmount. But Obama had become adept at addressing these potential issues of discomfort directly, often with a comic wit. Indeed, during his Democratic National Convention Keynote Address of July 2004, Obama's first major speech before the entire American nation, he addressed his eclectic background within the first minutes of his speech. In his very second sentence, he told the viewing public, "Tonight is a particular honor for me because, let's face it, my presence on this stage is pretty unlikely. My father was a foreign student, born and raised in a small village in Kenya. He grew up herding goats, went to school in a tin-roof shack. His father, my grandfather, was a cook, a domestic servant." Obama went on to recast the dialogue, speaking about his life experiences as if they were an example of a quintessential American immigrant story. Later in the speech, he alluded to himself as "a skinny kid with a funny name who believes that America has a place for him, too." His words had the intended effect: Obama acknowledged the elephant in the room head-on and not only quelled any associated concerns, but also turned that particular elephant into a source of strength. Obama's words endeared him to millions of supporters and accelerated his trajectory to the White House.

Time and again, Obama has shown that acknowledging elephants in the room can be a wise tactic that can help to tear down barriers and create the space to convey vision. From there, leaders can identify or establish areas of common ground with those they seek to influence, focusing attention on areas of commonality in an effort to make others more receptive to their vision.

Common Dreams and Aspirations

Another technique that aids Obama greatly as he seeks to convey vision and to encourage a wide variety of people to embrace his vision is his practice of stressing commonalities rather than differences among those he is addressing. He does this in four key ways: by drawing attention to common dreams and aspirations, common values or principles, common history, or common experiences.

Consider, for instance, Obama's 2004 Democratic National Convention Keynote Address, when he uttered initial remarks to help prepare an environment that might be more receptive to his vision. Obama helped to create common ground, telling listeners that his uncommon background was quite recognizable through the lens of the classic American immigrant experience. Rather than allow his father to be defined by the mud hut and the small African village where he was raised, Obama focused on the dreams of his father—a young man willing to leave his home country to gain education in the United States, and whose aspirations reflect a story common to many U.S. immigrants. Obama spoke:

> [I] finally took my first trip to his tiny village in Kenya and asked my grandmother if there was anything left from [my father], she opened a trunk and took out a stack of letters, which she handed to me.
>
> There were more than thirty of them, all handwritten by my father, all addressed to colleges and universities across America, all filled with *the hope of a young man who dreamed of more for his life.* And his *prayer was answered* when he was brought over to study in this country.[8] [Emphasis provided]

In the remarks above, Obama focuses our attention on the hope of a young man and the prayers that were answered, things to which typical Americans can relate. The aspects of his father's experience that would serve to separate him from most Americans—the mud hut and developing country—fade in our minds as Obama steers our attention to the areas of commonality. Aspiring leaders can learn much from this approach. When you are preparing remarks, consider: What elements make up the common ground that you can bring to the fore to establish ties to your audience? The more extensive the ties and greater the sense of common ground, the more hospitable an environment can be for the productive communication of ideas.

As Obama united diverse segments of the American population in support of his vision and goals during his 2008 U.S. presidential campaign, he also employed a practice of drawing attention to shared dreams—a desire for education, a better life for one's children, economic prosperity, etc.—as the basis for relating to a broad swath of the American public. Consider his remarks at the AP Annual Luncheon in Washington, DC, in April 2008:

> People may be bitter about their leaders and the state of our politics, but beneath that, they are hopeful about what's possible in America. That's why they leave their homes on their day off, or their jobs after a long day of work, and travel—sometimes for miles, sometimes in the bitter cold—to attend a rally or a town hall meeting held by Senator Clinton, or Senator McCain, or myself. Because they believe that we can change things. Because they believe in that dream.
>
> I know something about that dream. I wasn't born into a lot of money. I was raised by a single mother with the help of my grandparents, who grew up in small-town Kansas, went to school on the GI Bill, and bought their home through an FHA loan. My mother had to use food stamps at one point, but she still made sure that through scholarships, I got a chance to go to some of the best schools around, which helped me get into some of the best colleges around, which gave me loans that Michelle and I just finished paying not all that many years ago.
>
> In other words, my story is a quintessentially American story. It's the same story that has made this country a beacon for the world—a story of struggle and sacrifice on the part of my forebearers and a story of overcoming great odds. I carry that story with me each and every day. It's why I wake up every day and do this, and it's why I continue to hold such hope for the future of a country where the dreams of its people have always been possible.[9] [Emphases provided]

In his remarks above, Obama joined himself firmly to the diverse American audience he was addressing, with an emphasis on their shared American dream. Closely related to this technique, Obama stresses shared values as he seeks to convey his vision. In May 2009, when he needed to persuade the American public to accept his nominee to the U.S. Supreme Court, Judge Sonia Sotomayor, Obama introduced Sotomayor as much more than a woman who might become the first Latina named to the Supreme Court. He presented her as a woman who represented the values Americans cherish—hard work, integrity, determination, persistence, fairness. He presented her success as a very recognizable American success story, as an example of the American dream come true. In publicized remarks on May 26, 2009, Obama explained how Sotomayor's parents had come to New York from Puerto Rico during the Second World War:

> Sonia's parents came to New York from Puerto Rico during the Second World War.... her mother [w]as part of the Women's Army Corps.... Sonia's mother began a family tradition of giving back to this country. Sonia's father was a factory worker with a third-grade education who didn't speak English. But like Sonia's mother, he had a willingness to work hard, a strong sense of family, and a belief in the American Dream.
>
> When Sonia was nine, her father passed away. And her mother worked six days a week as a nurse to provide for Sonia and her brother—who is also here today, is a doctor and a terrific success in his own right. But Sonia's mom bought the only set of encyclopedias in the neighborhood, sent her children to a Catholic school called Cardinal Spellman out of the belief that with a good education here in America all things are possible.

With the support of family, friends, and teachers, Sonia earned scholarships to Princeton, where she graduated at the top of her class, and Yale Law School, where she was an editor of the *Yale Law Journal,* stepping onto the path that led her here today.

The words were highly effective. In stressing the cherished values and common dreams, Obama made Judge Sotomayor instantly recognizable as an American success story. He scored a win in promoting his vision of an inclusive Supreme Court, in part by shifting attention away from whether Sotomayor might be an "activist" judge, toward highly favorable commentary about how she represented values most Americans support. The press coverage during the ensuing days was highly positive toward this historic nominee, and she was ultimately confirmed for a seat on the Supreme Court.

Shared History

Obama also stresses shared history as a way of creating a positive environment for presenting his vision and ideas. On June 4, 2009, for example, when Obama delivered his famous Cairo speech to the Muslim world, he drew attention to America's historic ties to the Muslim world.

> ...Islam has always been a part of America's story.... [S]ince our founding, American Muslims have enriched the United States. They have fought in our wars, served in government, stood for civil rights, started businesses, taught at our Universities, excelled in our sports arenas, won Nobel Prizes, built our tallest building, and lit the Olympic Torch.... Much has been made of the fact that

an African-American with the name Barack Hussein Obama could be elected President. But my personal story is not so unique. The dream of opportunity for all people has not come true for everyone in America, but its promise exists for all who come to our shores—that includes nearly seven million American Muslims in our country today who enjoy incomes and education that are higher than average. Moreover, freedom in America is indivisible from the freedom to practice one's religion. That is why there is a mosque in every state of our union, and over 1,200 mosques within our borders. That is why the U.S. government has gone to court to protect the right of women and girls to wear the hijab, and to punish those who would deny it.

Obama's reference to shared history was masterful in this speech. He succeeded in illuminating common ground where many of his listeners had not previously realized any existed. The Middle Eastern commentary that flowed in the aftermath of this speech reflected how Obama's words had helped him win many hearts and minds.

Similarly, during his presidential bid, as he sought to sell his vision of the future of America, Obama first sought to sell himself and his eclectic background to the American public. Seeking to establish that he was like any other American, Obama acknowledged that his father was from Kenya, but shifted attention to the history that his family shared with most American families—the experience of the Depression, Patton's Army, and World War II, and work on the bomber assembly line at Fort Leavenworth. Drawing attention to these details enabled Obama to establish himself as being "just like any other American." Obama projected himself as firmly a part of the "we"—part of the same team as most Americans, striving for the same goals. This created the space for his vision to enjoy warm reception.

Shared Experiences

Obama leverages shared experiences to build rapport and to create a fruitful environment for sharing his vision and ideas. At times, he's found that common experiences, rather than shared histories or values, provide the most fruitful means for establishing a connection, even if those shared experiences are only "tangential." Consider, for instance, when Obama spoke before a group of working women in Albuquerque, New Mexico, on June 23, 2008. Clearly, Obama is not a working woman! But, he took time to consider how he could relate to the group. *What is the basis of our common experiences? How can I elaborate on those common experiences?* Obama created a connection magnificently as he referenced his experiences as the son of a working woman and as the husband of a working woman:

> It's great to be back in New Mexico, and to have this opportunity to discuss some of the challenges that working women are facing. Because I would not be standing before you today as a candidate for President of the United States if it weren't for working women.
>
> I am here because of my mother, a single mom who put herself through school, followed her passion for helping others, and raised my sister and me to believe that in America, there are no barriers to success if you're willing to work for it.
>
> I am here because of my grandmother, who helped raise me. She worked during World War II on a bomber assembly line—she was Rosie the Riveter. Then, even though

she never got more than a high school diploma, she worked her way up from her start as a secretary at a bank, and ended up being the financial rock for our entire family when I was growing up.

And I am here because of my wife Michelle, the rock of the Obama family, who worked her way up from modest roots on the South Side of Chicago, and who has juggled jobs and parenting with more skill and grace than anyone I know. Now Michelle and I want our two daughters to grow up in an America where they have the freedom and opportunity to live their dreams and raise their own families.[10]

In the approach above, Obama stressed shared experiences. He broke down barriers and built bridges, creating a more receptive environment in which to convey his vision for the future.

Together, his techniques for establishing common ground and creating a more fruitful environment for transmitting his ideas have helped Obama convey his vision with a high degree of effectiveness. As you seek to convey your vision, remember to prepare the ground as much as possible. Take meaningful steps to create common space, a place for your vision to be well received and embraced.

RECOGNIZE OTHERS MUST "SEE" TO BELIEVE: WORDS THAT RESONATE

Another technique that has enabled Obama to communicate his vision effectively and successfully—securing buy-in—is his practice of using words that will resonate with listeners. The precise words used to convey vision are key. Obama takes care to employ specific words that evoke an "Ah-ha, he really knows" reaction.

"He's really with us." In the process, he connects more deeply with listeners, reinforcing the sense that he and they are on the same team, which can make listeners much more prone to accept the vision he puts forth.

What will resonate with one group of listeners will, of course, depend on multiple factors—the audience, the purposes, the topics at hand, prevailing circumstances. To choose words excellently, leaders must first gain a solid understanding of the audience they seek to influence, and draw upon that knowledge in selecting their words. Obama does this, peppering his remarks with well-chosen words. At times, Obama refers to valued principles, maxims, or biblical truth. At other times, he references circumstances familiar to an audience. He sometimes leverages other people's words—often, the words of American iconic figures—to underscore his message and vision. At times, he employs words from valued lexicons, referencing cherished aspects of such things as a business culture or the mission of a particular group. Each of these approaches aids Obama in conveying his vision successfully.

Reference Principles and Widely Accepted Truths

Let's consider how Obama creates a good environment for conveying his vision as he references widely accepted principles, maxims, and truths. There are many examples. For instance, as a Christian who cherishes his faith, Obama often sprinkles his public remarks with words that evoke the faith of other Christians. *Faith in things not seen. I am my brother's keeper.* Many people hold dear these biblical truths and principles that have stood the test of time. For broad segments of the American population, hearing such language establishes a certain level of connectedness. The verses are familiar to many ears and resonate in the heart. Referring to them helps Obama to build bridges among highly disparate groups. Consider this excerpt from his 2004 Democratic Convention Keynote Address, in which he weaves in both a biblical reference and a reference to a widely accepted truth:

> For alongside our famous individualism, there's another ingredient in the American saga. A belief that we are connected as one people. If there's a child on the South Side of Chicago who can't read, that matters to me, even if it's not my child. If there's a senior citizen somewhere who can't pay for her prescription and has to choose between medicine and the rent, that makes my life poorer, even if it's not my grandmother. If there's an Arab American family being rounded up without benefit of an attorney or due process, that threatens my civil liberties. *It's that fundamental belief—I am my brother's keeper, I am my sister's keeper*—that makes this country work. It's what allows us to pursue our individual dreams, yet still come together as a single American family. *"E pluribus unum." Out of many, one.* [Emphases provided]

Obama used references to biblical truth again in this same speech, as he summarized his vision for America:

> In the end, that is *God's greatest gift to us*, the bedrock of this nation; *the belief in things not seen*; the belief that there are better days ahead. I believe we can give our middle class relief and provide working families with a road to opportunity. I believe we can provide jobs to the jobless, homes to the homeless, and reclaim young people in cities across America from violence and despair. I believe that as we stand on the crossroads of history, we can make the

right choices, and meet the challenges that face us. [Emphases provided]

Similarly, in his seminal "A More Perfect Union" speech in Philadelphia in March 2008, Obama's biblical references served him well:

In the end, then, what is called for is nothing more, and nothing less, than what all the world's great religions demand—*that we do unto others as we would have them do unto us*. Let us be *our brother's keeper, Scripture tells us. Let us be our sister's keeper*. Let us find that common stake we all have in one another, and let our politics reflect that spirit as well."[11] [Emphases provided]

Leverage Other People's Words

When seeking to convey vision effectively, Obama sometimes draws on the carefully chosen words of American icons, which can also help create a sense of common ground that promotes a more receptive environment for transmitting his ideas. Obama has quoted at key times such laudable leaders as Abraham Lincoln, Martin Luther King, Jr., and John F. Kennedy, among others. A couple of weeks before Obama announced his run for the presidency in 2007, for instance, Obama addressed 3,500 students at George Mason University. He conveyed his vision of the future for them, invoking the words of Martin Luther King, Jr. He urged his young listeners to realize they had the power to influence U.S. military involvement in Iraq. He quoted King, who

> When seeking to convey vision effectively, Obama sometimes draws on the carefully chosen words of American icons, which can also help create a sense of common ground that promotes a more receptive environment for transmitting his ideas.

had stated in a powerful speech that, "the arc of the moral universe … bends towards justice." Obama personalized the sentiment, speaking passionately to his young audience. "Here's the thing, young people, it doesn't bend on its own, it bends because you put your hand on that arc and you bend it in the direction of justice," Obama said, in a voice that resonated with deep belief. "Think about all the power that's represented here in all of you.… If you all grab that arc, then I have no doubt, I have absolutely no doubt, that regardless of what happens in this presidential year and regardless of what happens in this campaign, America will transform itself." The room exploded with enthusiastic applause. Obama had used the words with great effect, and his vision of the future and the role of young people in it was extraordinarily well received.

Similarly, during his presidential campaign, when Obama conveyed his vision of how a unified, grassroots effort could help transform American politics, he again leveraged the words of Martin Luther King, Jr., excellently. He stated:

And on the eve of the bus boycotts in Montgomery, at a time when many were still doubtful about the possibilities of change, a time when those in the black community mistrusted themselves, and at times mistrusted each other, King inspired with words not of anger, but of an urgency that still speaks to us today: "Unity is the great need of the hour" is what King said. Unity is how we shall overcome.

What Dr. King understood is that if just one person chose to walk instead of ride the bus, those walls of oppression would not be moved. But maybe if a few more walked, the foundation might start to shake. If a few more women were willing to do what Rosa Parks had done, maybe the cracks would start to show. If teenagers took freedom rides from North to South, maybe a few bricks would come loose. Maybe if white folks marched because they had come to understand that their freedom too was at stake in the impending battle, the wall would begin to sway. And if enough Americans were awakened to the injustice; if they joined together, North and South, rich and poor, Christian and Jew, then perhaps that wall would come tumbling down, and justice would flow like water, and righteousness like a mighty stream.

Unity is the great need of the hour—the great need of this hour.[12]

Draw on Relevant Lexicons

Obama's practice of weaving the language of relevant lexicons into his remarks also facilitates his efforts to transmit his vision effectively. The familiar terminology and language of a specific field can ring well in the ears of listeners. When Obama addressed the nation in his 2004 Democratic National Convention Keynote Address, for instance, he drew on familiar words from America's political lexicon. He commented:

Tonight, we gather to affirm the greatness of our nation, not because of the height of our skyscrapers, or the power of our military, or the size of our economy. Our pride is based on a very simple premise, summed up in a declaration made over two hundred years ago, *"We hold these truths to be self-evident, that all men are created equal. That they are endowed by their Creator with certain inalienable rights. That among these are life, liberty and the pursuit of happiness."*

That is the true genius of America, a faith in the simple dreams of its people, the insistence on small miracles.

That we can tuck in our children at night and know they are fed and clothed and safe from harm. That we can say what we think, write what we think, without hearing a sudden knock on the door. That we can have an idea and start our own business without paying a bribe or hiring somebody's son. That we can participate in the political process without fear of retribution, and that our votes will he counted—or at least, most of the time.

This year, in this election, we are called to reaffirm our values and commitments, to hold them against a hard reality and see how we are measuring up, to the legacy of our forebearers, and the promise of future generations. And fellow Americans—Democrats, Republicans, Independents—I say to you tonight: we have more work to do....
[Emphases added]

The words not only evoked patriotic sentiments and sounded pleasantly familiar to the American audience, but they also helped produce a more hospitable setting in which to put forth his vision and ideas.

This practice is relevant for leaders in a wide variety of fields. When appropriate, consider using words from a relevant lexicon that can help you portray your vision as a continuation of successful efforts of the past. For example, the new leader of a company that for decades operated successfully with the pithy motto "Always push the envelope and remember the customer is king," might wish to reference these words from the company's business lexicon as she presents her vision of the future. How does her new vision for the company stay true to these words that have guided the company to success and have become part of the cherished lexicon of that particular company? Many listeners and observers may wish to know. Leveraging key words from a valued lexicon can help leaders make tremendous strides in articulating a vision in a way that will resonate well with listeners.

Reference History and the Familiar

Another technique Obama employs as he conveys vision is the technique of referencing "the familiar." When placing his ideas in a familiar or historical context, Obama makes them more digestible. They are placed in a context listeners can more readily understand. At times, the vision can be seen as an extension, or as the next evolutionary step of, a successful history. Consider this example, when Obama communicated the vision he had of an America in which citizens were highly mobilized and diligently addressing social issues such as homelessness, violence, living wages, health care, and education. Obama skillfully placed his ideas in a historical context, referencing the American iconic leader Robert Kennedy:

> I was only seven when Bobby Kennedy died. Many of the people in this room knew him as brother, as husband, as father, as friend....
>
> ... [T]he idealism of Robert Kennedy—the unfinished legacy that calls us still—is a fundamental belief in the continued perfection of American ideals....
>
> Robert Kennedy reminded us of this. He reminds us still. He reminds us that we don't need to wait for a hurricane to know that Third World living conditions in the middle of an American city make us all poorer. We don't need to wait for the 3000th death of someone else's child in Iraq to make us realize that a war without an exit strategy puts all of our families in jeopardy. We don't have to accept the

diminishment of the American Dream in this country now, or ever.

It's time for us to meet the whys of today with the why nots we often quote but rarely live—to answer "why hunger" and "why homeless," "why violence" and "why despair" with "why not good jobs and living wages," "why not better health care and world-schools," "why not a country where we make possible the potential that exists in every human being?"[13] [Emphases provided]

In linking his ideas not only to history, but also to a laudable historic American leader, Obama helped substantiate his ideas in the minds of some listeners. He made his vision seem familiar, as well as more understandable, increasing the odds listeners might find it both desirable and acceptable. Leaders in all fields can benefit from this approach. A leader of a religious organization seeking to fulfill a mission of alleviating poverty among people in developing countries, for example, can place her vision for her organization in the context of the historic actions taken by her organization, which can help her to project her own vision as an extension, continuation, or advancement of those efforts. A leader taking the helm of a rapidly growing entrepreneurial venture can reference the company's past work and achievements, placing his vision for the future in that context to help substantiate it and make it more attractive. As you seek to convey vision in ways that are highly effective and increase the probability that others might see the vision as desirable and attainable, consider using words that evoke cherished parts of the history or culture of your organization or team. Speak in language that resonates so that the seeds of your vision and ideas might find their way to fertile ground.

⇥ HELP PEOPLE "SEE": ⇤
USE WORDS THAT PAINT A PICTURE

Creating a sense of common ground and a fruitful environment for conveying ideas are important steps as Obama seeks to communicate his vision effectively. Obama also makes a practice of employing very descriptive words as he conveys his vision, recognizing that *how* you convey your vision—literally, the words chosen—can impact the likelihood of whether your vision will be well received. Obama understands that others must be able to "see" your vision in order to be highly inspired to embrace it. He has mastered the art of using well-chosen descriptive words—words that paint vivid pictures and call to mind rich images, helping people to see his vision.

> Obama understands that others must be able to "see" your vision in order to be highly inspired to embrace it. Obama has mastered the art of using well-chosen descriptive words—words that paint vivid pictures and call to mind rich images as effectively as any visual aid.

Several things make certain words rich in descriptive power. Some words are powerful in the specific image they call forth. They don't simply "tell," they "show." They create imagery and hence can aid in conveying vision. Some descriptive words are highly *symbolic*, eliciting an emotional reaction. For example, referring to a flag draped over a coffin evokes patriotism, notions of loyalty and sacrifice to country. The net effect of such well-chosen words is that they increase the power of remarks and can make efforts to convey vision much more effective. Words rich in *corollary meaning* can also aid efforts to convey vision. Such a word is multidimensional in the ideas and images it evokes; it can be one word that "implies 20 others." In my book, *Say It Like Obama and Win!* I explore these and other descriptive words in greater detail. Obama's practice of using highly descriptive words aids his efforts to convey vision effectively.

Let's explore below a few more practices that enable Obama to convey vision so well.

Dynamic Words

Understanding that it is difficult to achieve a vision if others cannot see it, Obama often paints a vivid picture by using very dynamic words. During his presidential campaign, for example, Obama often indicated he intended to bring change and success "brick by brick, block by block, calloused hand by calloused hand." These dynamic words helped create moving images in the mind, making them resonate more strongly. Since assuming the presidency, Obama has continued to leverage the power of dynamic words, commenting on May 20, 2009, at the signing of the Helping Families Save Their Homes Act and the Fraud Enforcement and Recovery Act, that "Step by step, I believe we're moving in the right direction."

Details

Obama also understands that when seeking to convey vision, he should calibrate the number and type of details he offers, so that listeners will have a strong sense of his vision and the direction he is seeking to set. When seeking to communicate to others that he understands a situation well and that the matter is of great importance, for example, Obama will employ excellent detail in describing the issue at hand. During his address to Congress on September 8, 2009, for instance, Obama provided excellent detail to describe why health care reform remains so important. He explained:

> But the problem that plagues the health care system is not just a problem of the uninsured. Those who do have insurance

have never had less security and stability than they do today. More and more Americans worry that if you move, lose your job, or change your job, you'll lose your health insurance too. More and more Americans pay their premiums, only to discover that their insurance company has dropped their coverage when they get sick, or won't pay the full cost of care. It happens every day.

One man from Illinois lost his coverage in the middle of chemotherapy because his insurer found that he hadn't reported gallstones that he didn't even know about. They delayed his treatment, and he died because of it. Another woman from Texas was about to get a double mastectomy when her insurance company canceled her policy because she forgot to declare a case of acne. By the time she had her insurance reinstated, her breast cancer more than doubled in size. That is heartbreaking, it is wrong, and no one should be treated that way in the United States of America.

In providing this solid level of detail, Obama demonstrates he understands the issues and lays the foundation for elaborating upon how his vision can help address the critical situation.

Anecdotes

When substantiating his vision with detail, Obama knows how to offer well-considered anecdotes. Anecdotes—brief accounts of specific events or incidents—can serve as powerful tools for conveying vision and enable Obama to go into greater depth as he crystallizes his vision. When explaining his hope for a new, unified support base seeking to promote change during his 2008 campaign, Obama offered this anecdote:

There is a young, 23-year-old white woman named Ashley Baia who organized for our campaign in Florence, South Carolina. She had been working to organize a mostly African-American community since the beginning of this campaign, and one day she was at a roundtable discussion where everyone went around telling their story and why they were there.

And Ashley said that when she was nine years old, her mother got cancer. And because she had to miss days of work, she was let go and lost her health care. They had to file for bankruptcy, and that's when Ashley decided that she had to do something to help her mom.

She knew that food was one of their most expensive costs, and so Ashley convinced her mother that what she really liked and really wanted to eat more than anything else was mustard and relish sandwiches. Because that was the cheapest way to eat.

She did this for a year until her mom got better, and she told everyone at the roundtable that the reason she joined our campaign was so that she could help the millions of other children in the country who want and need to help their parents too.

Now Ashley might have made a different choice. Perhaps somebody told her along the way that the source of her mother's problems were blacks who were on welfare and too lazy to work, or Hispanics who were coming into the country illegally. But she didn't. She sought out allies in her fight against injustice.

Anyway, Ashley finishes her story and then goes around the room and asks everyone else why they're supporting the campaign. They all have different stories and reasons.

Many bring up a specific issue. And finally they come to this elderly black man who's been sitting there quietly the entire time. And Ashley asks him why he's there. And he does not bring up a specific issue. He does not say health care or the economy. He does not say education or the war. He does not say that he was there because of Barack Obama. He simply says to everyone in the room, "I am here because of Ashley."

"I'm here because of Ashley." By itself, that single moment of recognition between that young white girl and that old black man is not enough. It is not enough to give health care to the sick, or jobs to the jobless, or education to our children.

But it is where we start. It is where our union grows stronger. And as so many generations have come to realize over the course of the 221 years since a band of patriots signed that document in Philadelphia, that is where the perfection begins.[14]

The anecdote demonstrates in great detail the power of small changes in mind-set and the choice to unite across traditional societal divisions. It conveys well Obama's vision by focusing on one person listeners can relate to—Ashley.

⇥ ACKNOWLEDGE THE TERRAIN ⇤

Obama's success in conveying vision, as he has inspired millions of people to support his vision, is also attributable in part to his practice of "acknowledging the terrain." After he has established a sense of we-ness and common ground, he often addresses the relevant question: Is his vision achievable? When leaders articulate a vision, observers may ponder whether they have

COMMUNICATE YOUR VISION EFFECTIVELY 59

considered the challenges and devised reasonable ways of meeting and overcoming those challenges. Is the vision viable? Or does it merely represent pie-in-the-sky dreaming? Obama makes certain to nod to history and acknowledge the terrain, a practice that helps quell concerns about whether a particular vision he presents can be achieved.

> Is the vision viable? Or does it merely represent pie-in-the-sky dreaming? Obama makes certain to nod to history and acknowledge the terrain, a practice that helps quell concerns about whether a particular vision he presents can be achieved.

During his third primetime news conference as U.S. president on April 22, 2009, for example, Obama laid forth his vision for economic reform. But he took care to acknowledge the terrain, which included the large economic burden he had inherited and the difficult road ahead, before elaborating on his ideas. He noted:

> I want to give everyone who's watching tonight an update on the steps we're taking to move this economy from recession to recovery, and ultimately to prosperity.
>
> Now, it's important to remember that this crisis didn't happen overnight, and it didn't result from any one action or decision. It took many years and many failures to lead us here. And it will take many months and many different solutions to lead us out. There are no quick fixes, and there are no silver bullets. That's why we've put in place a comprehensive strategy designed to attack this crisis on all fronts.
>
> ...The road to that prosperity is still long, and we will hit our share of bumps and setbacks before it ends. But we must remember that we can get there if we travel that road as one nation, as one people....
>
> ...We'll recover from this recession, but it will take time, it will take patience, and it will take an understanding that,

when we all work together, when each of us looks beyond our own short-term interest to the wider set of obligations we have towards each other, that's when we succeed, that's when we prosper, and that's what is needed right now.

Only in the context of these acknowledgments of the tough terrain did Obama then elaborate on the main fixtures of his economic plan, which included a strategy for job creation, tax relief, and plans to help restart the flow of credit from banks to families and businesses. This particular mix, whereby he acknowledged the challenges in achieving a vision and then detailed his ideas about how to address the challenges, went far to help persuade some observers to give his approach a chance. To them, Obama's vision seemed well considered and viable. Obama received strong reviews even from some pundits who had once been his harshest critics, such as national commentator Tavis Smiley.

⇥ DEMONSTRATE YOUR LOGIC ⇤

> [Obama] communicates his vision in ways that make "compelling sense."

When seeking to present his vision effectively, Obama makes certain to demonstrate the logic of his ideas: he communicates his vision in ways that make "compelling sense." *Say It Like Obama and Win!* goes into depth in assessing Obama's many rhetorical techniques that serve this purpose well. I highlight three here: his practices of sequencing his ideas, addressing objections, and enumerating.

Sequence Ideas

In his quest to persuade others that his vision is desirable and worthy of support, Obama, like other orators skilled in the art of persuasion, takes care to create a strong sense of logic to his ideas. Clarity of reasoning is important. One key to creating a strong sense of logic involves sequencing ideas—presenting them in a logical, persuasive order. There is no "right" order as such, only an effective order. The listener must be able to understand the flow of thoughts and find that this flow makes logical, compelling sense. This lays the foundation for agreement.

In his public remarks, Obama sequences his ideas and themes well. At times, he sequences ideas within a single sentence or concise series of sentences. For example, during his 2004 keynote address, Obama sequenced his ideas in a way that conveyed logic and strong determination. He stated emphatically, "We have real enemies in the world. These enemies must be found. They must be pursued, and they must be defeated." Whether in a single sentence or expounded upon in much greater length in a sequenced construction, the practice of presenting a vision in words that demonstrate such a sensible logic serves Obama well.

Address Objections

As he elaborates on his vision, Obama also understands the value of addressing objections. This technique, known as *procatalepsis*, is a useful rhetorical device and an excellent persuasion tool. By airing a potential objection and responding to it, leaders can persuade listeners by providing sound reasons why key counterarguments should be dismissed. Addressing objections demonstrates awareness of key counterarguments and provides leaders with opportunities to illustrate why their chosen positions are more sensible. In addressing key counterarguments, leaders can skillfully undercut those arguments, strengthening their own positions. When seeking to persuade people of the value of your vision, consider whether you can benefit from drawing attention to key counterarguments and explaining why your vision is best.

Enumerate

As Obama has taken the helm as Commander-in-Chief, he has used the technique of enumeration to provide a strong sense of logic and reason to his ideas, which helps him convey his vision effectively. Enumeration enhances a sense that ideas are well considered and prioritized. Notably, on the 2008 presidential campaign trail, Obama rarely enumerated his ideas, because this particular technique dampens efforts to establish strong emotional bonds with listeners, something that Obama sought to do during his campaign. Enumeration is businesslike, lending itself to a sense of order. As Commander-in-Chief, Obama has found the technique useful. It allows him to demonstrate a depth of knowledge, command of issues, and strong sense of direction.

For example, in his remarks about the American automotive industry on March 30, 2009, Obama commented:

> First, we will ensure that Recovery Act funds to purchase government cars get out as quickly as possible and work through the budget process to accelerate other federal fleet purchases, as well. Second, we'll accelerate our efforts through the Treasury Department's Consumer and Business Lending Initiative. And we are working intensively with the auto finance companies to increase the flow of credit to both consumers and dealers. Third, the IRS is launching a campaign to alert consumers of a new tax benefit for auto purchases made between February 16th and the end of this year—if you buy a car anytime this year, you may be able to deduct the cost of any sales and excise taxes.

And this provision could save families hundreds of dollars and lead to as many as 100,000 new car sales.

Obama has employed this technique in many other speeches of note, from his historic talk in Egypt to his remarks about the swine flu pandemic during his third primetime news conference. As you seek to convey vision effectively, in a manner that will encourage others to embrace your vision, consider the many techniques at your disposal that can help others perceive your ideas as viable. Employ them to help others believe your vision makes compelling sense.

⇥ Elicit a Nod: Skillful Persuasion ⇤

In presenting his vision, Obama is always seeking to drive to "yes," eliciting a nod from listeners, which is the affirming gesture indicating they are embracing his vision and ideas. To this end, as he speaks of his vision and ideas, Obama employs a full range of rhetorical tools that can help him "get to yes." He employs the art of persuasion, with its many tools. His hallmark techniques include the use of juxtaposition and antithesis.

> Obama is always seeking to drive to "yes," eliciting a nod from listeners which is the affirming gesture indicating they are embracing his vision and ideas.

Through juxtaposition, Obama places opposing ideas side by side, crystallizing his ideas for listeners as he compares or contrasts those ideas. Consider this example, on March 19, 2009, as President Obama spoke before the Los Angeles Town Hall, Miguel Contreras Learning Center:

We also want to do this because it serves the most important goal we have today, which is to rebuild our economy in a way that's consistent with our values—an economy that rewards hard work and responsibility, not high-flying financial schemes; an economy that's built on a strong foundation, not one that's propelled by an overheated housing market or everybody maxing out on their credit cards. We need to bring about a recovery that endures. That's how we'll bring about a recovery that endures.

The use of juxtaposition enabled Obama to paint a lucid picture of the old versus the new, aiding listeners in their understanding of his vision and direction. Obama's use of juxtaposition as a rhetorical tool was equally effective during his March 30, 2009 comments about the American automotive industry. Obama remarked:

> The pain being felt in places that rely on our auto industry is not the fault of our workers; they labor tirelessly and desperately want to see their companies succeed. It's not the fault of all the families and communities that supported manufacturing plants throughout the generations. Rather, it's a failure of leadership—from Washington to Detroit—that led our auto companies to this point.

Similarly, through antithesis, Obama places ideas, concepts, or beliefs side-by-side and contrasts them: He presents clear "counterpropositions" that are useful in his efforts to persuade others. During his November 4, 2008, presidential victory speech, Obama commented, "…our stories are singular, but our destiny is shared…" In that same speech he observed, "…the true strength of our nation comes not from the might of our arms or the scale of our wealth, but from the enduring power of our ideals: democracy, liberty, opportunity and unyielding hope."

The use of antithesis construction has served Obama well, allowing him to offer crisp, lucid expressions of his vision.

Obama employs other rhetorical tools to facilitate his effort to convey vision and to persuade others to accept his ideas. For example, he often poses rhetorical questions—questions whose answers are considered obvious and therefore are not answered explicitly by a speaker. Rhetorical questions emphasize points and crystallize attention around important issues. Obama employs rhetorical questions effectively, using them to fix audience attention firmly on key issues or topics, as seen in *Say it Like Obama and Win!* He then proceeds to speak at greater length about his designated topics, clarifying key elements of his vision.

Asking a nonrhetorical question—one he answers—is another valuable technique Obama employs as he seeks to persuade listeners to accept and support his vision. Nonrhetorical questions allow listeners to feel as if Obama is raising and addressing commonly held concerns. Referred to as *hypophora*, the practice enables Obama to sound as if he is vetting key questions from the audience. A well-developed answer demonstrates depth of knowledge and aids effective knowledge sharing. Nonrhetorical questions also focus attention on key concerns and make remarks more engaging.

Barack Obama has shown great skill in employing nonrhetorical questions. Before he delivers his remarks, Obama seems to often consider: What does the audience most want to know and learn about my vision? What will listeners most doubt or question? The next task: ask and answer.

Consider this example, as Obama spoke of Robert Kennedy at the Robert F. Kennedy Human Rights Award Ceremony on November 16, 2005. Obama asked: "Why is it that this man who was never president, who was our attorney general for only three years, who was New York's junior senator for just three and a half, still calls to us today?" Obama proceeded to elaborate about the relevant attributes of Kennedy. As he often does when using this technique, Obama answers the question at length to underscore his points and crystallize his vision. In asking a germane question and then answering it, Obama succeeds in advancing his key points.

Together, these techniques enable Obama to convey vision effectively. In his role as U.S. president, Obama faces leadership challenges on a new scale and size. His leadership practices above can give him the tools to successfully convey vision that addresses the social and economic challenges America faces.

EMPLOYING THE LESSONS

Barack Obama's ability to articulate his vision excellently has served as a key factor in his success as a leader. The practices and principles he employs allow him to articulate a clear vision that other people find understandable, desirable, and attainable. Focused on the clear vision he presents, Obama's teams and organizations benefit from a shared vision and can focus on end goals. Obama's ability to convey vision effectively also allows him to attract high levels of support beyond the teams he leads.

As you think about the practices that allow Barack Obama to communicate his vision effectively, consider how these practices can enhance your own ability to convey vision excellently. Bear these questions in mind:

- How well do I communicate vision?
- Do I take the time to know my purpose and my target audience, steering attention to common ground?
- When communicating my vision, do I use excellent communication techniques and language that allows others to "see" and ultimately believe in the vision? How can I improve the ways in which I communicate vision?

- When I communicate my vision to others, do I adequately acknowledge and address challenges we will face? Do I explain convincingly how we can overcome those challenges?
- In which ways can I draw on more effective language and communication practices to create a strong vision that others will understand and ultimately embrace?
- Do I demonstrate a strong logic to my ideas as I articulate my vision?
- Do I employ adequate "skillful persuasion" as I attempt to convey my vision?

PART II

FORM A WINNING TEAM

CHAPTER 3

LEVERAGE A STRONG REPUTATION

"They keep slinging mud at him, but nothing seems to stick."

"They keep taking shots at him, but the shots seem to just bounce off."

"He went through such fire, but he emerged unscathed."

This is what we mean by Teflon. Barack Obama has built his reputation Teflon strong. By *Teflon*, I mean a reputation so sterling and so solid, and so strongly backed by deeds, that it's hard for detractors to make much of a chink as they pursue efforts to tarnish that reputation. Teflon—a strong reputation—helps leaders to persuade people during good times, and serves as an

> Teflon—a strong reputation—helps leaders to persuade people during good times, and serves as an outer layer of protection during periods of adversity or controversy.

outer layer of protection during periods of adversity or controversy. For Obama, his strong reputation allowed him to persuade millions of Americans that he did indeed represent *change* and that even though he was a relative newcomer to the national political stage, they could trust electing him to the highest office in the land. Since assuming the presidency, Obama's strong reputation has also meant that, even amid all the heated fervor surrounding the 2009 health care debate, he has weathered storms much better than many other leaders could. Indeed, his personal approval among the American public remains high, even though concerns about his policies have at times grown.

As we will see, Obama has reaped the benefits of a strong reputation throughout his career. He has been able to leverage his strong reputation when it counted, capturing significant opportunities to advance his goals and career. After he was elected to his first public office as an Illinois state senator, for example, the strong reputation Obama had built in law school and while practicing law in Chicago spurred Judge Abner Mikva, who had considered hiring Obama as a law clerk, to urge Illinois Senator Emil Jones to give Obama a chance to spearhead bipartisan legislation for ethics reform. This represented a difficult, but high-profile and in some ways career-defining opportunity.[1] From Obama's success in this effort, other opportunities flowed. The stronger Obama's reputation became, the more the old adage applied: his reputation began to precede him. Obama's strong reputation created fruitful ground as he persuaded others to support his goals and partner with him on key efforts.

Obama has built and continually strengthened his Teflon through consistent practices and actions. Let's explore some of these successful practices and principles below.

⇥ UNDERSTAND THE IMPORTANCE OF TEFLON ⇤

It is useful to think of *reputation* in terms similar to how we think of first impressions, second impressions, and third impressions: people tend to think back on your reputation at key moments. They mull your reputation through their minds, for instance, when they weigh decisions

It is useful to think of *reputation* in terms similar to how we think of first impressions, second impressions, and third impressions: people tend to think back on your reputation at key moments.

such as whether to follow your lead, whether to partner with you and whether to give you a chance in the midst of controversial circumstances. Your reputation reflects a cumulative product of your efforts and actions over time, and the many impressions you have created. When you have built your reputation strong—when it is "sterling," positive, and a tremendous asset—your reputation can function as excellent Teflon. When a leader hits tough times, the presence or lack of a strong reputation tends to become exceedingly apparent. Consider, for instance, when President Bill Clinton faced accusations of an affair with Monica Lewinsky. He had little Teflon to protect him from allegations of philandering, because his actions up until that point—multiple extramarital affairs—had contributed to his reputation as "Slick Willie." With so little Teflon to buffer him, many observers tended to believe with ease the accusations of a Lewinsky affair.

On the contrary, some leaders have succeeded in building their Teflon excellently. Few observers would believe easily, for instance, that Senator John McCain could engage in acts of disloyalty to America. The first, quick response of many people to such an assertion would simply be, "Never." Any accuser would have a high hurdle to overcome, because McCain's great sacrifices to

America during the Vietnam War are well known. We are acquainted with the hardships and torture he endured as a POW. His Teflon is strong and insulates him from accusations of disloyalty.

Similarly, a public figure such as Oprah Winfrey found that she could withstand intense scrutiny in the face of the controversy surrounding James Frey, whose "memoir" *A Million Little Pieces* was soon dubbed "A Million Little Lies" because it contained fabricated stories. When Winfrey came forward, asserting she had not known the work contained untruths when she chose the work as an Oprah Book Club selection, the public believed her. Her years of frank honesty on her syndicated television show paid off. Her Teflon was strong.

> Knowing that a strong, positive reputation is priceless, all leaders should ask themselves, "How strong is my reputation? In hard times, how well would it protect me?"

Knowing that a strong, positive reputation is priceless, all leaders should ask themselves, "How strong is my reputation? In hard times, how well would it protect me? In good times, does it aid me in advancing my goals or persuading others?" How well your reputation serves as an armor of protection or aids you in advancing your causes is a product of your actions and the degree to which others have viewed your deeds as consistently reinforcing a positive reputation. Let's explore some of the practices and principles that have allowed Obama to build a strong "layer of protection."

⇥ CONVEY STRONG ETHICS ⇤

Obama's practice of consistently conveying his strong ethics to others has helped him build and maintain a strong reputation. Obama has built an image as a highly principled man because he speaks of his commitment to admirable principles often. When leaders succeed in conveying strong ethics and substantiate those words consistently through deeds, they increase the likelihood that people will respond during periods of controversy and negative accusations with responses such as, "No, that is not who I have seen all of this time." They are more likely to await an explanation and give a leader a chance.

When leaders succeed in conveying strong ethics and substantiate those words consistently through deeds, they increase the likelihood that people will respond during periods of controversy with responses such as, negative accusations with responses such as, "No, that is not who I have seen all of this time."

In his public pronouncements, Barack Obama takes opportunities often to convey his high ethical standards and commitment to principled values. When he was running for the U.S. Senate, for instance, he could be heard stating, "There are a set of principles that I care about. And there are people I'm fighting for in this campaign."[2] Consider also his remarks during his 2007 Announcement for President in Springfield, Illinois:

> [L]et me tell you how I came to be here. As most of you know, I am not a native of this great state. I moved to Illinois over two decades ago. I was a young man then, just a year out of college; I knew no one in Chicago, was without money or family connections. But a group of churches had offered me a job as a community organizer for $13,000 a year. And I accepted the job, sight unseen, motivated then by a single, simple, powerful idea—that I might play a small part in building a better America.
>
> My work took me to some of Chicago's poorest neighborhoods. I joined with pastors and laypeople to deal with communities that had been ravaged by plant closings. I saw that the problems people faced weren't simply local in nature—that the decision to close a steel mill was made by

distant executives; that the lack of textbooks and computers in schools could be traced to the skewed priorities of
politicians a thousand miles away; and that when a child
turns to violence, there's a hole in his heart no government
alone can fill.

It was in these neighborhoods that I received the best
education I ever had, and where I learned the true meaning of my Christian faith.[3]

In offering this short summary of these life choices and values,
Obama underscored his morality, commitment to community,
and principled values. Obama takes the opportunity to present
such information about himself frequently, and he backs the
words with consistent deeds. This has served as a foundation for
the strong reputation he enjoys.

⇥ BE A STRAIGHT SHOOTER ⇤

Obama's practice of telling things "as they are" and remaining
transparent has also aided him in building his strong reputation.
He presents himself as a straight shooter
and engages in actions consistent with this.

> Obama's practice of telling things "as they are" and remaining transparent has also aided him in building his strong reputation.

Consider, for instance, the very personal
matter of his indiscretions as a youth.
While some politicians have tried to deny
allegations that they experimented with
drugs as youth (only to have revelations emerge later), Obama
was candid from the beginning. In a televised interview, Obama
made no effort to hide his past mistakes. "I think it was typical
of a teenager who was confused about who he was and what his
place in the world was, and thought that experimenting with
drugs was a way to rebel," he explained. "It's not something that

I'm proud of." Obama proceeded to explain why he was so candid and truthful about the matter. "I think one of the things about national politics is this attempt to airbrush your life. And it's exhausting, right, you know. 'This is who I am. This is where I've come from.' And you know, if we have problems in this campaign, I suspect it's not gonna be because of mistakes I've made in the past. I think it's gonna be mistakes that I make in the future."[4] Obama's candid admission had the effect of disarming detractors from using his youthful indiscretions against him. Most of the American public accepted that everyone makes mistakes and seemed to appreciate Obama's frank admission of his own mistakes.

Obama's reputation as a straight shooter has served him well in many of his endeavors. When he first tried to set in motion his work as a community organizer in Chicago in the mid-1980s, for example, Obama chose to be candid during an early meeting with church leaders. He was a recent college graduate and "wet behind the ears," and others knew it. Yet he was tasked with organizing seasoned leaders of institutions such as notable churches. Rather than try to hide or sugarcoat his lack of direct experience in community organizing, Obama acknowledged it head on. According to Dan Lee, a deacon at a Catholic church, Obama commented without reticence, "I know you all think I'm a young whippersnapper...." He continued with confidence, "Let me set your fears to rest. We're going to learn together."[5] His frank admission of his inexperience, ironically, inspired community leaders to give him a chance.

During the 2008 presidential campaign as well, Obama reinforced his reputation as a straight shooter through many of his political choices. In the midst of the Jeremiah Wright controversy, for example, Obama chose not to sidestep the complex issues of race that Reverend Wright had stirred with his fiery comments.

David Axelrod recalled that amid the firestorm of controversy, Obama instructed his aides to clear time. Axelrod remembers Obama saying, "You know what? I'm gonna make a speech about race and talk about Jeremiah Wright and the perspective of the larger issue.... And either people will accept it or I won't be president of the United States. But at least I'll have said what I think needs to be said."[6]

Obama delivered a historic speech about American race relations, spelled out the areas in which America still needed to strive to "perfect itself," and challenged Americans to make more progress. As David Plouffe noted, this "was a moment of real leadership. I think when he gave that race speech in Philadelphia, people saw a president."[7] Indeed, Obama's reputation as a straight shooter and honest broker has bolstered his leadership and helped him win the respect of millions.

⋊ OFFER AN OPEN EAR, WIELD A FAIR HAND ⋉

Obama's practice of offering an open ear to others, even to those with whom he disagrees on key issues, represents another practice that has strengthened his reputation. As Obama states often, he developed the powerful skill of listening during his days as a community organizer in Chicago. Back then, Obama would conduct some 30 conversations or interviews with community members per week in an effort to understand the needs of residents of the Altgeld Gardens low-income housing community.[8] Obama learned that listening could be a potent tool in connecting with others, pinpointing key issues and discerning areas of common ground. His willingness to listen and use information in key ways to advance causes impressed Chicago community leaders. Reverend Alvin Love, of Lilydale First Baptist Church, indicated it was a key reason he chose to work with Obama. When Obama ran for the Illinois State Senate, he employed similar tactics, going door to door to meet with South Side residents.[9] He later commented, "I learned that if you're willing to listen to people," he explained, "it's possible to bridge a lot of the differences that dominate the national political debate."

As Gerald Kellman, who hired Obama for the position as a Chicago community organizer in the mid-1980s, notes, "Obama is tied to the principles ... but he's not tied to how you get there. That's very much out of organizing. You're there to do a job, and you're there to get things done."[10] Obama keeps an eye on the broader principles and goals, but seeks to work with others with open ears as much as possible.

During his tenure as *Harvard Law Review* president, also, Obama's reputation for listening to others served him well. Harvard Law School Professor Laurence Tribe noted Obama's winning interpersonal skills, explaining, "He's able to build upon what other students say and see what's valuable in their comments without belittling them."[11] One observer called this a "thoughtful and inclusive approach."[12] Obama could listen, draw on words, and push discussion forward. This approach helped Obama forge consensus and "heal factions."

Abner Mikva, a former congressman and one of Obama's mentors, observed, "he's not looking for how to exclude the people who don't agree with him. He's looking for ways to make the tent as large as possible."[13] Listening is key for this. Listening helps Obama "nuance" his positions to make them as appealing to as many people and groups as possible.

Obama's positive reputation for listening to others has been strengthened by his practice of showing respect to others and acting with fairness toward them, even when he is at odds with

Obama seeks win-win situations and has become known for "wielding a fair hand."

them over significant issues. Obama seeks win-win situations and has become known for "wielding a fair hand."

In spite of a willingness to listen and act fairly, however, Obama is not reticent to criticize the ideas of others. As *Harvard Law Review* president, for example, he would send back articles with handwritten notes all over them to students who had hoped to have their work considered for publication. But the *constructive* nature of his criticism met with approval and won him many supporters.[14]

Obama carried this leadership approach forward. As he engages people at odds with him on various issues, Obama listens and engages them constructively, in a nonconfrontational style, with civility and fairness. As he has stated, "We can have a strong disagreement, passionate disagreements about issues without—without resorting to name-calling. We can maintain civility."[15] His willingness to engage others and act with a high degree of fairness has strengthened Obama's reputation as a trustworthy leader among both those who agree with his positions and those who do not. As Bradford Berenson, a Harvard Law School contemporary who was a member of the so-called conservative faction noted, "Whatever his politics, we felt he would give us a fair shake."[16] Obama's reputation as a fair leader who listens has yielded positive results throughout his career.

⇥ BE TRUE TO YOUR WORD, ⇤
BUILD A CONSISTENT RECORD

Jean Rudd, executive director of the Woods Fund and a community leader familiar with Obama, believes, as do many others, that "His honesty is refreshing."[17] Obama enjoys a strong, positive reputation in part because he seeks to remain true to his word. When he makes a promise, he tries hard not to back out on it. When he articulates issues of key concern to him, he tries earnestly to pursue activities and legis-

> Obama enjoys a strong, positive reputation in part because he seeks to remain true to his word.

lation consistent with his articulated stance. In the Illinois Senate, for example, Obama strengthened his reputation by pursuing legislation consistent with his stated areas of concern, such as ethics reform, poverty, women's rights, and health care. He helped to expand children's health care, provide greater access to health care for people in Illinois, and promote legislation supporting victims of domestic violence and women's equal pay. Obama also spearheaded a bill mandating that police videotape interrogations and confessions in potential death penalty cases. Importantly, as Obama delivers on his promises, he says so, reminding people that he is committed to the principle of keeping his word.

Obama's deliberate efforts to remain true to his promises have yielded noteworthy results. It became common to hear leaders such as Johnnie Owens, an activist who eventually became the executive director of the Developing Communities Project, praise Obama's principled leadership. "Anyone who knows me knows that I'm one of the most cynical people you want to see..." Owens stated. "I've lived in Chicago all my life. I've known some of the most ruthless and biggest [con people] out there, but I see nothing but integrity in this guy."[18]

Obama's reputation as a man of great honesty and integrity has reinforced his ability to forge strong relations, even with leaders with whom he does not agree on notable issues. They may not like all of his stances, but he has earned their respect on a

> Obama's reputation as a man of great honesty and integrity has reinforced his ability to forge strong relations with leaders with whom he does not agree on notable issues. They may not like all of his stances, but he has earned their respect on a personal and leadership level.

personal and leadership level. As such, Obama has garnered fans among the conservative right, in spite of his views on abortion. He has earned support from gay activists who would prefer he adopt more assertive positions on homosexual rights. Honesty and integrity have helped thicken Obama's Teflon, enabling him to gain friends and influence a large set of people.

↦ GIVE LOYALTY ITS DUE PLACE ↤

Obama also gives loyalty a strong place in his values set. He does not, as he calls it, "throw people under the bus." He demonstrated this clearly during the Reverend Jeremiah Wright scandal, when in the 2008 presidential campaign season, videotapes surfaced of Wright making remarks many Americans deemed offensive. While Obama agreed the comments seemed unpatriotic and at times racially charged, he was slow to denounce Wright, who had been a long-time pastor and friend. In explaining why he was so slow to publicly distance himself from Wright, Obama acknowledged loyalty played a large role. Over decades, Obama he had seen Wright lead many positive, praiseworthy activities among a poverty-stricken and often hope-deprived urban community. Obama acknowledged the politically expedient thing to do amid the videotape controversy would have been to denounce Wright quickly and completely. But he explained that loyalty and a sense of ethics had prevented him from throwing Wright "under a bus."

Similarly, when Obama's pick for U.S. Treasury Secretary, Timothy Geithner, came under tremendous criticism in 2009 for mistakes on his tax returns, Obama refused to replace Geithner. He stood up for Geithner's character and gave him a chance to weather the intense criticism. Regardless of whether an observer agrees with Obama's choices with regard to Wright, Geithner, or other instances, many observers believe they see integrity behind Obama's actions. He places great value on loyalty and displays the courage to choose loyalty over political expediency. This has served to strengthen his overall reputation.

⇥ REMAIN HUMBLE ⇤

Another principle that has bolstered Obama's reputation is his conscious practice of remaining humble in spite of his many academic, personal, and professional successes. As far back as Harvard Law School, when Obama became the first African American president of the *Harvard Law Review*, the mass media dubbed him a "rising star." The amount of press coverage Obama received after he became the *Review*'s president has been described by some as "almost embarrassing." The attention could have caused dissension and backlash from envious *Review* colleagues. Yet, Obama greeted the attention with what has become his trademark humility. He was quoted as saying, "For every one of me, there are thousands of young black kids with the same energies, enthusiasm, and talent that I have who have not gotten the opportunity because of crime, drugs, and poverty. I think my election does symbolize progress but I don't want people to forget that there is still a lot of work to be done."[19] This tactic of exuding humility helped Obama to continue functioning effectively as a leader of the *Review*, and helped him avert unnecessary conflicts with law students who might have resented the tremendous attention he received.

Humility continued to serve Obama well. He began his U.S. Senate tenure after his highly publicized 2004 Democratic National Convention Keynote Address. The national media were still showering attention on him, calling him once again a rising star. The public and press treated Obama, as others would term it, as a "rock star." Realizing this attention could make long-tenured senators feel upstaged, Obama took steps to keep a lower profile and focus his attentions on building meaningful relationships with other senators. He successfully forged relations he was able to leverage when he ran for U.S. president.

On the whole, when Obama has achieved great successes, you can hear him giving credit to others, rather than accepting the credit for himself. His humility has served him well.

⇥ STAY ABOVE THE FRAY ⇤

Obama adheres consistently to the notion that people should "stay above the fray." By this, he means more than simply, "Never hit someone below the belt." He means also that one should find the higher ground and attempt to stand on it.

Obama adheres consistently to the notion that people should "stay above the fray." By this, he means more than simply "Never hit someone below the belt." He means also that one should find the higher ground and attempt to stand on it.

The American public witnessed one of the most shining examples of this during the 2008 presidential campaign, when the mainstream media began to focus attention on the out-of-wedlock pregnancy of Bristol Palin, daughter of Republican vice presidential candidate Sarah Palin. Obama could have tried to capitalize on the situation, using the circumstances to undercut any notion that Palin and the Republicans represented "good family values." Instead, Obama responded in a way that quickly quelled the media attention and quite probably prevented it from blossoming into a larger story. He told reporters, "I think people's families are off-limits, and people's children are especially off-limits. This shouldn't be part of our politics." Obama's choice to speak these words did not flow from a political calculation. In the eyes of many viewers, Obama went above and beyond, providing a wonderful example of a leader committed to staying on higher ground. He strengthened his Teflon.

In the same vein, Obama's response about negative campaigning also displayed his commitment to staying above the fray. When Steve Kroft pointed out to Obama during a CBS 60 Minutes interview that Senator Hillary Clinton's primary advertising campaign against him had turned decidedly negative, Kroft followed the observation with a query: "Is there a point at which you go to the closet and pull out Clinton's skeletons?" Obama responded, "No. We don't play that. Yeah, I mean, one of the rules that I laid down very early in this campaign was that we will be fierce competitors but we will have some ground rules. And one of the ground rules for me is that we battle on policy differences. And that if we draw a contrast between Senator Clinton and myself, then it is based on fact." Obama clarified further, "We're not gonna fabricate things. We're not gonna try to distort or twist her positions." He held to this emphatically, stating, "Not only is it offensive to me personally, but I think it's bad politics for me. That's not who I am. That's not what my supporters are looking for."[20]

Similarly, Obama conveyed a commitment to remaining above the fray whenever he criticized his campaign opponents in 2008. When criticizing presidential candidate John McCain, for instance, he would usually first affirm McCain's service to the country. This helped him to avoid an image of "mudslinging." For instance, Obama said:

> In just a few short months, the Republican Party will arrive in St. Paul with a very different agenda. They will come here to nominate John McCain, a man who has served this

country heroically. I honor that service, and I respect his many accomplishments, even if he chooses to deny mine. My differences with him are not personal; they are with the policies he has proposed in this campaign.[21]

Obama's care in modeling good behavior and staying above the fray has served to strengthen his strong reputation and aided him on the road of success, allowing him to build successful leadership around notions that he represents "leadership you can trust" and "change you can believe in."

⇥ DISPLAY STRENGTH ⇤

Significantly, Obama realizes that when some people seek to act in principled ways, other people sometimes perceive them as weak. He understands, therefore, that as he demonstrates principled leadership he must also exude strength. In consciously demonstrating strength, Obama underscores that his willingness to offer open ears or a fair hand does not represent weakness or an inclination to relinquish deeply held principles. Similarly, Obama makes clear that he does not fear confrontation, but prefers to avoid negative behavior that can burn bridges.

> In consciously demonstrating strength, Obama underscores that his willingness to offer a fair hand does not represent weakness or an inclination to relinquish deeply held principles.

Obama has demonstrated strength in multiple types of ways. When he came under intense criticism for not denouncing Reverend Jeremiah Wright for his incendiary comments in 2008, Obama chose to denounce Wright but displayed great strength as he took a strong stand on America's many continuing racial challenges. Viewers did not see a man pressured into denouncing an old friend out of weakness, but a leader willing to do what he perceived as the right thing while still standing strong in his convictions.

As U.S. president, Obama has indicated a willingness to speak to the leaders of countries considered in recent years to be enemies of America. He has explained why his position does not represent weakness. He has stated, for example

> Here's what I said. We can't tolerate al Qaeda having base camps and safe havens where they are planning attacks against U.S. targets. That's not acceptable. If we have a high value al Qaeda target in our sights, then we need to make sure that if the Pakistanis are unwilling or unable to go after them, that we do. That's common sense. And I think that's appropriate.... Yes. I think that a nuclear armed Iran is not just a threat to us, it's a threat to Israel. And it is a game changer in the region. It's unacceptable. And that's why I've said that I won't take any options off the table, including military, to prevent them from obtaining a nuclear weapon. But I do think that it is important for us to use all the arrows in our quiver. And we have not applied the kind of tough diplomacy over the last eight years that I think could have made a difference.[22]

The strength Obama has shown has helped him earn and retain a great deal of respect. In combination with the principles he demonstrates, millions of people have come to view him as a highly capable and strong leader.

⇥ DEMONSTRATE SUPERIOR PREPAREDNESS ⇤

The record Obama has established as a leader who addresses issues with great preparedness also strengthens his reputation. This aspect of his reputation stretches far back to his days as a community organizer in Chicago. At that time, he was known to prepare intensely for meetings between Altgeld Gardens public housing residents and authorities from whom they would be seeking resources. In efforts to help residents realize their demands, Obama would meet with residents and coach them on how to speak with authorities, guiding them as they prepared statements or talking points. He then allowed the residents to go to the forefront, speaking in their own capacities. In the aftermath of meetings, Obama would debrief residents, reviewing successes and shortcomings, knowledge he could later put to use.

Obama's reputation for preparedness carried through to his law school years, when law school colleagues commented on how insightful and brilliant they considered him to be, given his strong performance in class. He became widely known as having a "first-rate legal mind," which facilitated his efforts to become president of the prestigious *Harvard Law Review*.

When Obama was running for the U.S. presidency, Jesse Jackson also commented on how impressive he found Obama's "mental preparedness." Obama had studied and developed a mastery of the key issues America faced. This adoration for his preparedness carried on. Following Obama's comments on his 100th day in office as U.S. president, for example, he garnered praise from pundits who had once been highly critical of him. Tavis Smiley, for instance, praised Obama for how well he vetted questions from the press, addressed complex issues, and demonstrated a sophisticated understanding of America's most pressing problems. Obama's record of preparedness has amplified his reputation as a capable leader.

⇥ REMAIN COOL UNDER FIRE ⇤

Obama's ability to remain "cool under fire" stands out as a quality that impresses many people. As Obama himself observed during the presidential campaign, "It turns out that even under this kind of stress I've got a pretty even temperament. I don't get too high, I don't get too low."[23]

The importance of an even temperament can be more apparent when contrasting public reaction to leaders who have failed to display such even keels. Recall the widely publicized scream that Howard Dean uttered during the 2004 presidential campaign. The misstep cost Dean his political future, as Americans concluded they could not trust the presidency to a man who had demonstrated erratic behavior, even though the scream represented a momentary lapse. Senator John McCain also weakened his reputation when he displayed fits of anger in public, and when he appeared agitated during a presidential debate against Obama in 2008. Some media referred to this as the "hothead" element of McCain's personality and questioned whether he could be trusted to keep calm when making critical national decisions, particularly decisions affecting U.S. military operations and relations with other nations.

Obama became known long ago for keeping his cool under pressure. As former Representative Abner Mikva, a mentor to Obama who helped him make a name for himself in the Illinois Senate, observed: "I have never seen anybody in the political arena who can be as deliberate and cool as he is on decisions. In all the years I've known him, I've never seen him emotionally angry. I'm sure he's been—I mean, I could tell he was upset at times, but the emotions never went into the decisional process."[24]

In observing how cool Obama remained under pressure, many Americans concluded they could trust him as an Illinois state senator, as a U.S. senator, and ultimately as U.S. president. He has benefited from the

In observing how cool Obama remained under pressure, many Americans concluded they could trust him as an Illinois state senator, as a U.S. senator, and ultimately as U.S. president.

notion that leaders who remain calm will make better, wiser choices. Indeed, following his first 100 days in office as U.S. president, many commentators complimented Obama on the calming effect he'd had on the American public that, at the end of the Bush administration, had lacked optimism in the future and feared an economic collapse. As David Gergen, a tenured Harvard professor and co-director of Harvard's Center for Public Leadership, commented, "How Obama maintains his equanimity is one of the mysteries of the day, but he has an inner calm—almost a Hawaiian Zen—that is calming for the country. FDR and Reagan brought a contagious optimism to the job that gave people hope; Obama brings a calm that helps to banish fear and gives people strength for the journey."[25]

Similarly, when ABC News anchor George Stephanopoulos asked his guests "What is the most important thing you've learned about President Obama and his administration in the first 100 days?" political commentator Donna Brazile observed, "His demeanor, his calm... he has given the American people a glimmer of hope... a sense that he knows what the light looks like at the end of the tunnel."[26] Obama's temperament and ability to maintain calm under difficult circumstances have strengthened his reputation as a highly capable leader.

EMPLOYING THE LESSONS

Through multiple examples, we have seen the importance Barack Obama places on building and maintaining a strong reputation. Obama has built carefully a strong reputation for highly ethical behavior, and this has served as a solid foundation for his leadership. His strong Teflon has enabled him to persuade millions of people to support his vision and has helped him to face and overcome controversy.

As you think about how the practices and principles that have enabled Barack Obama to build and leverage a strong reputation might enhance your own leadership and style, consider these questions:

- Have I built up my Teflon adequately?
- Do I convey strong ethics?
- Do others perceive me as a straight shooter? Would my leadership benefit from this?
- To what degree do people perceive me as someone who has an open ear, wields a fair hand, and shows respect to others? To what degree do people perceive me as loyal? Would my leadership benefit from this?
- Am I known for "staying above the fray"? Would my leadership benefit from this?
- Do I place enough emphasis on exuding strength as I also try to pursue principled leadership?
- Do I always come across as well prepared for issues at hand?
- Can I improve my ability to appear "cool under fire"?
- In light of how Barack Obama's strong reputation has helped him to weather storms and thrive in their aftermath, what steps can I take to strengthen my reputation as a highly ethical and dependable leader?

CHAPTER 4

MAKE FRIENDS IN UNUSUAL PLACES

Some leaders live by the mantra "The enemy of my enemy is my friend." Barack Obama asks instead, "Why have any enemies at all?"

Various observers have poked fun, calling Obama's philosophy "utopian," "unrealistic," "naïve." Obama's point of view even made him a target for satires, all in fun, from groups such as JibJab, which offered a popular caricature of Barack Obama straddled atop a bright white unicorn, flying over a rainbow and promising change away from "divisive exchange." But for Barack Obama to date, the approach of extending a hand and seeking common ground has yielded notable positive results. Who could have imagined, otherwise, that Obama's ascension to the presidency of the *Harvard Law Review* would be due in part to the support of conservative editors? Who could have predicted either that prominent personalities as diverse as Al Sharpton, Pat Buchanan, Warren Buffett, Maria

Shriver, and Colin Powell would all have in common support for Barack Obama? Indeed, it once would have tested the imagination to think of conservative evangelical Pat Robertson offering such glowing words of a Democratic president-elect, as when he commented on election night in November 2008, "Obama is absolutely *brilliant* and I'd like to make a prediction. He can be one of the great presidents of the United States." Robertson went on, months later, to denounce fellow conservative Rush Limbaugh for "hoping Obama fails" as president, stating he was "remarkably pleased" with Obama's performance in the early months of his presidency.

While others may be surprised by Obama's success in gaining such a wide range of support, Obama remained confident all along of the positive outcomes. He has promoted the practice of reaching out to others and forging friends in unusual places throughout his career. Obama has underscored his view of the importance of relationships, explaining that "forming relationships a lot of times was more important than having all the policy talking points in your arsenal.... [M]ost of the time people at the state level—and in the U.S. Senate—are moved as much by whether or not they trust you and whether or not they think your values are sound as they are by graphs and charts and numbers on a page."[1] Obama reiterated his ambition to make friends in unlikely places during his presidential campaign in February 2008, noting that "We are bringing together Democrats and Independents, and yes, some Republicans... There's one right there, an Obamacan, that's what we'll call them."

Obama's pragmatic view of the need to make "friends" in both traditional and nontraditional places stretches back to his days as a community organizer in Chicago. Gerald Kellman, who hired Obama for work with his Calumet Community Religious Conference in an effort to organize community leaders and residents in one of Chicago's impoverished South Side neighborhoods, recalled Obama's viewpoint at the time. He noted Obama wished to learn from the mistakes of his father, who attained a Harvard Ph.D. education but failed to realize his goals upon returning to his home of Kenya, given his inability to work successfully within the prevailing political circumstances. Kellman noted that Obama "talked about what happens to you if you're not practical in finding ways to do things effectively."[2]

Loretta Augustine Herron, a founding member of Obama's Developing Communities Project in Chicago, explained how Obama viewed his opponents back in the 1980s. 'They're not enemies,' he used to tell us. 'They're both working for their constituents, and they have to do this.' He did not take their acts of opposition personally. "Whoever can help you reach your goal, that's who you work with.... There are no permanent friends, no permanent enemies."[3]

But far greater than the pragmatic need to make friends and leverage them is Obama's genuine desire to unite people and bring about win-win solutions whenever possible—a mentality that earned him a reputation at Harvard Law School as a leader who could "heal the *Review*'s partisan divisions," and among "Generation Y" as a "new kind of politician."[4]

Obama's approach in securing the support of friends in unusual places has borne fruit over the years as his network of friends has grown. During his eight years in the Illinois Senate, for example, Obama worked arduously to build a formidable network of connections and friendships that served him excellently as he worked across party lines to pass legislation addressing key concerns, brokering compromises that members of both parties could ultimately accept. His network of friends also served him wonderfully when he sought a seat in the U.S. Senate.

As Obama moved forward in his career, his ability to win friends in unusual places became a distinct strength of his leadership.

As Obama moved forward in his career, his ability to win friends in unusual places became a distinct strength of his leadership—enabling him to court former Clinton backers effectively after he won the Democratic presidential nomination, gain support among young conservative evangelicals, and sway broad segments of young people. Perhaps in the future we will see more limits to this approach as Obama continues his efforts in difficult areas such as Middle East peace. But to date, his philosophy of extending a hand and befriending people in both traditional and nontraditional places has been a winning approach, providing Obama with an ever-expanding, diverse set of supporters. Making friends in unusual places has become a signature of his leadership.

The results speak for themselves. Obama's ability to secure friends in unusual places helped him as a community organizer in Chicago to gain employment training services, playgrounds, and after-school programs. This ability facilitated his work across party lines in the Illinois Senate to bring about the first campaign finance reform in over two decades. It also served him well as he worked with police groups and other law enforcement agencies to bring about hallmark legislation addressing racial profiling and requiring officials to videotape homicide interrogations.

More recently, in the 2008 presidential election Obama's ability to gain friends in unusual places helped facilitate the large crossover of Republican support for his candidacy. Websites such as republicansforobama.org sprang up as early as 2006. So many Republicans began to offer their public support that they were dubbed Obamacans. The conservative endorsements, some assert, were the most numerous given to a Democratic candidate in decades, and included influential conservative and Republican figures such as General Colin Powell, the former secretary of state; William Donaldson, the chairman of the U.S. Securities and Exchange Commission under President Bush; Paul O'Neill, U.S. secretary of the treasury under President George W. Bush; Ben Bernanke, former chairman of the Federal Reserve; Francis Fukuyama, a notable academic; William Well, former governor of Massachusetts; James Brady, former White House press secretary under President Ronald Reagan; Scott McClellan, former White House press secretary under President George W. Bush; and Christopher Buckley, author and son of William F. Buckley, Jr., among others. Notable right-leaning newspapers also endorsed Obama's presidential bid, including the *Chicago Tribune*, which had never before endorsed a Democrat; the *Economist*; the *New Haven Register*; the *Denver Post*; the *Salt Lake Tribune*; the *New York Daily News*; the *Pasadena Star*, and the *Orlando Sentinel*.

Let's explore the practices and principles that have allowed Obama to make so many friends in unusual places.

⇥ EMPLOY A POWER ANALYSIS: ⇤
THE PRAGMATIC SIDE OF FRIENDS

Barack Obama is committed to the ideal of unity and seeks to build coalitions as broadly as possible as he addresses issues of concern. But he also recognizes the practical importance of engaging effectively people with power to help bring about his goals. Obama's work as a community organizer introduced him to the value of assessing power holders— people, groups, and organizations of potential support, influence, and power.

Barack Obama is committed to the ideal of unity and seeks to build coalitions as broadly as possible as he addresses issues of concern. But he also recognizes the practical importance of engaging effectively people with power to help bring about his goals.

When he taught others about community organizing, for instance, Obama counseled that leaders should learn early—with regard to the work they must do and the groups they must influence—who possesses power and why and how they have that power. "I want to break this down," he was quoted as saying. "We talk 'they, they, they' but don't take the time to break it down. We don't analyze. Our thinking is sloppy. And to the degree that it is, we're not going to be able to have the impact we could have," he explained.[5] Leaders should also learn to identify who is the person with "real power" and who is " just a third-string flak catcher."[6]

> Assessing power holders and learning to gain their support became one of the sharp tools in Obama's skills set.

Assessing power holders and learning to gain their support became one of the sharp tools in Obama's skills set. Over his career, we see how Obama puts this into practice. He successfully built a formidable network of supporters—diverse, traditional and nontraditional, and fiercely loyal. For example, Obama entered the Illinois Senate during a period of Republican control in a city where insider politics was considered essential for any sort of progress. Specifically, Republicans dominated the senate 37–32, and power was concentrated in the positions of senate president, house speaker, and the two chamber minority leaders. In this context, old-style politics was seen as the only viable way to make gains. Understanding this, Obama secured the mentorship of the Democratic leader in the Illinois Senate, Emil Jones, someone who knew how to work the Chicago political network.

Obama recognized Jones could help him, given his lack of long-standing Chicago roots and the fact that his "black experience" differed greatly from the typical African American experience, and hence some people questioned his "blackness." A strong association with Jones gave him credibility. Obama cultivated and nurtured this relationship. It paid off when Obama ran for the U.S. Senate. He sought Jones's support early on, explaining that as president of the Illinois Senate, Jones could help persuade the mayor, labor groups, and the governor to support him, or at least neutralize any opposition from those camps.[7] Jones lent his support to great effect.

⇥ Go Where Friends Are ⇤

One principle Obama embraced that helped him to make a wide range of influential friends, was to "go where the friends are." He consistently put himself where people of influence were. When Obama

> Obama has displayed consistently his philosophy of putting himself where people of influence are.

returned to Chicago after law school, for instance, he realized he might pursue a political career. Knowing his future ambitions, he selected his law firm very deliberately. Obama met with Judson H. Miner, a head of Miner, Barnhill & Galland, during his third year of Harvard Law School in Chicago in 1991.[8]

Miner recalled how clear Obama was in his desire to learn from him "the political lay of the land," since Miner had helped Harold Washington, Chicago's first black mayor, become elected in 1983. Miner had also served as Washington's corporation counsel. As Miner recounts, Obama sought him as a mentor and was also seeking avenues to become introduced to the power players of Chicago.[9] Miner, Barnhill & Galland was an ideal law firm for Obama, given his interest in eventually running for the Illinois Senate to represent Hyde Park, a community that includes both the University of Chicago and bordering impoverished African American neighborhoods.[10] Given the firm's reputation,

Obama's choice to work with Miner, Barnhill & Galland sent a message that he sought to be seen as an independent—an appropriate choice if seeking election from Hyde Park.[11] Given the prestige of the firm, it also provided him with exposure to power players in the city and state.

Miner served as a very willing mentor and introduced Obama to many of the notable power holders in Chicago.[12] He brought Obama along for a regular poker game, attended by notables of the city.[13] Through his work for Miner's firm, Obama also forged relationships with influential leaders such as Bishop Arthur M. Brazier, the pastor of an 18,000-member black church and the head of the Woodlawn Organization, which worked to better the impoverished neighborhoods near Hyde Park; and Marilyn Katz, who had extensive ties to activist networks.[14]

Obama began playing tennis at Chicago's East Bank Club, cultivating relationships with leaders there.[15] Obama also socialized at events such as Chicago Symphony Orchestra performances with power players such as Newton N. Minow, who had worked in the Kennedy administration and was a head of Sidley Austin, a top-tier law firm.[16] He expanded his networks with top business leaders and also forged ties to Reverend Jeremiah A. Wright Jr.'s activist United Church of Christ in Chicago.[17]

During his days in the Illinois Senate, Obama devoted considerable effort to building relationships in useful places. He spent time on the golf field. "An awful lot happens on the golf course," he was quoted as saying.[18] Obama also joined the board of two influential nonprofits, the Woods Fund and the Joyce Foundation, extending his network further. Each step of the way, he continued to be guided by influential mentors, such as Abner Mikva.

⇥ NEVER LIMIT YOURSELF TO EXPECTED ALLIES ⇤

As Obama seeks to build a broad network of support and friends in many places, two of his central tenets stand out. They can be summed up simply as, "Never limit yourself to friends in usual places" and "Be willing to make friends in unusual places."

The mindset stems from his personal background. Born the son of a black African father and a white mother from Kansas, raised in Hawaii and Indonesia, and living

[T]wo of Obama's central tenets stand out. They can be summed up simply as, "never limit yourself to friends in usual places" and "Be willing to make friends in unusual places."

for a time with an Asian stepfather and white grandparents, Obama learned to thrive amid diversity. He learned to see that people have multiple sources of commonalities and when you tap into them, people often respond and are willing to transcend and render nearly irrelevant traditional lines of division. Obama learned from an early age how to develop a broad range of friends and cultivate a wide variety of relationships.

In his career, this desire to make a range of friends translated into Obama's refusal to partake in extreme politics. Manifested as early as his leadership at Harvard Law School, Obama refused to openly support staunch conservatives or agitate too aggressively for race-related issues such as the call for more diverse faculty hiring, an issue over which African American professor Derrick Bell resigned.[19]

A refusal to limit himself was also seen in Obama's determination to actively seek and attain well-placed mentors and support among powerful personalities who concurred with his views. Obama always set his sights high, never giving in prematurely to a notion that a potential mentor was out of reach. When he served as a lowly senator in the Illinois congress, for example, Obama sought the mentorship and support of powerful players including Emil Jones. When he began his bid as a presidential candidate, Obama again aimed high, landing Peggy Pritzker, a member of the wealthy Pritzker family, as his key fundraiser. Obama even secured the public support of Oprah Winfrey, who proudly pronounced on her television show, "This is my senator— my *favorite* senator." By May 2008, Warren Buffett, one of the world's wealthiest businesspersons—owner of a billion-dollar business and aptly referred to as the "Sage of Omaha"—endorsed Barack Obama. Since he is known for picking winners, Buffett's endorsement went a long way.

During his presidential campaign, Obama again aimed high, seeking the public endorsement of prominent members of the Kennedy family, in spite of the long-standing friendship between the Kennedys and Clintons. In 2008, Senator Edward Kennedy and Caroline Kennedy, the daughter of John F. Kennedy, provided well-publicized, moving endorsements of Obama, indicating he could unify the country and expressing adoration for his bipartisan efforts. Through their actions, the public perceived that the Kennedy family passed the Kennedy "torch" to Obama—something exceedingly significant. Caroline Kennedy went so far as to write in her July 27, 2008, *New York Times* article entitled "A President Like My Father":

> Over the years, I've been deeply moved by the people who've told me they wished they could feel inspired and hopeful about America the way people did when my father was president.... All my life, people have told me that my father changed their lives, that they got involved in public service or politics because he asked them to. And the generation he inspired has passed that spirit on to its children. I meet young people who were born long after John F. Kennedy was president, yet who ask me how to live out his ideals.

Sometimes it takes a while to recognize that someone has a special ability to get us to believe in ourselves, to tie that belief to our highest ideals and imagine that together we can do great things. In those rare moments, when such a person comes along, we need to put aside our plans and reach for what we know is possible.

We have that kind of opportunity with Senator Obama.

During his presidential bid, Obama also courted the support of Governor Bill Richardson, one of the most successful Hispanic legislators in the United States. He did this in spite of the popular belief that the Hispanic community would not support an African American candidate, given the history of African American-Hispanic conflict in some parts of the United States. Obama succeeded in gaining Richardson's endorsement, showing the value of his determination to never foreclose options or limit himself in cultivating "friends in unusual places."

This principle has borne great fruit as Obama has approached supporters on "the other side of the political fence." As far back as his work in the Illinois Senate, Obama established a strong record of securing bipartisan support to achieve designated goals. As *Newsweek* recounted:

Back in the Illinois Senate, Obama made a name for himself as someone who could work both sides of the aisle. He befriended an eclectic group of lawmakers, including Kirk Dillard, a conservative Republican. Dillard specifically recalls Obama's work to reach a compromise on the death penalty. Governor George Ryan had commuted every death sentence in the state after a series of flawed cases had come to light; the legislature was deeply split. Conservative law-and-order types were incensed, while black legislators, in particular, thought it was about time that the state stopped executing prisoners who had been wrongly convicted. Obama was handed the Herculean task of reaching a compromise. He did so by getting conservatives to embrace the idea of videotaping police interrogations and suspects' confessions. Among Obama's toughest opponents: Illinois state Senator Ed Petka, a former prosecutor who had put so many men on death row that his friends called him Electric Ed. "Ed Petka was the hardest person for Obama to convince that he was the real deal, but even Petka became an Obama convert with respect to these criminal-law issues," says Dillard.[20]

Obama's success in reaching across the aisle also continued during his time as a U.S. senator and presidential candidate. Obama enjoyed one of the broadest Republican crossovers of support in presidential campaign history. He benefited from many well-publicized Republican endorsements, including that of Republican Colin Powell, who endorsed Obama during the key weeks leading up to the November 2008 presidential election, calling Obama a "transformational figure" during a nationally televised interview on October 19, 2008.

⇥ EMPLOY A WIN-WIN, "BOTH–AND" MIND-SET ⇤

Another distinct aspect of Obama's approach as he cultivates friends in unusual places is his choice to embrace a win-win and a (in his words) "both–and" mind-set.

Another distinct aspect of Obama's approach as he cultivates friends in unusual places is his choice to embrace a win-win and a (in his words) "both–and" mindset. Obama explained his philosophy: "I learned that if you're willing to listen to people, it's possible to bridge a lot of the differences that dominate the national political debate. . . . I pretty quickly got to form relationships with

Republicans, with individuals from rural parts of the state, and we had a lot in common."[21]

Abner Mikva, a former congressman who supported Obama's efforts in the Illinois Senate, has explained that Obama is "not looking for how to exclude the people who don't agree with him. He's looking for ways to make the tent as large as possible."[22] This is what *The New York Times* dubbed "the politics of maximum unity."[23] *The New York Times* also described Obama as "the ultimate pragmatist, a deliberate thinker who fashions carefully nuanced positions that manage to win him support from people with divergent views."[24] As Obama himself summed up, "It is very much a both–and as opposed to an either–or approach."[25]

This does not mean Obama fails to stick to his principles. Quite the opposite. As Obama has noted, "There are a set of principles that I care about," and he defends those principles as he seeks to build consensus and broker acceptable win-win solutions. Obama's success in seeking and conveying win-win solutions and persuading others that such solutions and approaches are viable has aided him directly in his efforts to secure the support of friends in unusual places.

⇥ MEET ON COMMON GROUND ⇤

While the principle of gaining friends in unusual places is important, how can you do that specifically? One technique that aids Obama in his efforts to win friends in unusual places is his practice of identifying and highlighting common ground, which helps people believe that a mutually beneficial alliance can flourish. Obama has demonstrated keen skill

> One practice that aids Obama in his efforts to win friends in unusual places is his practice of identifying and highlighting common ground, which helps people come to believe that a mutually beneficial alliance can flourish.

in bringing people of widely diverse backgrounds together, helping them to see commonalities. He succeeds in creating a sense of "we" where often others only ever saw before an "us" and a "them." Several practices have allowed Obama to build those bridges, inspiring people in unusual places to support him, move beyond traditional divisions, or look beyond past grievances.

For example, when nurturing friends in unusual places, Obama highlights common experiences, common aspirations, common values, and/or common histories. Even beyond this, Obama knows he must be clear in his own mind about the areas of commonalities and must articulate and sell his view to skeptical listeners. He must explain convincingly why—in spite of the differences, and even amid the differences—the common ground he highlights is enough, and the parties can work together to yield a win-win outcome. Obama has done this time and again excellently.

One outstanding example of his skill in securing once-reluctant friends occurred after he won the Democratic presidential primary and began courting Hillary Clinton's former supporters. After Clinton conceded that Obama had won the Democratic presidential primary, she and Obama spoke before approximately 200 of her top donors and fund-raisers at the Mayflower Hotel in Washington in June 2008. This preceded a public appearance they would make the next day in Unity, New Hampshire, a location chosen for the significance of its name and its New Hampshire location. Clinton's supporters were still smarting, with feelings bruised and emotions high. They had backed Clinton passionately and felt she had not received a fair shake. They believed she faced sexism during the race, particularly during a debate or two, when male moderators seemed to barrel her unfairly with aggressive manners they had not shown her male counterparts. Obama reached out and befriended Clinton's backers in a masterful way—first affirming Clinton and the struggles of women and then highlighting common ground, creating a sense of "we-ness" and a sense of shared struggle.

To this end, Obama used two carefully chosen anecdotes to acknowledge the talents and significance of Hillary Clinton's presidential bid and to create common ground, laying the foundation for his new "friendships." He began with a story about how his grandmother reacted watching such a strong, talented woman run for the White House in such an extraordinary campaign. Obama's maternal grandmother, who helped raise him and had once worked on a bomber assembly line during the Second World War, had not been able to attend college. As she watched the Democratic primary race, Obama explained to the Mayflower audience, "she was rooting for her grandson," but she believed that Clinton had been treated harshly in the press. Obama recounted his grandmother's words: "[W]hen I see that instinct of hers to fight on behalf of those who need a champion, she reminds me a little of me." Obama provided the story as an example of "the ability of Hillary Clinton to inspire passion on behalf of those who have been left out in the past." His words helped to woo Clinton's supporters, as he acknowledged that for many women, including his own grandmother, Hillary Clinton was an inspiration.[26]

Obama also recounted a tale about his nine-year-old daughter Malia, who also understood the historic nature of the Democratic presidential primary race between an African American man and a woman. Malia had noted that if either ascended to the U.S. presidency, history would be made with the first woman or first African American president in U.S. history. Obama recounted how she acknowledged this, then said, "it's about time, and rolled over and went to bed." The story brought laughter in the room. Obama underscored, "Between my grandmother's generation and my young daughter, there's a testimony to the challenges that are hard won and hard fought. To the point that my 9-year-old takes for granted that of course we can have a woman president. Of course we can have an African American president. But that doesn't come just by the passage of time. It comes because people are consistently working and fighting."[27]

With his words, Obama created a sense of we-ness in the room. He created the space for fruitful relationships with Clinton's donors. Obama pressed his cause further as he revealed that he had instructed his top donors and supporters "to get out their checkbooks and start working to make sure Senator Clinton—the debt that's out there needs to be taken care of." He also helped create an atmosphere for strong relations through his humility. He noted, "I recognize that this room shared the same passion that a roomful of my supporters would show. I do not expect that passion to be transferred. Senator Clinton is unique, and your relationships with her are unique." At the same time, he encouraged this support, noting, "Senator Clinton and I at our core agree deeply that this country needs to change.... I'm going to need Hillary by my side campaigning during this election, and I'm going to need all of you."[28]

Obama proved equally effective in using common aspirations, goals, and values to help forge valuable alliances "across the aisle." As *The New Republic* noted on June 25, 2008, some of Obama's policy stances and goals—urging a quick resolution to the Iraq conflict and opposition to elements of the Patriot Act—helped him garner support among conservatives. In their article entitled "The Rise of the Obamacons," the *Economist* noted that "For many conservatives, Mr. Obama embodies qualities that their party has abandoned: pragmatism, competence, and respect

for the head rather than the heart. Mr. Obama's calm and collected response to the turmoil of Wall Street contrasted sharply
with Mr. McCain's grandstanding. . . ." Similarly, conservative
publications such as *Insight Magazine* (July 2007) and *The
Atlantic* (January 2008) expressed adoration for Obama's character. Obama's ability to convey a sense of common values and
goals paid off.

Obama's work with HIV/AIDS provides an example of how
he has steered attention successfully to shared goals and values
in order to build relations with unlikely allies. On the issue of
HIV/AIDS in the developing world, Obama has echoed the
view of Pastor Rick Warren, who asserts that where common
goals exist, you can and should work with people you don't agree
with on all issues. Obama has appealed to religious conservatives, noting that although they differ in their perspectives on
the issue of abortion, their shared commitment to eradicating
the scourge of HIV/AIDS among impoverished communities
around the world provides an opportunity to work together for
positive outcomes. Obama has persuaded many key leaders and
worked with them in addressing HIV/AIDS.

Obama has employed this approach also in the foreign policy
arena. During his historic June 4, 2009 speech to the Muslim
world, as he sought to forge common ground, Obama drew
attention to America's ties to the Muslim world. He said:

> I have come here to seek a new beginning between the
> United States and Muslims around the world; one based
> upon mutual interest and mutual respect; and one based
> upon the truth that America and Islam are not exclusive, and
> need not be in competition. Instead, they overlap, and share
> common principles—principles of justice and progress;
> tolerance and the dignity of all human beings.

… I am convinced that in order to move forward, we must say openly the things we hold in our hearts, and that too often are said only behind closed doors. There must be a sustained effort to listen to each other; to learn from each other; to respect one another; and to seek common ground. As the Holy Koran tells us, "Be conscious of God and speak always the truth." That is what I will try to do—to speak the truth as best I can, humbled by the task before us, and firm in my belief that the interests we share as human beings are far more powerful than the forces that drive us apart.

… Islam has always been a part of America's story. The first nation to recognize my country was Morocco. In signing the Treaty of Tripoli in 1796, our second President John Adams wrote, "The United States has in itself no character of enmity against the laws, religion or tranquility of Muslims." And since our founding, American Muslims have enriched the United States. They have fought in our wars, served in government, stood for civil rights, started businesses, taught at our universities, excelled in our sports arenas, won Nobel Prizes, built our tallest building, and lit the Olympic Torch. And when the first Muslim-American was recently elected to Congress, he took the oath to defend our Constitution using the same Holy Koran that one of our Founding Fathers—Thomas Jefferson—kept in his personal library.

… That does not mean we should ignore sources of tension. Indeed, it suggests the opposite: we must face these tensions squarely.

With these words, substance won the day. Obama successfully demonstrated the shared history, highlighting ties that many people had been unaware of, and he shifted the tone of the dialogue, laying a foundation for more extensive cooperation and "friendships" with many leaders and countries of the Middle East.

⇥ SPEAK IN UNDERSTANDABLE WAYS ⇤

Closely related to his practice of highlighting shared values, experiences, or histories is Obama's practice of speaking to potential friends in language that resonates with them. This practice enhances his ability to connect with listeners. In *Say It Like Obama and Win!*, I explore Obama's key techniques in detail. Through countless examples, Obama draws on meaningful language that helps strengthen his foundation for making friends in unusual places successfully.

For instance, as Obama speaks to Christian groups, he draws on the religious language of his faith. Consider this example, when Obama underscores his belief he can work on issues such as HIV/AIDS with various Christian groups that are opposed to his views on abortion. He has said: "While we will never see eye-to-eye on all issues, surely we can come together with one voice to honor the entirety of Christ's teachings by working to eradicate the scourge of AIDS, poverty, and other challenges we all can agree must be met."[29] In his explicit reference to Christ, Christ's teachings, and the Christian call to help address poverty and disease, Obama spoke a language that cut straight to the heart of his Christian listeners. While some listeners still remained opposed to cooperating with him, Obama swayed some conservative Christians. He has demonstrated remarkable skill in using this same technique in a wide range of settings, from comments before women's groups, to addresses before veterans.

⇥ KEEP AN EYE TO THE FUTURE ⇤

Another principle Obama embraces as he courts friends in unusual places is "keep an eye to the future."

"Keep an eye to the future." This principle has guided Obama as he has forged friends in unusual places. Obama alluded to this philosophy when he spoke of conservative Harvard Law School students. "These are the people who will be running the country in some form or other when they graduate. If I'm talking to a white conservative who wants to dismantle the welfare state, he has the respect to listen to me and I to him."[30]

As Gerald Kellman, who hired Obama to serve as a community organizer in the mid-1980s, explained, "[I]t was strategic that he would not have fallouts with people he disagreed with because he realized that he had to work with them not just on one particular issue, but on other issues down the road."[31] Consistent with this, Obama adopts a nonconfrontational style when at all possible, knowing he may need to work in other situations with the very people who might oppose his immediate goals. Obama does not fear confrontation or assertive actions, but tries to never burn a bridge.

At Harvard Law School, this translated into Obama's reluctance to partake in extreme politics—supporting staunch conservatives, or agitating too assertively on race-related issues such as the call for more diverse faculty. Obama tried to stay above the fray as much as possible, becoming known as a unifier and a "healer" of divisions at Harvard Law School and beyond.

⇥ SHOW RESPECT FOR YOUR POTENTIAL FRIENDS ⇤

When cultivating relations with potential friends in unusual places, Obama consciously shows respect to others, even those with whom he disagrees on major issues. How you make potential friends feel, he understands, is key to gaining support from them.

Few things can get in the way of a productive relationship as much as disrespect.
When potential friends feel disrespected,
walls go up and heels dig in.

In Obama's view, showing respect to
those with whom you do not fully see eye-

> Obama understands that how
> you make potential friends feel
> is a key to gaining support from
> them. Few things can get in the
> way of a productive relation-
> ship as much as disrespect.

to-eye is not tantamount to abandoning deeply held principles,
values, or beliefs. Respectfulness and acceptance are two different
things. Obama acknowledges differences of view and holds firm
to his principles, but simultaneously shows willingness to cooper-
ate with others in areas of commonality. His choice to show
respect to those with whom he does not fully agree underlies his
ability to gain their cooperation and work with them successfully.
Where grievances already exist, showing respect functions like
placing a salve on a smarting wound, and can begin a process that
ultimately leads to alliances and fruitful partnerships.

An examination of Obama's career provides many examples of
how his choice to show respect to others helped him to win friends
and wield influence. Reverend Alvin Love, pastor of the Lilydale
First Baptist Church, recalled how, as a community organizer in the
mid-1980s, Obama first showed up looking very inexperienced, but
also showed respect by coming with open ears. Obama "asked what
I wanted to see get done and what was important in this
neighborhood,"[32] Love explained. "He was interested in finding out
what I thought could be done in the community about issues like
public safety and employment, rather than giving me some long-
winded spiel." With a willingness to show respect for the hard work
community leaders were already doing, Obama succeeded in
recruiting some fifteen ministers, and mobilizing their efforts on
issues such as job trainings and drugs in the community.

During his second year in law school, Obama's classmates
began to urge him to run for president of *Harvard Law Review*.
Obama had shown a great deal of respect to those he did not

agree with. As a Harvard Law School colleague, Christine Lee, recalled, "He's willing to talk to [the conservatives] and he has a grasp of where they are coming from."[33] As Berenson summed up, "What really set him apart from the people who had roughly the same views he did is that he did not demonize the people on the other side of the dispute." For example, as Berenson recalled, "He was not the sort to accuse people of being racist for having different views of affirmative action." Obama gained the support of dedicated conservative *Review* editors, who believed that in spite of his liberal leanings, he would treat them fairly."[34]

After assuming the role of U.S. president, Obama continued to use respect as a means of influencing others and making friends in unusual places. For example, in his historic June 2009 speech to the Muslim world, Obama began with words that spoke volumes and set the tone:

> I am honored to be in the timeless city of Cairo, and to be hosted by two remarkable institutions. For over a thousand years, Al-Azhar has stood as a beacon of Islamic learning, and for over a century, Cairo University has been a source of Egypt's advancement. Together, you represent the harmony between tradition and progress. I am grateful for your hospitality, and the hospitality of the people of Egypt. I am also proud to carry with me the goodwill of the American people, and a greeting of peace from Muslim communities in my country: *assalaamu alaykum.*

Listeners in Egypt and throughout the Muslim world heard respect, a desire to reach beyond old barriers, and a willingness to extend a hand. Obama proceeded in that vein, stating

> As a student of history, I also know civilization's debt to Islam. It was Islam—at places like Al-Azhar University—

that carried the light of learning through so many centuries, paving the way for Europe's Renaissance and Enlightenment. It was innovation in Muslim communities that developed the order of algebra; our magnetic compass and tools of navigation; our mastery of pens and printing; our understanding of how disease spreads and how it can be healed. Islamic culture has given us majestic arches and soaring spires; timeless poetry and cherished music; elegant calligraphy and places of peaceful contemplation. And throughout history, Islam has demonstrated through words and deeds the possibilities of religious tolerance and racial equality.

He chose to convey respect—by paying tribute to the many contributions of the Muslim world, highlighting Muslim ties to America, and acknowledging (though not necessarily validating) grievances. Obama laid a foundation for greater progress on issues such as terrorism prevention and Middle East peace.

⇥ RECOGNIZE A PICTURE SAYS A THOUSAND WORDS ⇤

Obama embraces the view that the task of making friends is a dynamic process. That is, making one friend here can lead to another friend there, as a new friend wields influence to bring other supporters on board. With this notion in mind, Obama

> Obama embraces the view that the task of making friends is a dynamic process: that is, making one friend here can lead to another friend there.

recognizes that image matters. At opportune times, he takes steps to make the support of unexpected allies highly visible. Obama's actions reflect the idea that, "If you've got the support, flaunt it at the right times." When done well, this can create a snowball effect: as you make friends in unlikely places, other nontraditional allies can be inspired to give you a serious look and assess the viability of a fruitful partnership with you.

Obama has made his support from friends in unusual places highly visible at key times. Whether the friend in an unusual place was a highly influential Democrat who chose to endorse Obama over his Democratic primary rival Hillary Clinton, or a prominent leader from across the aisle, Obama has shown adeptness in show-casing the support at ideal times. Senator Edward Kennedy's pub-lic endorsement of Obama exemplifies the point. Kennedy, longtime friends with both Bill and Hillary Clinton, chose to endorse Obama over Hillary Clinton during the 2008 presidential campaign—something of great importance. As Democratic Rep-resentative Bill Delahunt explained, "The America of Jack and Bobby Kennedy touched all of us. Through all of these decades, the one who kept that flame alive was Ted Kennedy. So having him pass on the torch [to Obama] is of incredible significance. It's historic." Obama made certain to publicize the endorsement well.

Similarly, Obama's choice to appear so visibly with renowned economic advisers during his presidential campaign—including such respected personalities such as former Treasury Secretary Paul O'Neill, former Federal Reserve Board Chairman Paul Volcker, former Treasury Secretary Robert Rubin, and Warren Buffett—also exemplifies the value he places on showcasing his friends in unusual places and using their support to enhance his credibility and extend his network further.

Obama's skill in illuminating his alliances with respected conservative leaders also contributed to the strong Republican crossover support he ultimately received in his presidential cam-paign. Take the example of Obama's choice to attend the Sad-dleback Conference on HIV/AIDS in 2006, hosted by one of America's most prominent evangelical pastors and author of *The Purpose-Driven Life*, Rick Warren. Obama's visible friendship with Warren helped him solidify his image of a Democrat with Christian values. Warren insisted Obama was a "friend," and the images of Warren welcoming Obama warmly on stage for his talk served Obama well.

⟶ LEVERAGE FRIENDS, EXPAND YOUR NETWORK ⟵

In accordance with his view that making friends is a dynamic process and that "making a friend here can lead to making a friend there," Obama embraces the idea that a successful leader leverages his or her friends excellently to build an expanding network that can help achieve designated goals.

> Obama embraces the idea that a successful leader leverages his or her friends excellently to build an expanding network and achieve designated goals.

Obama has shown over time his adeptness in persuading his friends to open doors, extend their networks, and go to bat for him. In 2003, for example, when Emil Jones became president of the Illinois Senate, Obama persuaded Jones to help him gain greater opportunities to spearhead legislation, something that benefited Obama's career. When Obama got ready to run for the U.S. Senate, he also sought support from Senator Terry Link, who played poker and golf with Obama. Link served as the chairman of the Lake County Democratic organization, and Obama hoped he would persuade that group to back him. Link obliged. When Link informed the Lake County Democratic organization that he was instructing them to back Obama, Link recalled the group reacted something like, "You're nuts! We can't support him." Link expressed his confidence, assuring them, "When you know him like I know him, you'll all support him." Link recalls proudly that Obama's most significant primary percentage of support ultimately came from his county, where Obama won every precinct.[35]

Obama's ability to leverage his friends can also be seen in his success persuading highly influential or wealthy friends to support his bid for U.S. president. He rallied the support of Peggy Pritzker, chair of Classic Residence by Hyatt and Transunion, and a member of Chicago's Pritzker family, one of the wealthiest American families. She leveraged her contacts and raised major sums for him. Obama inspired media mogul Oprah Winfrey to cast aside her long-standing practice of nonendorsement of presidential candidates. Winfrey backed Obama for president on CNN's "Larry King Live" even before Obama announced a presidential run. She continued to publicly endorse him even though her TV ratings suffered for a while. In Winfrey's words, Obama was "worth going out on a limb for." Winfrey followed this up with a 2008 all-star fund-raising dinner for Obama, and multiple appearances at Obama campaign rallies, including a very important one preceding Super Tuesday. Obama's skill in persuading and inspiring his traditional and nontraditional friends to open their networks to him has provided him key support at critical junctures throughout his career.

⇥ HOLD NO GRUDGES ⇤

Obama has made certain not to hold grudges against people who at one point or another had failed to support him or chose to explicitly oppose him or his work.

Another principle of tremendous importance that has directly aided Obama's ever-expanding network of friends is his philosophy that can be summed up succinctly as "Hold no grudges."

Obama has made certain not to hold grudges against people who at one point or another had failed to support him or chose to explicitly oppose him or his work. His unwillingness to take things "personally" and his refusal to hold grudges have meant that Obama has made friends of many powerful personalities who at one point have been at odds with him. When such personalities have "come around," Obama has woven them into his network of friends and relied on them for fruitful work. There are many instances of the productiveness of his approach.

Consider the example of Warren Buffett. He provided a public endorsement of Obama very late in the Democratic presidential primary race, waiting until it appeared certain Hillary Clinton would lose the Democratic nomination. Buffett is a highly respected "look to" business personality, whom millions of people trust for opinions on topics from the economy and business trends, to the significance of political events. Employing his philosophy of "hold no grudges," Obama happily extended an open hand to Buffett and it paid off, providing Obama greater credibility within business circles.

Obama embraced this philosophy during his time in the Illinois Senate also. Many African American state legislators in Illinois, including Democratic senators Donne E. Trotter and Rickey R. Hendon, were known for giving Obama a hard time. They asserted Obama was not "truly black" given his multiracial background and the privileges he had enjoyed, such as a Harvard education. State Senator Kimberly Lightford recalled, "We could barely have meetings in [the black] caucus because Donne and Rickey would give him hell." Many observers attributed the conflict to envy of Obama's charisma, education, and high popularity. Obama, however, held no grudges and worked with these policy makers as he spearheaded landmark legislation in Illinois. He eventually won most of them over, and they provided useful support during his bid for a U.S. Senate seat.

Perhaps the best example of the fruit Obama's philosophy of "hold no grudges" can yield is manifested in Obama's relationship with former U.S. President Bill Clinton. Many observers of the

2008 presidential race readily recall that as Obama fought for the Democratic nomination for U.S. president, Bill Clinton issued biting words, calling Obama's candidacy a "fairy tale" and levying what some considered a racial insult as he likened Obama's viable candidacy to civil rights leader Jesse Jackson's multiple previous bids for the White House by—campaigns that were never viable. To many observers, the comparison was one based solely on race and had been intended to demean Obama. With this series of events, many other leaders would have considered the hatchet buried, with no possibility of anything other than further enmity between the parties. Not so with Obama. He did not hold a grudge and instead forged a productive relationship with Bill Clinton.

This is all the more impressive when considering the broader context of Obama's relationship with Bill Clinton. While conflict between the two leaders during the 2008 campaign received ample attention, less well known is the history between the leaders that extends back to when then-President Bill Clinton delivered a fatal blow to a younger, greener Obama, Obama was running for the first time for national office, seeking to unseat Congressional House member Bobby Rush. A nervous Rush asked Clinton for a public endorsement, something Clinton was known not to do in primary races. Yet, Clinton obliged, putting a final nail in the coffin for Obama's bid for a House seat. Rush ultimately carried the primary with over 61 percent of the vote, a stunning 2:1 loss for Obama.

For many leaders, this early history of conflict would have sown seeds of resentment that would have festered for years. Yet, sticking to his principle of not holding grudges, Obama reached out to Bill and Hillary Clinton after he won the Democratic nomination for U.S. president in 2008. He understood the significance an endorsement from both Hillary and Bill Clinton could have for his candidacy and for uniting the Democratic Party. Hillary Clinton came around more quickly than her husband. Bill Clinton took notably longer, almost an embarrassing length of time, before he finally endorsed Obama. Rather than cling to any sense of resentment, Obama kept the door open. The dividend paid well as the Democrats closed ranks and Obama won the U.S. presidency by the largest percentage of the popular vote since Eisenhower in 1952. Obama went on to cultivate a positive relationship with Bill Clinton. He was later able to rely on Bill Clinton to help win the freedom of two American journalists held captive in North Korea and to open the door for an easing of tensions that had been building over the prior months between the United States and North Korea, as a belligerent North Korea flouted international prohibitions and tested nuclear missiles. Obama continued to nurture his relationship with Bill Clinton, addressing the Clinton Global Initiative in September 2009. Moreover, Obama draws on the unique perspectives Clinton possesses. The two have met over lunch. As White House spokesman Robert Gibbs explained, the two have "a very strong relationship," and because very few people understand fully the demands and challenges of the U.S. presidency, "President Obama values the type of advice that President Clinton has."[36]

EMPLOYING THE LESSONS

Throughout his successful career, Barack Obama has demonstrated the value of making friends in unusual places. His ability to reach out and gain the support of unlikely allies has helped him to gain key support, broaden his bases of support, and forge multiple roads to success.

As you think about the practices and principles that allow Obama to make friends in unusual places, consider whether your own leadership might benefit from these practices and principles. Keep these questions in mind:

- Do I limit myself to friends in expected places?
- Am I aware of who holds power to help bring about the goals I seek? Have I paid adequate attention to a "power analysis"?

- What friends in unusual places could potentially help me to enhance my effectiveness as a leader or help ensure the success of my work?
- Do I "go" where the potential friends are?
- Do I have a "both–and" and "win-win" mind-set?
- What common ground can I highlight to help forge productive relations with friends in unusual places?
- Do I keep an "eye on the future" as I think about what friends to cultivate in unusual places?
- Do I show respect to potential friends in unusual places?
- Do I understand that "a picture says a thousand words" and make sure to leverage that principle excellently to make the support of "unexpected" friends visible when needed?
- Do I leverage effectively the network of my friends in unusual places?
- Do I hold a grudge? If so, what additional friends would I have if I did not? Would my leadership benefit from the support of those friends?
- How can I better leverage the allies I find outside of traditional places?

CHAPTER 5

BUILD AND LEAD
A WINNING TEAM

*"And to my campaign manager, David Plouffe… my chief strate-
gist, David Axelrod … to the best campaign team ever assembled in
the history of politics—you made this happen, and I am forever
grateful for what you've sacrificed to get it done."*

Barack Obama spoke these words triumphantly within the
first minutes of his victory speech on election night, November 4,
2008. He had just achieved the unthinkable—winning election
to the office of U.S. president only forty years after Martin Luther
King, Jr., had delivered his "I Have a Dream" speech, in a country
still beset at times by notable racial tensions. The event was hailed
a watershed moment in U.S. history. Yet, this success was only
one of many Obama has enjoyed as a result of his ability to build
and steer high-performing teams.

Obama's record of achievement is not "accidental." For Barack
Obama, there is no such thing as accidental organizational

For Barack Obama, there is no such thing as accidental organizational culture or accidental strong team performance.

culture or accidental strong team performance. His success in leading an organization as a community organizer, guiding the *Harvard Law Review*, running a record-breaking presidential campaign, and "hitting the ground running" as U.S. president has shown that time and again Obama knows how to form and lead winning teams.

In the case of his 2008 campaign, the excellence of his team manifested itself in multiple achievements—growing the U.S. electorate, remaking the American political map, leveraging leading-edge technology, and managing a nationwide decentralized organization with millions of supporters, among others. Obama displayed exceptional skill in aligning the work of his team and organization with his vision and goals. Observers praised the execution of his campaign, which delivered Obama's message with great precision, capitalized on new opportunities, and managed crises excellently. Very notably also, his team displayed very little internal conflict. The press has widely noted that Obama's campaign was uniquely unified, with few reports of infighting or backbiting, few leaks to the press, no major staff overhauls, no major change in themes or broad strategies, and no notable campaign-related scandals.[1]

Obama's success in forming winning teams over the course of his career is the product of much more than good fortune. It has flowed from the highly effective leadership practices and principles that he employs. How has Obama managed to build such strong teams during multiple periods of his career? What leadership practices and principles have enabled him to create winning teams? Let's explore the practices and principles that have helped bring success.

⇥ PAY ATTENTION TO STYLE AND TEAM CULTURE ⇤

As we discussed earlier, a team is more than a group of people; a team is distinguished by the focus of its members on a shared goal. Obama's success demonstrates that a leader seeking to create teams of the highest caliber should not only take steps to articulate clear goals, but should also build, spread, and sustain a strong team culture that supports the work of the team. By *culture* I mean the shared values, beliefs, attitudes, ethics, philosophies, behavior patterns, and atmosphere that characterize an organization, group, or team. For Obama, there has been no such thing as "accidental culture." He deliberately makes his team culture an extension and reflection of his core beliefs, with an expectation that those working directly with him will be on board with those beliefs, ethics, and attitudes.

> Obama's success demonstrates that a leader seeking to create teams of the highest caliber should not only take steps to articulate clear goals, but should also build, spread, and sustain a strong team culture that supports the work of the team.

This is particularly important to Obama because he prides himself on acting with "principled leadership." He is very *values-driven*. When first contemplating deeply a run for the U.S. presidency, Obama stated his aim: "We could try some things in a different way and build an organization that reflected my personality and what I thought the country was looking for."[2] While he is open to differing ideas and working with people from vastly varied backgrounds, when creating an optimal team he seeks to work with others who are willing to uphold his core values, as well as to ensure the team reflects his worldview, style, and aims.

One of his core values is that he seeks to pursue *win-win solutions* when at all possible. He puts a high premium on the unity and consensus building that can lead to win-win situations. This is a trait that has characterized his leadership from the earliest days. A community leader who worked with Obama in Chicago in the mid-1980s, Reverend Alvin Love reflected on this trait, noting, "Everything I see reflects that community organizing experience. I see the consensus-building, his connection to people and listening to their needs and trying to find common ground. I think at his heart Barack is a community organizer. I think what he's doing now [seeking national office] is that. It's just a larger community to be organized."[3]

Obama is also very *no-nonsense* in his approach. This is shorthand for "reasonable, deliberate, methodical, focused, and cool." He does not accept or promote game-playing. He chooses to "be straight" and above the fray. As such, he does not court "screamers" to be a part of his team, because he places too much value on harmony and nonconfrontation as key elements of his teams and the associated culture. In Obama's words, "...I have a low tolerance of nonsense and turf battles and game-playing, and I send that message very clearly."[4] He frowns on divisiveness, saying, "We can have a strong disagreement, passionate disagreements about issues without—without resorting to name-calling. We can maintain civility."[5]

Obama *expects excellence* of himself and others. Complacency has no place in his work. We see signs of this point of view throughout his career. As a law school professor, for example, he explained to students he expected rigorous thinking and he set a high bar. Complacency has no part of his teams' cultures.

Obama promotes *high levels of effectiveness and efficiency* in his work, with particular emphasis on meeting the needs of citizens or other "customers." Chief Operating Officer Betsy Myers noted that "He said he wanted to run our campaign like a business." And this means that the customer would be treated excellently.[6]

Other values Obama prizes are *innovation* and *rigorous thinking*. He enjoys being on the leading edge. He likes to question assumptions, asking the question, "Why not?" He likes to push the envelope with novel but well-reasoned ideas—always assessing creative or unorthodox solutions for their viability, using history to understand challenges and opportunities in implementing new ideas. This trait is discernible throughout his career. Even while he served as a law professor at the University of Chicago, one need only skim his final examinations to see how Obama encouraged rigorous thinking among his students, prodding them to assess and challenge traditional assumptions and to think outside of the box. This became a hallmark of his leadership style. Certainly, his commitment to innovation made a significant mark on the progress and success of his 2008 presidential campaign.

In his decision making, Obama is *fact-driven*. He does not allow emotions to override his choices. Susan Rice, his choice for U.S. Ambassador to the United Nations, noted this as she explained why Obama had taken more time than other leaders to state a position about Russia's decision to move troops into Georgia in 2008. In Rice's words, "He didn't look at the initial reports and view them through the prism of preconceived notions about Russia or Georgia."[7] Obama evaluates decisions methodically. David Axelrod concurs with this view of Obama, indicating, "He's very methodical in how he evaluates decisions. He asks a series of questions. He'll engage you in dialogue on the options. And then he'll make a decision. And he doesn't look back at that decision."[8]

Obama is also known for his *intense planning*. He has long been known for running meetings with great efficiency, using well-developed agendas and keeping discussions on point.

Colleagues recall that during his community organizing work in Chicago, Obama prepared meticulously for meetings between residents of the Altgeld Gardens public housing project and authorities from whom they hoped to gain resources. Obama outlined talking points, highlighted ideas or remarks that could be useful, and coached them. In the aftermath of meetings, he debriefed residents, assessing successes and shortcomings of their meetings—knowledge he could put to use subsequently.

Finally, Obama remains dedicated to focusing on setting a strong and clear vision for his teams and organizations. He develops a solid "big picture" and designates goals, and he fleshes out viable steps to get to his goals. Preferring to stay focused on big-picture issues, Obama prefers to work with team members who can work with *high levels of autonomy*. He once told the host of Meet the Press, Tim Russert, "I'm not an operating officer." He explained further what this meant when he thought about the U.S. presidency. He said, "[B]eing president is not making sure that schedules are being run properly or that paperwork is being shuffled effectively. It involves having a vision for where the country needs to go."[9] Obama is known for selecting strong leaders and empowering them, so that he preserves his ability to focus on setting strong vision and ensuring his team overall is making ardent strides toward designated goals.

Perhaps more than many leaders, Obama is acutely aware of his values, worldview, leadership style, and aims. He pays attention to these factors as he chooses team members. He knows that building an exceptional team reflects more than determining what skill mix the team needs and identifying talented personnel who possess those skills. For success, he chooses team members who affirm his values, worldview, and aims and who can work in a manner that fits with his own leadership style.

⇥ IDENTIFY KEY PRIORITIES ⇤

Obama demonstrates that another key step in forming a winning team is to identify the key priorities of your team or organization early on. What goals must be met in order to achieve your mission or vision? Obama was clear in his aim in 2007–2008: he sought to win the U.S. presidential election through a successful grassroots campaign for change. Obama had a strong sense of direction from the start, which aided him in developing a fundamental sense of key issues and priorities he'd need to address through the leadership team he assembled.

> Obama had a strong sense of direction from the start, which aided him in developing a fundamental sense of key issues and priorities he'd need to address through the leadership team he assembled.

As Valerie Jarrett remembers, Obama said that "if he were to do this, he wanted to make sure that it was a different kind of campaign and consistent with his philosophy of ground up rather than top down."

"As somebody who had been a community organizer," Obama explained, "I was convinced that if you invited people to get engaged, if you weren't trying to campaign like you were selling soap but instead said, 'This is your campaign, you own it, and you can run with it,' that people would respond and we could build a new electoral map."[10] With this vision, Obama understood he would need among his top advisers a highly capable head of fund-raising, skilled campaign manager, outstanding campaign strategist and marketer, and technology expert. He recruited accordingly.

Once he assumed the presidency, Obama showed equal skill in highlighting his high-level priorities and determining key responsibilities to be addressed. He pinpointed as priorities matters such as economic recovery, financial stabilization, health care, technology, and environmental affairs. When an adequate official position did not exist to address a particular matter, Obama created one. Thus, we saw Obama create the position of chief technology officer, to which he named Aneesh Chopra. Similarly, Obama adjusted positions to reflect new priorities, such as when he elevated to the cabinet level the position of U.S. Ambassador to the United Nations, reflecting his desire to enter, as he referred to it in his U.N. address on September 23, 2009, "a new era of engagement" in the world. With a clear sense of his priorities, Obama moved forward to build a winning team.

⇥ DETERMINE THE IDEAL SKILLS MIX ⇤

Another technique that has enabled Obama to form outstanding teams is his practice of considering what ideal skills mix his teams need to forge a path to success. Among the relevant elements are professional experience, professional achievement, education, and life experiences. Obama also considers, as was the case with his pick of Senator Joe Biden for vice president, in which ways a particular leader might supplement his own skills and experience. Biden's strength and experience in foreign policy helped to address Obama's relative inexperience in foreign affairs.

As we examine the teams Obama has formed at various points in his career, we can see how he tapped leaders who, together, brought a winning combination of skills, experiences, and traits.

As we examine the teams Obama has formed at various points in his career, we can see how he tapped leaders who, together, brought a winning combination of skills, experiences, and traits. At a meeting in late 2006 that Obama convened to discuss his potential presidential run, for example, his choice of leaders in attendance reflected his thinking about the ideal team skills mix. Those in attendance included skilled strategists David Axelrod and David Plouffe; Robert Gibbs (who would handle communications); Pete Rouse, Tom Daschle's former chief of staff and a Capitol Hill insider; Marty Nesbitt; Steve Hildebrand (Plouffe's deputy); and Valerie Jarrett, a close Obama family friend who had worked for Chicago Mayor Richard M. Daley. Many of these dynamic personalities were people whom Obama had worked with before—he knew and trusted them. They were "seasoned veterans" and brought a great deal to the table. David Axelrod and Valerie Jarrett had provided advice to Obama in prior campaigns. Plouffe, Axelrod's business partner, had ample experience, including work with former House Democratic leader Dick Gephardt. Steve Hildebrand had worked with former Senate majority leader Tom Daschle. Pete Rouse, Daschle's former chief of staff, had served as chief of staff in Obama's Senate office. Robert Gibbs, who had served for a time with John Kerry, had also worked with Obama. In bringing together this mix of skills and experience, Obama set himself off in a good direction.

⇒ STAFF FOR EXCELLENCE: TARGET THE BEST, ⇐ VALUE EXPERIENCE

An old adage says, "You're only as strong as your weakest link." This adage reflects Obama's thinking. He is known for surrounding himself with leaders of the highest caliber. Obama explained his philosophy of picking the best people: "…I've got a good nose for talent," he said. "So I hire really good people. And I've got a pretty healthy ego, so I'm not scared of hiring the smartest people, even when they're smarter than me. … If you've got really smart people who are all focused on the same mission, then usually you can get some things done."[11]

David Axelrod has observed the same, noting that when it came time for Obama to pick a vice presidential running mate, "…there were those who said, 'Well, you don't want Joe Biden because Joe has been around a long time. He's got a lot of opinions. He's a strong personality.'" And Obama said, "'No, that's exactly what I want.' He's completely comfortable with very bright people. He doesn't mind being challenged. He enjoys it."[12]

It is no great surprise, then, to see Obama pinpoint people he considers the best in their fields and attempt to court them to work alongside him. He has done this consistently throughout his career. During his first electoral campaign for a seat in the Illinois State Senate, for example, Obama specifically inquired about who was the best civil rights attorney to lead a challenge of signatures on the nominating petitions of his Democratic political opponents. The excellence of the attorney helped bring the desired results, and Obama disqualified all of his Democratic rivals. Obama carried through to his presidential campaign this habit of working with the very best in a field, as exemplified when he recruited cofounder of Facebook Chris Hughes and partnered with Apple to secure an iPod campaign tool for his supporters. Since he assumed the role of U.S. president, Obama has continued to adhere to this principle. We note the high-caliber leaders in his administration; included in their ranks are Nobel Prize winners, Rhodes Scholars, Ivy League graduates, and some of the most successful and innovative leaders in policy and business.

> It is no great surprise to see Obama pinpoint people he considers the best in their fields and attempt to court them to work alongside him.

⇥ PROMOTE SMOOTHER SAILING ⇤
WITH CULTURE AND VALUES

While Obama seeks to work and partner with people who represent "the best" and who have proven records of experience and success, he pays close attention to each potential team member's commitment to his values and team culture. He seeks to find all in one. "It was very important to have a consistent team," Obama explains,

While Obama seeks to work and partner with people who represent "the best" and have proven records of experience and success, he pays close attention to each potential team member's commitment to his values and team culture.

"a circle of people who were collaborative and non-defensive." When hiring someone, Obama is clear from the start about the importance of culture and shared values.[13] For him, the values team culture "fit" is a potent part of any calculation when choosing team members.

An examination of some of Obama's closest advisers confirms the importance Obama places on values and team culture elements. As *Newsweek* termed it, "Axelrod was a seer and a good listener, though not much for glad-handing and schmoozing."[14] This fits well with Obama's style and the culture he seeks to build in his teams. Obama's presidential campaign manager David Plouffe is considered "calm and a little nerdy himself. … Plouffe reflected the cool self-discipline of the candidate, and the two of them [Obama and Plouffe] set the ethos of the campaign, which staffers dubbed "No-Drama Obama."[15] When discussing Barack Obama, Chris Hughes commented, "I connected to Barack as an individual first. It just so happened that he was in politics."[16] For both Obama and Hughes, that strong values–culture connection made a difference.

Notably, Obama leaves little to chance. During the vetting process, he makes sure to communicate clearly to potential team

> Obama makes sure to communicate clearly to potential team members his expectations and to weed out from his team any member who does not wish to sign on to the core values and modus operandi he sets forth.

members his expectations and to weed out from his team any member who does not wish to sign on to the core values and *modus operandi* he sets forth. Obama often meets one-on-one with potential team members to inform them of his team's operating values and culture, including the "no drama" mantra, and his insistence on excellence, nonconfrontation, and collaboration. Susan Rice, a foreign policy adviser to Obama during his presidential campaign who now serves as U.S. Ambassador to the United Nations, mentioned that when Obama hired her, he made it clear that he expected her to adhere to his "no drama" culture. She explained, "That means that people check their personal histories and their personal baggage at the door. There's no tolerance for people biting at each other, trying to tear each other down."[17] The norm is that no one violates this, as there is low tolerance for deviating greatly from the articulated culture.

Similarly, when Obama conferred with Betsy Myers in January 2007 before she took the position of chief operating officer of his presidential campaign, he put forth three principles for her: "Run the campaign with respect; build it from the bottom up; and finally, no drama."[18]

Obama's insistence that team members embrace the team's core values and culture has borne good fruit. As *Time* magazine observed, during the 2008 presidential campaign, "The team that Obama put together was a mix of people who, for the most part, had never worked together before but behaved as if they had." They acted as if they had because the vetting process worked excellently. Obama was clear about his team culture, communicated expectations excellently, and weeded out and chose personnel appropriately. In doing so, he ensured a high level of loyalty to the culture from the beginning, which helped to provide smoother sailing.

According to Michael Froman, a friend of Obama's who met him during his Harvard Law School days, Obama "laid out his theory that, if he ran, he wanted to have a campaign with a relatively tight-knit group of people." He recalled Obama stressed that "No matter how chaotic the campaign got that there'd be—he used the words–'an island of tranquility.'"[19] With his leadership practices, he succeeded in creating this. He has also taken steps to sustain it, as needed. For instance, when one of Obama's workers (a "low-level staffer") caused a stir during the presidential campaign by referring to Senator Hillary Clinton by an inappropriate name, Obama chastised his staff member: "I don't want you guys freelancing and, quote, *protecting me* from what you're doing," he clarified. "I'm saying this loud and clear—no winks, no nods here." He stood by his insistence that his team run a campaign largely free of mudslinging. He stated, "I'm looking at every one of you. If you think you're close to the line, the answer isn't to protect me—the answer is to *ask* me."[20]

Obama's ability to ensure his team members embrace his core values and team culture has repeatedly helped him create highly unified, cohesive teams.

⇥ WHEN ALL ELSE IS EQUAL, SEND A MESSAGE ⇤

Another practice that has helped Obama build winning teams is that, when all else is equal, he chooses team members who—by nature of their backgrounds or experiences—send a message to others the team seeks to work with or court. Consider, for instance, when Obama was considering who to tap to help spearhead his new media work within the Obama campaign. The choice of Chris Hughes, the 24-year-old cofounder of

Facebook, met the key criteria: Chris possessed the right skills mix, represented the best of his field, and would embrace the campaign's core values, culture, work style, and vision. When choosing between a candidate such as Chris Hughes and some other candidate who also meets the key criteria, Obama has shown great skill in discerning when a potential pick will help "send a message" to others. In the case of Hughes, Obama was able to signal as he hired Hughes that the best of the young generation of voters was willing to partner with him. It functioned nearly as an endorsement. He also signaled that he was in touch with the new cyber world that characterizes the world of young people, and that his campaign would reflect leading-edge technological advances. The benefits of these signals were many. For instance, they helped garner the attention of young people; they attracted mainstream publicity; and they helped reinforce the theme of change that Obama sought to advance.

Obama has continued this practice since assuming the position of U.S. president. When selecting a U.S. ambassador to the United Nations, for instance, Obama chose Susan Rice, a woman who also met all his key criteria. Notably, choosing her sent additional important messages to other leaders around the world. Rice, a Rhodes Scholar who achieved the highest accolades in the academic world from Stanford and Oxford, and who learned outstanding business skills at McKinsey & Company, represents an empowered woman, and Obama seeks to support the empowerment of women as he advances women's rights around the world. Rice is also a young mother who sometimes took her baby with her to the State Department (and breast-fed him there) while she served as assistant secretary of state for African affairs, giving an interview in which she stated bluntly she did not care what anyone else had to say about this. In this alternate way, she also represents an empowered woman of the sort Obama seeks to support in his efforts around the world.

Imagine, in light of this background, the powerful message Obama has already sent even before a meeting is held with the leaders of countries known for suppressing women's rights. Additionally, Rice's schooling amid so many international students at Oxford gave her a deep understanding of other cultures and other perspectives from around the world. In selecting her as U.S. ambassador to the UN, Obama also signaled to the world a desire to engage on the world stage. Rice's selection, in and of itself, has sent messages and in some ways advanced Obama's agenda well before Obama or Rice convened any meetings with world leaders.

We see this pattern in many of Obama's other appointments, including the selection of Sonia Sotomayor, the first Hispanic member of the Supreme Court, whose pedigree is sterling and whose appointment sent a message of inclusiveness to minority populations. There is also Hilda Solis, the daughter of Hispanic immigrants, who was appointed to serve as labor secretary; her choice signaled Obama's commitment to issues surrounding immigration. Obama's choice of Nobel Prize winner Steven Chu to serve as secretary of the Department of Energy signaled his commitment to innovation and rigorous approaches to pressing environmental issues.

⇥ BENEFIT FROM MIGHTY BRAINSTORMING ⇤ (INNOVATION AND YOUR "TEAM OF RIVALS")

Another reason why Obama's teams prove successful is because they embrace innovation, drawing on novel ideas to address effectively long-standing issues or complex problems. The high levels of innovation that often characterize Obama's teams flow from multiple sources. For one, Obama enjoys

> Obama's teams prove successful because they embrace innovation, drawing on novel ideas to address effectively long-standing issues or complex problems.

including on his teams people with varied life experiences and perspectives, prompting some observers to say he likes to convene a "team of rivals." Additionally, Obama creates environments that encourage participation, rigorous thinking, and sharing of varied ideas. Obama thrives on hearing different perspectives and on testing assumptions, and he benefits from the "mighty brainstorming" he leads among a highly talented and accomplished set of team members. With these practices, innovation becomes a central pillar of his teams.

> Obama thrives on hearing different perspectives and testing assumptions, and he benefits from the "mighty brainstorming" he leads among a highly talented and accomplished set of team members.

However, there is a caveat here. Suggestions that Obama seeks to build a team of rivals, in which he brings highly accomplished leaders together who harbor widely divergent views, are somewhat overstated. As we have seen, Obama insists his team members embrace the core values and team culture he holds dear. Team members share a commitment to his core values and vision. Within that context, however, Obama has benefited from a relatively high diversity of team member opinions and experiences: he benefits from drawing on the diversity of viewpoints among highly talented individuals who are focused on the same goals and who share a passionate commitment to the team and overall mission.

⇥ EMPOWER THE LEADS, MAKE ROLES ⇤ AND RESPONSIBILITIES CLEAR

Obama has also experienced success in building winning teams because he has made certain to structure his teams in ways that fit well with his own leadership style. Obama likes to focus on the "big picture." He enjoys gaining superior knowledge of the issues

> Obama has also experienced success in building winning teams because he has made certain to structure his teams in ways that fit well with his own leadership style.

at hand. He then sets a vision for addressing the issues and identifies steps to progress toward goals. As he keeps an eye on overall
progress toward goals, Obama strives to remain attentive to the big
picture and does not delegate this. He seeks, therefore, to work
with highly capable leaders whom he can empower and to whom
he can give a great deal of autonomy to get their jobs done.

Certainly, there is no one-size-fits-all way in which roles and
responsibilities should be structured in a team or organization.
The key to Obama's success is not that he has developed the
ideal leadership structure for all leaders in all circumstances, but
that he has structured roles and responsibilities to fit with his
leadership style, the culture of his teams, and the mission at
hand. For him, decentralization of roles and responsibilities
serves these purposes well.

During his 2008 presidential campaign, it became common
to hear key figures in his staff comment, as Chris Hughes did,
that he did not meet with Obama on a day-to-day basis. Hughes
revealed that after the campaign gained great momentum, he
did not confer often with Obama because "He knew who we
were and that what we were doing was working."[21]

The high decentralization and autonomy of his leaders work
for Obama because he defines roles and responsibilities clearly
and builds accountability into his organizations. There is clarity
around who "owns" a particular task and what the metrics for
success are. During the campaign, if marketing seemed to falter,
for instance, the structures of responsibilities indicated clearly
who must answer for the state of affairs. As leaders seek to build
high-performing teams, they can benefit greatly from the simple
principles of defining roles and responsibilities clearly and
ensuring leaders are held accountable for their performances.
Obama's success shows how essential these practices can be in
helping to yield a highly disciplined, effective team.

EMPLOYING THE LESSONS

Barack Obama's success as a leader is in part attributable to the outstanding work of the winning teams he has led. Obama has mastered the art of building winning teams. In doing so, he employs many best practices—knowing his priorities, pinpointing key responsibilities, identifying the best skills mix for tasks at hand, valuing relevant experience, and empowering his leads, among others—which together enable him to consistently form teams that produce excellent results.

As you think about the practices and principles that allow Barack Obama to build winning teams, consider whether your own leadership might benefit from these practices and principles. Keep these questions in mind:

- Do I know my priorities?
- Am I aware of my leadership style? Am I mindful of the culture I hope to create?
- Have I considered adequately how my leadership style and the key elements of the team culture I hope to create should influence the type of team members I target?
- What are key responsibilities for the work I seek to achieve? Have I identified the key skills mix required for a team's success? Have I chosen team members who together bring the ideal mix of skills?
- Have I targeted the best team members? Do they have ideal experience?
- Have I ensured I will be exposed to varied vantage points that will enable me to weigh an adequate range of perspectives? With the team members I have chosen, will I benefit from a "mighty brainstorm"?
- Have I empowered key leaders? Are their roles and responsibilities clear?
- Do I send a good message to others through my choice of team members?

CHAPTER 6

MOVE BEYOND "HIGH PERFORMANCE" TO "ALL HANDS"

"All hands on deck!"

We have all heard the familiar cry—a call summoning every-one together to help in an urgent situation, when important work must be done within a very short time frame. For many of us, we hear the words and conjure in our minds crew members clad in uniforms, moving as quickly as they can onto a ship's deck. Hearing urgency in the tone, each crew member knows every moment counts, as does every effort. An energized, focused team, they await attentively the command of their leader. They stand poised, their sleeves rolled up, ready to work diligently toward a common goal. In this scenario, we might also imagine that even the smallest of the lot—a tiny crew member at the tail end of the line—bounces with anticipation knowing that whatever muscle he can give might be that tiny extra effort the crew needs to get the job done. Sure it might be true, he knows, that he might not be able to do *as much* as the others. But he also realizes that even his bit can make the difference between whether the team succeeds or does not.

It's this particular vision of teamwork that underlies the notion that Barack Obama knows how to create not just a "high-performing" team culture, but also what I refer to as an "all-hands" team culture—a culture characterized by a high degree of passion, energy, unity, dedication, and intense willingness among team members to leverage their skills and talents in pursuit of a designated goal.

As we saw earlier, for Barack Obama there is no such thing as "accidental" organizational culture. He understands the key importance of organizational culture and team culture in fostering environments that support the attainment of designated goals. Obama methodically introduces key elements into the culture of his teams, enabling his teams to focus squarely on the end goals while also reflecting his values. In Chapter 5, "Build and Lead a Winning Team," we explored key practices and principles that have allowed Obama to build cultures that support high-performing teams. In this chapter, we focus on a facet of organizational culture associated in particular with Obama's 2008 presidential campaign—the all-hands element of his team culture.

Obama believes passionately in the abilities of the ordinary person and has, through his leadership, sought to inspire ordinary citizens to take action on important issues, to "take ownership" of their efforts, and to empower them to bring change. Obama embraced this approach as far back as the mid-1980s, when he worked as a community organizer in Chicago. He demonstrated firm commitment to coaching residents of the Altgeld Gardens public housing project to go before public officials in organized efforts to secure greater resources and programs to meet their needs.[1] As Loretta Augustine-Herron, who served on his Developing Communities Project board in Chicago, recalled, "Obama would say: 'You've got to do it right... Be open with the issues. Include the community instead of going behind the community's back'—and he would include people we didn't like sometimes. You've got to bring people together. If you exclude people, you're only weakening yourself. If you meet behind doors and make decisions for them, they'll never take ownership of the issue."[2]

Similarly, in his 2008 presidential campaign, Obama stressed how he wished to create a widespread grassroots movement that would inspire a large number of energized people to come forward to help create change. He wanted to create a highly participatory campaign, one decentralized enough to allow enthusiastic participants to take ownership of key work locally as they strove toward common goals. The all-hands culture he built, spread, and sustained within the Obama campaign became one of its most distinguishing features and helped pave a path to successive victories.

> Obama has shown he knows how to build winning team and organizational cultures. The all-hands culture he built, spread, and sustained within the Obama campaign became one of its most distinguishing features.

What factors distinguish an all-hands culture? Why did an all-hands culture help yield success for Obama during his presidential bid? What leadership practices and principles allowed him to build, spread, and sustain that culture so effectively? What might we learn? Let's consider these questions below.

⇥ UNDERSTAND KEY ELEMENTS OF ⇤ AN ALL-HANDS CULTURE

We explored in Chapter 5, "Build and Lead a Winning Team," Obama's skill in building a winning team culture. With regard in particular to the Obama campaign, we can also see how Obama cultivated an all-hands culture that served his purposes excellently. Several elements distinguish an all-hands culture. For instance, a high level of passion and commitment among team members helps distinguish all-hands cultures. Passion and energy were indeed defining characteristics of Obama's campaign supporters. After winning the Democratic nomination, Obama commented on this striking aspect of his campaign and its supporters. When Steve Kroft asked him if he had truly thought the historic victory would happen, Obama replied, "...I never doubted that it could happen. I never doubted that if we were able to mobilize the energy that you saw in that stadium."

> A high level of passion and commitment among team members helps distinguish all-hands cultures.

Another striking aspect of all-hands culture is the deliberate steps leaders take to make all participants feel welcomed in the tasks at hand. In doing so, all-hands cultures give people a sense that their perspectives and efforts are valued. Obama does this particularly well. As Susan Rice, a foreign policy adviser to Obama who now serves as U.S. ambassador to the United Nations, explained, Obama "makes everybody feel as though their viewpoint has been heard and appreciated. So even if you happen to be on the losing end of a decision, you feel like your perspectives have been valued, which makes it much more easy for you to be enthusiastic in supporting the decision he ultimately makes."[3] Unique or dissenting opinions are welcomed and are not viewed negatively. As we have learned, Obama welcomes dissenting opinions and seeks to learn from new or differing ideas. He encourages people to speak up in a positive environment. An all-hands culture reflects these preferences well.

An all-hands culture also encourages and helps participants to leverage their unique talents and traits in pursuit of the mission or designated goals. Participants and team members come to believe firmly their contributions, both large and small, can make a meaningful difference. Notably, all-hands cultures remain free of "up-or-out" mentalities. Rather, organizers encourage team members and participants to keep strengthening their skills and talents, and provide the means to do so when possible. The overall message of an all-hands culture is, "Everyone together, eyes on the goals, leverage your talents in the ways you are able."

An all-hands culture also encourages and helps participants to leverage their unique talents and traits in pursuit of the mission or designated goals.

While the all-hands elements of team culture were particularly evident in Obama's presidential campaign, he has long believed that the principles associated with an all-hands culture can unleash unlimited potential in efforts to mobilize people to achieve notable goals. Obama has sought to mobilize people to create change since his days working with the student anti-apartheid movement in college and since his days as a community organizer in Chicago. He once remarked:

> We must find ways to channel all this energy into community building. … Now an agenda for getting our fair share is vital. But to work, it can't see voters or communities as consumers, as mere recipients or beneficiaries of this change. It's time for politicians and other leaders to take the next step and to see voters, residents, or citizens as producers of this change. … Our goal must be to help people get a sense of building something larger.[4]

For onlookers impressed with the high level of unity, enthusiasm, loyalty, and cohesion among participants in the Obama campaign, we point out that all-hands culture can become self-reinforcing. By encouraging participation, all-hands cultures nurture enthusiasm and build loyalty; with loyalty and enthusiasm come greater participation and commitment. Additionally, given the way in which all-hands cultures encourage participants to develop their skills and provide the means to do so when possible through training or other avenues, all-hands cultures also increase the numbers of skilled participants who can engage effectively and who, equally importantly, can recruit and teach others to participate in meaningful ways also.

The presence of an all-hands culture within the Obama campaign helped to produce a highly energized campaign with passionate supporters, who took ownership of key work, gained skills to keep doing their work better, and enthusiastically recruited others to contribute in equally meaningful ways. The exponential growth of support for Obama was in many respects due to the impact of the effective ways in which this all-hands culture was cultivated and harnessed.

> The presence of an all-hands culture within the Obama campaign helped to produce a highly energized campaign with passionate supporters, who took ownership of key work, gained skills to keep doing their work better, and enthusiastically recruited others to contribute in equally meaningful ways.

Let's look at some of the specific practices that helped Obama create and sustain an all-hands culture.

⇥ PROMOTE CULTURE THROUGH CUSTOMS ⇤ AND PRACTICES, BIG AND SMALL

One approach that aided Obama's efforts to cultivate and spread an all-hands culture was his practice of promoting that culture through actions both large and small. For example, Obama communicated in terminology consistent with an all-hands state of mind. He stressed repeatedly that small actions, such as forwarding an e-mail to a group of friends or attending a campaign rally, could ultimately have a large impact, and he never belittled small efforts. He consistently challenged people to be a part of the creative process, even in the small actions.

Obama also promoted and sustained an all-hands culture by communicating to his staff clear expectations about acceptable actions and asking them to reinforce the culture. Obama campaign staffers were trained to seek out and train others to play increasingly large roles in the campaign—

> Obama also promoted and sustained an all-hands culture by communicating to his staff clear expectations about acceptable actions and asking them to reinforce the culture.

part of an all-hands state of mind. Obama campaign representatives were also taught to help others identify their talents or ways they could help, and to facilitate efforts to leverage these.

⇥ PROVIDE AFFIRMATION ⇤

Another practice that aided Obama as he created, spread, and maintained an all-hands culture was his success in promoting the notion that each individual can make a difference. This practice reflected his long-standing leadership style. As a law professor at the University of Chicago, for instance, Obama was known for encouraging bashful students to speak up, rephrasing their words more eloquently if necessary in order to weave their ideas into class discussion. The result: *affirmation*. He succeeded in creating in his classroom an atmosphere where students felt encouraged to contribute and were prodded to continually strengthen their performances. The style made him a very popular professor.

Obama encouraged this approach within his campaign. David Plouffe acknowledged the great effect, as participants felt affirmed in assisting with even the smallest of efforts. Plouffe noted, "We've all worked in campaigns a lot and volunteerism in politics is a dying thing. And to see this many people getting involved, giving $25, manning phone banks, becoming neighborhood team captains, you know, hasn't been seen in a very long time. And I hope that that is the legacy of this campaign."[5]

⇥ MATCH SKILLS AND INTERESTS, ⇤ MAKE DIFFERENCES A STRENGTH

If an all-hands culture thrives on the notion that each person can make a difference, determining substantively what this means for each participant is a key step in enabling an all-hands culture to bear good fruit. In *which way* can each participant make a difference?

If an all-hands culture thrives on the notion that each person can make a difference, determining substantively what this means for each participant is a key step in enabling an all-hands culture to bear good fruit. In *which way* can each participant make a difference? Obama trained his staffers to help identify how willing supporters could help.

As Jeremy Bird, the Ohio General Election Director for Obama's presidential campaign, recalled, supporters were not viewed as "just there for the grunt work." Efforts to match participant skills and interests to the tasks at hand became a key part of staffers' work.

Embedded within these efforts, of course, is a belief that differences can be a source of strength. This notion, in itself, helps to bolster a sense of camaraderie among participants who might be very different in terms of life experiences, skills, and talents. The simple principle of working with willing participants to identify what they are "comfortable with" and leveraging the ways they could contribute had profound outcomes for Obama's campaign and its productivity. As Zack Exley, a campaign participant, observed:

… Team leaders like Don have some latitude to shape roles around individual personalities. While not everyone has a volunteer coordinator, Don created that role for retired high school English teacher Marilyn Elsley, one of his recruits who wanted to lead but wasn't comfortable with the canvassing coordinator position.

After visiting my fourth or fifth team, it was painfully clear that an enormous amount of power is unlocked by this incredibly simple act of distributing different roles to people who actually feel comfortable taking them on. And I say "painfully" because I couldn't stop thinking about all the union and electoral campaigns I've worked on where we did not do this.

I thought about Patrick's story from high school when I met Jacob Manser, a 16-year-old who is serving as the canvass coordinator for his neighborhood team in the heart of Columbus. The team's FO, Steph Lake, took me by the beginning of an afternoon phone bank that the team was coordinating. All the team members were playing their different roles: The team's volunteer coordinator, a semi-retired software developer named Robert Hughes, had prepared the call lists in conjunction with the team's phone bank coordinator, Leslie Krivo-Kaufman, another high school student. Team leader Janeen Sands oversaw the whole event. And another volunteer, who was not even a team coordinator (yet) had donated her house for the event. …

Ryan… has six teams covering a wide swath of rural and exurban Southwest Ohio. He said, "It's great—it's like having six offices around town."[6]

The philosophy of "do what you are able" allowed Obama's team to capitalize on the strengths of participants and drove the quickly increasing numbers of engaged supporters.

⇥ REWARD EXCELLENCE ⇤

Matching skills with interests can encourage productivity, with all participants doing their parts: all hands are on the deck, even those of the little guys. What helps ensure these efforts can be effective? For Obama, two steps proved important: rewarding excellence and empowering participants with training.

To ensure an all-hands environment facilitates high performance, Obama makes sure to reward excellence among team members and participants. He recognizes that a key to inspiring excellence is expecting excellence, and a key to sustaining excellence is rewarding it. In the Obama campaign, one effective way to reward excellence was to give a high-performing worker greater responsibilities, which had the feel of a "promotion" and functioned as an incentive.

> Obama recognizes that a key to inspiring excellence is expecting excellence, and a key to sustaining excellence is rewarding it.

In the Obama campaign, the link between high performance and the "reward" of greater responsibilities always remained clear. Obama staffers methodically tested volunteers and other team members for "reliability" before they were assigned greater roles or responsibilities. Volunteers tell countless tales of how those in leadership positions were tested with tasks—first simple ones, then increasingly difficult ones. They were held accountable. Only after delivering results and demonstrating consistent reliability were they offered greater responsibilities.

Throughout the Obama campaign, as Obama reinforced and nurtured an all-hands culture, the practice of rewarding excellence helped encourage participants to perform excellently and also helped yield greater levels of participation, as volunteers expanded their work and reached out to others, ultimately recruiting additional volunteers, organizers, and leaders.

⇒ TRAIN WELL ⇐

As Obama cultivated an all-hands aspect to his organizational culture, he discerned that training represented a key ingredient for making the approach work well. He could extend greater responsibilities to volunteers successfully only if he helped ensure they had the skills and basic knowl-

As Obama cultivated an all-hands aspect to his organiza-tional culture, he discerned that training represented a key ingredient for making the approach work well.

edge to complete those responsibilities excellently. He viewed his work with his staff and volunteers as a two-way street: they offered their time, talents, and skills, and he invested in them, helping them develop their capacities. His enthusiastic staff and volunteers wanted to succeed. The two-way nature of the commitment made for a "can do" culture, and emphasis was placed on continual improvement. Just as with his work with Altgeld Gardens residents in Chicago in the 1980s, Obama trained strong leaders in the campaign, allowing them to own projects.[7] Training of staff and volunteers became key for the success of his innovative approach, and helped give rise to an organization that reflected the organizing mantra "Respect. Empower. Include."

The uniqueness of this approach was apparent from the beginning. Other organizations and campaigns failed to extend significant roles or responsibilities to volunteers, who were instead given mere grunt work. The Obama campaign sought to make volunteers into organizers and leaders who could organize others and multiply the number of other leaders. Jeremy Bird acknowledged the training could be costly, but "training is the most important thing." He placed a high priority on bringing "all of our organizers together and training them for a full weekend." They planned for the training to be more than a mere orientation. "We wanted to make sure that ours was a real, interactive, in-depth training."[8]

Select volunteers with strong, consistent records of excellent work were asked to attend Camp Obama meetings, where they received training on how to organize their communities. Camp Obama training sessions were held in cities including Burbank, Oakland, New York, Atlanta, St. Louis, and Phoenix. For Obama, this represented "empowering people in the field." Those trained volunteers would then return to organize their communities, allowing paid campaign staff to come into locales with infrastructure intact, ready to advance efforts further.

As the campaign's field director, Temo Figueroa, summed it up: "We decided that we didn't want to train *volunteers*... We want to train *organizers*—folks who can fend for themselves."[9] Participants would depart from training sessions organized into teams by Congressional district, and were tasked with helping to establish and build the local organization.[10] Within the early months of the campaign, estimates suggest Obama's team trained over 7,000 volunteers to serve as effective organizers in their communities.

At the local levels, further training occurred. Local leaders compiled training materials consistent with the national efforts. Bird and other national leaders also compiled a 280-page manual to help facilitate local organizing.

Reinforcing the key role training held within the campaign, Obama staffers set measurable goals. They used the numbers of volunteers trained as a key metric by which they measured their progress and success. Regional Field Director for Southwest Ohio, Christen Linke Young, offered a glimpse of the practices:

> We had a whole month where, on our nightly calls with headquarters, we did not report our voter contact numbers. We only reported our leadership building.... Headquarters wasn't paying attention to how many voters we registered or how many doors we knocked on that day—they were paying attention to how many one-on-one meetings we had, house meetings, neighborhood team leaders recruited, how many people we had convinced to come to this wonderful training in Columbus that we had.[11]

Special programs offered by the Obama campaign also emphasized the importance of training. A flier about the Obama Organizing Fellow program explained:

> The Obama campaign this summer is looking for students and recent graduates who share the senator's belief that real change comes from the ground up....
>
> Fellows will be trained on the basics of organizing, and campaign fundamentals. They also will be asked to commit to at least 30 hours weekly.
>
> Specifically, Fellows will be trained in field organizing, messaging and other activities; organize in a community, working alongside grassroots leaders and campaign staff; and continue to build the movement. Fellows will coordinate voter registration drives, organize phone banks, plan canvasses, and help with campaign events....

Although this is an unpaid position, Fellows can expect the self-satisfaction that comes from "reviving democracy in communities across the country," as Obama put it in a Web site video. (Fellows who demonstrate exceptional organizing skills and want to continue working with the campaign also get first dibs on paid positions in the fall.)[12]

Importantly, Obama and his team did not see training as a static, one-session-and-you're-finished event. They emphasized continual improvement and tried to offer avenues for improvement when a team member or participant fell short of expectations. For example, Field Director Jackie Bray revealed:

When we identify a volunteer or a potential volunteer we always hold a one-on-one meeting. Movements aren't built on individual people—they are built on relationships. Then we ask our volunteers to make deeper commitments. We coach new volunteers and facilitate the process for folks who are old hat at this stuff through an organizing activity.... Once someone has succeeded at an organizing activity we ask them to try their hand at leading a voter contact activity.... Training is a huge part of quality control and we need our leaders to be good trainers. If a potential leader is a successful trainer then we meet with them again to ask them to take that next step and become a Team Coordinator or Team Leader. If at any moment in this process a volunteer isn't successful our organizers are trained to spend time coaching them through getting better. We are an inclusive team here and our goal is always to make people better.[13]

Obama's efforts became distinguished, as strategist Donna Brazile put it, because he did not simply take donations from supporters; he also "gave them seats at the table and allowed them to become players."[14] As he promoted an all-hands culture, training helped to ensure that these ardent supporters who came "to the table" were empowered with key skills that would allow them to help Obama achieve success. The results were phenomenal, as the all-hands culture and the enthusiasm and participation it bred allowed the Obama campaign to build a presence within all fifty states.

⇥ KEEP THE "COMMUNITY THING" GOING ⇤

The impact of the all-hands aspect of the Obama campaign's culture was strong and positive. The empowerment and high camaraderie fed loyalty and fueled participants to continue to reach out to greater numbers of people. It is this level of commitment that is indeed striking about all-hands culture. As Christen Linke Young observed of the Obama campaign:

> I feel like people are committing more time this election because there's a community thing going on, and they're part of something that's local and social. But we're also more effective at harnessing volunteers because the teams do a lot of the training and debriefing themselves—it scales well. Everyone who goes out canvassing comes back with at least one story of someone they impacted. The team leaders are trained to give people time to tell those stories, and so everyone gets a sense of progress and they learn from each other how to be more effective next time.[15]

Obama promoted an all-hands culture excellently by continuing to encourage practices and customs that kept the sense of community thriving.

⇥ Usher Abrasives Out ⇤

Three practices, in particular, helped Obama to maintain the culture he successful created: ushering "abrasives" out, rallying the troops, and managing expectations well.

Just as Obama promoted effectively an all-hands culture, he also employed practices that helped sustain that culture. Three practices, in particular, helped him to maintain the culture he successfully created: ushering "abrasives" out, rallying the troops, and managing expectations well.

Obama realizes that when people do not embrace the fundamental values of a team or organization, their presence in a position of leadership or in large numbers within an organization can serve to undermine greatly the organization and its work. Obama values unity, nonconfrontational styles, and a willingness to foster consensus, among other key elements. He realizes that when he places someone in a key position who rejects these fundamental values, dissension can follow, causing demoralization among team members and considerable distraction from team goals. Moreover, Obama also knows a willingness to place someone in a position of key influence within his team or organization who rejects the fundamental elements of the team's culture could communicate to others that he himself does not hold those principles in high esteem.

Obama has striven to show he "walks the walk." He leads by example, affirming the values he has infused into his team culture whenever possible. He demands that those on his team do the same. When speaking of the 2008 campaign, an Obama aide noted that Obama had said firmly, "I don't want elbowing or finger-pointing," and "We're going to rise or fall together." Obama permits scant room for significant deviation from the principles and culture he seeks to promote. As such, you will find no "screamers" in his inner circle. Obama has, on the contrary, taken steps to usher the "abrasive" personalities out of key teams, knowing that such personalities can undercut culture and morale.

For example, after his presidential victory in November 2008, when Obama was considering whom to name as Treasury secretary, Lawrence Summers was reportedly on the short list. Certainly, Summers brought a lot to the table. Known for his intellectual excellence and economic acumen, he had a long résumé of impressive experience. He had already served as chief economist for the World Bank from 1991 to 1993. Between 1993 and 1999, he served as the Under Secretary for International Affairs and Deputy Secretary of the Treasury, directing the U.S. Treasury's international policy and guiding a successful response to the 1997 Asian financial crisis. The glaring negative factor that stood in Summers's way, however, was his reputation as a man whose abrasive style stirred bitter infighting.

As president of Harvard University, for example, Summers managed to sink himself in controversy, stoking a very public dispute with then-tenured Harvard professor Cornell West. The open, bitter conflict spurred West, one of the few tenured African American professors at Harvard, to resign and leave for Princeton, resulting in great discontentment and bruised feelings at Harvard. African Americans and minority populations, in particular, felt more alienated from the university. Summers stirred great controversy again during his tenure as Harvard president with his ill-advised statements about girls, questioning their abilities to perform as strongly as boys in the sciences. The statements created a firestorm of upset among faculty members, students, and alumni, and Summers was forced to resign as Harvard's president in 2006. Other people who had worked with Summers in different capacities complained his personal style left many people feeling belittled and his abrasiveness reduced both morale and productivity.

With this background, many observers remained concerned about Summers's contentious personality and how it might affect dynamics in an Obama cabinet. Ultimately, Obama chose Summers to serve as director of the National Economic Council, a White House position that would not require Senate confirmation and that kept him from the cabinet. The move enabled Obama to benefit from Summers's expertise while preserving a team environment in his cabinet that reflected his values. Obama took similar steps to ensure the key leaders of his presidential campaign also reflected the values he advanced through an all-hands culture. In this way, Obama helped to protect and sustain the all-hands culture that proved vital to the success of his campaign.

⇥ MANAGE EXPECTATIONS ⇤

Another practice that helped Obama sustain a strong all-hands culture in the Obama campaign was his practice of managing expectations and bolstering the spirits of his organization's workers in the face of setbacks.

Even beyond his campaign, Obama makes a good habit of managing expectations. When addressing the American public, for instance, he sets his ambitions high and articulates clear goals, but also clarifies when the road to success might be long, filled with turns, and difficult. During his presidential inaugural address, for example, following the euphoria and celebration surrounding his historic victory, Obama adopted a relatively somber tone and focused Americans on the many challenges ahead. He warned it might take time to see progress, and he emphasized that success would require that Americans pitch in and do their part.

Similarly, after assuming the presidency, Obama sought to manage expectations when encouraging Americans to see progress on key issues such as economic recovery and health care. For instance, when facing growing criticisms of his efforts to reform health care, Obama spoke words that helped set an expectation of slow progress and resistance, yet also shone a light on the successes to date. He said:

> Any time you try to do something big in Washington, there's gonna be controversy. Health care we've been debating since Theodore Roosevelt. But every time we've made progress, it's been because we've realized that the status quo was unsustainable, and somehow people of goodwill have come together after vigorous debate, sometimes angry debate, and gotten something done. And that's what happened in Social Security. You know, people said Social Security was a socialist program. Yet now it's the most important social program that we have to make sure that seniors are secure.
>
> Said the same thing about Medicare. That this is going to be a government takeover of Medicare. Well, it turns out that if it weren't for Medicare, a lot of seniors out there would be completely out of luck. And so I wanted to provide a context to explain to people: it's always hard for us to make progress, but this is the right thing to do. Now is the time to do it....

…one of my advisers early on in this process. He said, "I've been in this town a long time. I think this is the year we're going to get health care done. But I guarantee you this will be pronounced dead at least four or five times before we finally get a bill passed." And so in some ways we anticipated this was just going to be difficult. Look, you're talking about one-sixth of the economy. You've got a whole range of special interests out there that are profiting from the current system and don't want to see it change. You've got a continuing habit of polarization inside of Washington that's hard to break.

And so we knew this was going to be hard....

We have seen unprecedented movement by Congress. We've got four out of the five committees that have already done something. The fifth one is about to move. Just announced it. So we're further along than we ever have been.

The other thing that we've be able to achieve is we really have 80 percent of this package has some broad support across the spectrum in some very substantial areas."[16]

After public approval ratings had slipped, these words helped Obama bolster public morale. His efforts to manage expectations produced the positive effect he had hoped for.

Obama applies similar principles to his work with his teams and organizations. For example, before he won the Iowa primary, some of his biggest donors grew nervous with the increasingly negative nature of Hillary Clinton's campaigning against him, fearing her efforts were derailing his campaign efforts. Obama sought to quell their fears and bolster their morale by managing expectations. He told a roomful of his donors: "Can I see how many people in this room I told that this was going to be easy? If anybody signed up thinking it was going to be easy, then I didn't make myself clear.... We're up against the most formidable team in 25 years. But we've got a plan, and we've got to have faith in it."[17] Obama retained the support of his major donors, and campaign morale remained high. His efforts paid off as he won the Iowa primary and proceeded on to many more victories on the path to the White House. Throughout the 2008 campaign, the same type of tactics that brought this success allowed Obama to sustain the high levels of morale that characterized the all-hands culture at all levels of his organization.

⇥ RALLY THE TROOPS ⇤

Finally, to keep his all-hands culture strong, Obama and his team took deliberate steps to rally the troops. This involved explicit efforts to maintain the high levels of enthusiasm, loyalty, and commitment that characterized the all-hands culture of the Obama campaign. Staffers and volunteers would receive encouragement via special e-mails, for instance, touting successes and encouraging them to reach for greater goals. Successes were celebrated. Staff members and volunteers might be informed that they had raised another $1 million, and would also be encouraged to spread the word about the Obama message. Advances were cited and used effectively as means to continue motivating commitment and high performance.

EMPLOYING THE LESSONS

Barack Obama's ability to build an all-hands culture among the teams and organizations he leads has aided his success. The distinguished nature of the all-hands culture was particularly evident during his 2008 presidential campaign. As you think about the practices and principles that allow Barack Obama to build and sustain an all-hands culture, consider whether your own leadership might benefit from these practices and principles. Bear these questions in mind:

- Have I created a strong "teamwork" culture?
- Would my organization benefit from elements of an all-hands culture?
- Have I matched skills and interests in ways that will build a high-performing, all-hands team?
- Have I found ways—traditional or innovative—to inspire and reward excellence?
- Do I invest adequately in training?
- Do I pay adequate attention to morale?
- Have I taken steps to ensure a strong team culture flourishes?
- Have I ushered "abrasive" personalities out when needed?
- Have I set expectations well?
- Do I manage expectations in ways that help my team maintain high morale, weather setbacks, and celebrate successes?

CHAPTER 7

USE DIVERSITY AS A SOURCE OF STRENGTH

"Majority-minority. It's the first majority-minority Cabinet."

Many people found it hard to overlook this fact as President Barack Obama completed the appointments to his cabinet in 2009. *Majority-minority*, a term credited to political scientist Paul Light,[1] acknowledged that Obama's cabinet marked the first time more women and ethnic minorities made up a majority of a U.S. president's cabinet, a watershed moment in U.S. history.

When we examine the winning teams Obama has created consistently throughout his career, it becomes clear that this level of diversity is to be expected, because one of their distinguishing features has been their sheer diversity. His talented teams often include a rainbow of races, a broad mixture of ethnic groups—something that Obama considers desirable in and of itself, since it reflects his commitment to unity and inclusion. To focus exclusively on skin color, however, would miss the point in a notable way, because for Obama, diversity is more than skin-deep. It's more than just ethnic. Obama recognizes people can be "internally diverse," and he values diversity of life experiences, diversity of perspectives, and diversity of thought.

Indeed, in considering how Obama views diversity, it is important to know what diversity is *not* to him. It is not simply color. It is not about choosing unqualified team members simply because they possess "nontraditional" backgrounds. Obama rejects any notion that diversity and excellence can't be found together. He knows the two aren't mutually exclusive. Far from it: Obama believes adamantly that excellence comes in different hues, from different regions, from different ways of life. When you cast a net in rich waters, he believes, you can always find excellence *and* diversity. Obama proves the point: his team members are diverse and highly accomplished, too, and Obama has managed to harness a winning combination—leveraging networks and the creative thinking that comes from varied perspectives. Obama has sought to achieve such a notable degree of diversity because he believes from experience that diversity among team members can serve as a formidable competitive strength. When it is used well, diversity expands the "we"—a team's base of support—and can give rise to unprecedented levels of innovation. As Obama strives to select outstanding team members, therefore, he keeps an eye on bringing diversity to his team.

> Obama rejects any notion that diversity and excellence can't be found together.

> When it is used well, Obama believes diversity expands the "we"—a team's base of support—and can give rise to unprecedented levels of innovation.

With this frame of mind, Obama pledged prior to winning the U.S. presidency to make his cabinet one of the most diverse in history. He delivered on that promise well, drawing on diversity in all its key forms. He exceeded even President Bill Clinton, who had set records during his own time, appointing five women and six minorities in his first cabinet—something Clinton had proudly touted as reflecting his promise to form a cabinet that mirrored America.[2]

Under Obama, the top three positions—secretary of state, secretary of defense, and attorney general—are held by "diverse" picks, each diverse in her or his own way (gender, political affiliation, and race, respectively). Secretary of State Hillary Rodham Clinton became only the second woman in U.S. history to hold that influential role.[3] In Obama's cabinet, there are seven women, including Janet Napolitano as the secretary of homeland security, a bold choice. There are four African Americans, including Attorney General Eric Holder, the first African American to hold the post as the nation's top law enforcer. The cabinet also includes Asian Americans Gary Locke, secretary of commerce; Steven Chu, secretary of energy; and Eric Shinseki, secretary of veterans affairs. As Rahm Emanuel boasted in December 2008, "Based on what I can cull from records, we have more Hispanics in senior positions in this White House than under either President Bush or President Clinton."[4] Obama also named two Republican-affiliated men to his top team, including Robert Gates as secretary of defense (an Independent, but a holdover from the Bush administration) and Illinois Representative Ray LaHood as transportation secretary. Moreover, Obama's cabinet includes age diversity—with six cabinet members over the age of 60, eight over the age of 50, and seven over the age of 40—and to a lesser extent, regional diversity as well.[5]

Why does Obama go to such lengths to bring diversity into his teams? What are the specific benefits of diversity? What has allowed Obama to make diversity a source of team strength? What can other leaders learn about the ways in which diversity might benefit their own organizations or teams? Let's explore these questions below.

⇥ RECOGNIZE THE ARRAY OF DIVERSITY ⇤

Before moving on to discuss what Obama views as the benefits of diversity, we should take time to consider further how Obama defines diversity. As noted above, he sees diversity as being about more than just ethnicity and as more than skin-deep. He has held this perspective for decades. When he served as president of *Harvard Law Review*, Obama already indicated he viewed diversity as a broad attribute that could include factors such as varied life experiences, education, gender, political affiliation, age, geographic affiliation, and socioeconomic background. Some of his African American colleagues criticized him, in fact, for not selecting larger numbers of African Americans for top law review positions.[6] For Obama, however, he valued a broad type of diversity, believing that with diversity of life experiences and worldviews often comes diversity of perspective and thought—things that can enrich both learning and team environments.

Obama can see in others what has been referred to as "internal multiculturalism," and he recognizes *hidden immigrants*, a term that refers to people who grew up in highly diverse settings, such as children of military servicepeople or people who grew up outside of the United States, for

> Obama can see in others what has been referred to as "internal multiculturalism."

example, and therefore likely have a worldview defined by the diversity of their experiences. Obama values this experience, having spent the majority of his own youth outside of the continental United States. Significantly, several members of his inner team are "internally multicultural," including Treasury Secretary Tim Geithner, who spent parts of his youth in India, Thailand, China, Japan, and east Africa; National Security Adviser James Jones, who grew up in Paris; and Valerie Jarrett, who spent parts of her youth in Iran and England.[7] When Obama seeks teams that have diverse members, he means this in the broadest sense.

EMBRACE DIVERSITY'S BENEFITS—EXPANDED NETWORKS AND INNOVATION

Obama is also acutely aware of some key benefits that diversity can bring. Much has been made about who supported Obama in his bid for the presidency and thus to whom he might feel beholden. For example, African Americans provided almost unanimous support to Obama in the November 2008 presidential election, a greater percentage than to any other Democratic candidate in U.S. history. Latino voters delivered 67 percent of their votes to Obama, a 2:1 level of support over McCain. This proved particularly crucial in formerly "red" states such as Florida and Colorado. Given their support, some ethnic minority lobbies sought to persuade Obama he should allocate a good share of administration positions to people of their ethnicity. Early on, a coalition of national Latino organizations sat down with Obama to prod him to appoint large numbers of Latinos to key positions, and reminded him of the strong Latino support in the presidential election. They also reminded him of the dismal numbers: only 8 percent of the federal government workplace was made up of Latinos in recent years (compared to their 13 percent of the general workforce and 15 percent of the American population), and only 3.6 percent of government senior executives were Hispanic.[8]

For Obama, as with any public official, certainly calculations of this sort have a limited claim as he considers appointments. But for Obama, this was far from the driving factor in his push for diversity. Rather, three other motivations fueled his deep commitment to achieving diversity. First, Obama is passionate about the notion of inclusion and unity, and building a diverse team and administration fits well with this. Second, he knows from his own experience that when leaders draw on diverse teams, they can potentially harness and funnel high levels of innovation. Bringing together highly qualified people with varied perspectives can give rise to rich conversation and brainstorming, which in turn can produce creative solutions and ideas. Obama prizes this. A key example of this occurred during the Obama campaign, as Obama's team benefited greatly from the presence of Chris Hughes, a diverse team member (given his youth) who brought fresh ideas and new ways of addressing old issues and tasks. The results were magnificent, as Hughes guided the Obama campaign to use leading-edge technology as a core means of mobilizing voters.

Finally, Obama seeks to capitalize on the networks diversity can bring. Each diverse team member comes with a network—one that can be tapped or mobilized, expanding the reach of Obama's team and their work.

> Bringing together highly qualified people with varied perspectives can give rise to rich conversation and brainstorming, which in turn can produce creative solutions and ideas.

> Each diverse team member comes with a network—one that can be tapped or mobilized, expanding the reach of Obama's team and their work.

⇥ CAPITALIZE WHERE VALUES, TALENTS, ⇤ AND DIVERSITY COINCIDE

Another practice that allows Obama to use diversity as a strength is his habit of applying his typical vetting process to locate highly qualified team members who embrace his vision and values. From there, he culls his alternatives. He enjoys being able to select a team that includes diverse members. As Rahm Emanuel explained as Obama filled administration positions in late 2008 and early 2009, "I'm proud of the fact that it is a diverse staff. But most importantly, the quality is of a single standard... we got a great staff of seasoned people—both on the policy front and on the political front—who know their stuff."[9]

In a nutshell, Obama does not buy into the notion that ensuring a presence of diversity in a team must be tantamount to selecting "token" or unqualified candidates. He affirms that outstanding professionals come in all colors, from all regions, all religions, and all life experiences. He affirms that a differing perspective can often be an enriching one.

In considering the cabinet he has appointed, we see how these practices have played out. The cabinet members support Obama's stances on the large issues, such as withdrawing troops from Iraq, remaining vigilant in the war on terror, reforming health care, restoring America's moral standing in the world, engaging more on the world stage, and addressing the large economic ailments of the U.S. economy such as the housing and credit crises. In addition to embracing and affirming Obama's core values, vision, and policy stances, the cabinet members are seasoned leaders who have strong records of achievement in their respective fields. Indeed, experience enjoyed a high priority as Obama made his selections. Members of Obama's camp seemed very leery of repeating the trials of Bill Clinton's first administration, an administration some believe was beset with problems given its inexperienced staff. Obama named to his team professionals with ties to Wall Street or large corporations—highly experienced professionals with intimate knowledge of the institutions that seemed on the edge of financial collapse. He also filled his cabinet with some leaders with deep, relevant experience who hailed from outside of Washington's circles and brought fresh perspectives and ideas.

In assessing Obama's individual picks for his cabinet, he certainly did not compromise on quality in order to achieve a high level of diversity. Asian American Steve Chu is a Nobel Prize winner and physicist, representing the best of his field. He is known as a strong advocate of assertive action on climate change and global warming. Labor Secretary Hilda Solis, the first Hispanic woman elected to the California State Senate, is a highly accomplished leader known for strong commitment to labor causes and for fighting for the "everyday" person. As the daughter of a Mexican immigrant who served as a battery recycling plant worker in California and organized a Teamsters union, Solis brings diversity of heritage and a strong record of advocating for workers' rights, access to health care, and Medicare coverage increases.[10]

Secretary of State Hillary Clinton, the second woman to serve as secretary of state, had already established ties and clout among many world leaders. Her addition to the foreign policy team was considered a tremendous plus. U.N. Ambassador Susan Rice, an African American, brought a wealth of knowledge from her experience as assistant secretary of state for African affairs, along with her sterling academic credentials from Stanford and Oxford and her award-winning academic work focused on the United Nations. African American Eric Holder came with experience as a former federal prosecutor in the District of Columbia and a federal judge on the District of Columbia bench (Reagan appointee). He also had a strong record in the second highest Justice Department position during Clinton's presidency.

The net effect: Obama achieved impressive diversity. Certainly, room for improvement nearly always exists, and Obama had some gaps in representation. None of his cabinet members are openly gay, and none hail from South Asia—a growing population in the United States. Similarly, there are only two Republican-affiliated cabinet members. There are also no southerners except for Robert Gates of Texas. Some people assert, also, that too much emphasis is accorded to professionals with Ivy League educations.

Nonetheless, the array of diversity is the most extensive to date, and the caliber of his cabinet and overall administration picks is outstanding by any standard. As the host of ABC's This Week noted, "We have not seen this kind of combination of star power and brain power and political muscle this early in a cabinet in our lifetimes."[11]

⤜ DRAW TALENT FROM FRUITFUL SOURCES ⤏

For many leaders, a will to achieve diversity and a clear recognition of diversity's value and benefits still leave the question: How can they achieve diversity? That is, where shall they start to recruit talented individuals who can bring diversity to their ranks?

For Obama, several practices help ensure he draws from a large pool of qualified, diverse candidates. One principle that guides him can be summarized thus: "When you cast your net in rich waters, you will have a wealth of candidates from whom to choose."

One body of rich water includes the pool of candidates with direct, though likely lower-level, experience in a particular field. For Obama, this pool of candidates provided a wealth of people to choose from. In short, as he sought to diversify his administration, Obama had some help. Years before, former President Bill Clinton had set in motion what I refer to as a *silent revolution*, ensuring that many of the middle-echelon staff members of the Clinton administration were people of color and women. He had appointed so many talented minorities to lower-level staff positions that by the time Obama won the presidency, Obama had a wealth of highly qualified diverse candidates from whom to choose for higher-ranking positions.

In Obama's case, the private sector and private sector projects also played a role. For example, the Warren Institute at the University of California, Berkeley, Boalt Hall School of Law worked with philanthropists on the Talent Bank Project, which helped collect thousands of résumés of highly qualified people of color. With the leadership of notable academic stars such as University of California law school's Dean Christopher Edley, they worked together with Korn/Kerry, a leading headhunting (executive recruiting) firm to compile a "talent book" full of résumés to help with the process of identifying talent for the incoming administration.[12]

In his effort to diversify his administration, Obama has also chosen to "go where diverse candidates are." He knows how to tap the networks of companies, organizations, or universities that attract, recruit, and train talented, diverse candidates. For example, Obama tapped into the Black Client Service Staff (BCSS) network at McKinsey & Company, placing several

McKinsey alumni such as Tony Miller and Jim Shelton in prominent positions (as Deputy Secretary of Education, and Education Department Assistant Deputy Secretary for Innovation and Improvement, respectively). Obama has equally tapped the strong networks of top private and public universities. Moreover, he leverages the networks well. For example, if he taps someone from an institution with a strong alumni network such as Harvard, the University of Virginia, or UC Berkeley, members of his team often secure recommendations from them for names of other highly talented and diverse alumni who have the ideal skills and desire to work with the administration.

⇥ INVEST IN THE FUTURE: REMEMBER ⇤ THOSE LOWER ECHELONS

For organizations truly committed to achieving diversity for the long haul, Obama offers another lesson: plant seeds today that you hope to reap tomorrow. Invest in the future. People who have garnered lower-level experience in administrative positions or key policy positions may appear most qualified for the opening higher-level positions in the future. Therefore, if the lower echelons of an organization do not reflect diverse personnel, the pool of highly qualified, diverse candidates for higher positions down the road will be smaller. A key best practice: *remember those lower echelons.*

When you build diversity into the middle echelons of an organization, you potentially make an investment in the future diversity of the leadership of your organization. In government circles, for instance, since experience matters and top administration officials

> When you build diversity into the middle echelons of an organization, you potentially make an investment in the future diversity of the leadership of your organization.

are often culled from those with prior administration experience, creating diversity at those levels can prove a beneficial practice. This represents seeds that will produce good fruit. The principle holds for a wide variety of sectors.

Interestingly, as various ethnic groups lobbied Obama to try to secure representation in his administration, some openly asserted they were more concerned with middle-echelon positions. As Marie Blanco said, "We weren't so much thinking about top cabinet positions. There are a lot from that level down that are very important, that matter."[13]

Obama has taken good steps to diversify multiple layers of his administration. Typical of his appointments are outstanding professionals known for their excellence and innovation. For example, Obama named Jim Shelton, a Stanford graduate and McKinsey & Company alumnus known for being on the leading edge of education and innovation, was the key to the spot as Education Department Assistant Deputy Secretary for Innovation and Improvement. Shelton brought valuable experience as a program director for the education division of the Gates Foundation, guiding the foundation's work in the northeast United States. Obama so carefully layered multiple echelons in his administration with diverse talent that we also saw Nancy Sutley named to the chair of the White House Council on Environmental Quality; Louis Caldera, a West Point graduate who served as secretary of the army under Clinton, named head of the White House Military Office (he subsequently resigned, however, over a misstep involving a military test); Cecelia Muñoz, a 2000 winner of the $500,000 McArthur Foundation "genius grant," named House Office of Intergovernmental Affairs director; and Moises Vela, Vice President Al Gore's chief financial officer and senior adviser on Hispanic affairs, tapped as director of administration for the vice president.

⇥ Build Bridges on Common Ground ⇤

Finally, the way Obama builds a strong culture among diverse team members serves as a key to the success of his approach to diversity. As we saw in Chapter 2, "Communicate Your Vision Effectively," the way Obama draws attention to common ground is a hallmark of his leadership style. He also sets all eyes on the same goals, creating a strong sense of "we-ness." Obama puts those principles and practices to use as he forges a strong team with highly diverse team members. Moreover, he creates an atmosphere in which team members embrace core values and goals, but view differences of perspectives as valuable. In this environment, he creates a high-performing team of individuals willing to lend their ideas and networks. History attests to the fact that these techniques have brought Obama tremendous success and he has leveraged diversity excellently, bringing outstanding team outcomes.

EMPLOYING THE LESSONS

Barack Obama leverages diversity as a strength in his endeavors, drawing on diversity as a source of insights and coalition building. In seeking highly qualified and diverse team members, he draws talent from fruitful sources. Obama's skill in identifying multiple sources of "diversity," forming diverse teams, and building a strong sense of camaraderie among team members of differing backgrounds has served as a distinct aspect of his leadership strength.

As you think about the practices and principles that enable Obama to leverage diversity as a source of strength, consider whether your own leadership and work might benefit from the insights and networks of diverse team members. Keep these questions in mind:

- With regard to my work, what are the multiple sources of relevant diversity that might enhance my work and help me build a winning team?

- Have I used diversity as a source of strength in my work?
- Do I leverage the innovation and networks that often come with teams comprised of diverse members?
- What other benefits could diversity bring to my leadership or my work?
- In seeking to draw on the power of diversity, have I identified fruitful sources of outstanding professionals or candidates who can bring diversity to my team and my work?
- As I seek to prepare for the future, am I building diversity into the middle echelons of my organization?
- When building or leading diverse teams, have I taken adequate steps to illuminate areas of common ground and to build bridges among diverse team members? Have I established a sufficiently strong sense of camaraderie and respect for differences among team members?

PART III

ENABLE THE TEAM, SOLIDIFY A WINNING CULTURE

CHAPTER 8

MAKE TECHNOLOGY YOUR FRIEND

Rss feeds. iPod downloads. GPS locators. Podcasts. Webcasts. Online answer centers. These were among the technological tools Barack Obama employed to build and run a highly successful presidential campaign in 2008. It is difficult to discuss Obama's success in 2008 without reference to how excellently he leveraged technology in support of his efforts to enable a winning team, solidify his organizational culture, and drive effectively toward his organization's goal of winning the election for U.S. president.

In developing a technology strategy and tailoring the tools, Obama established a new gold standard, taking the use of new media and emerging technologies to a new level. Never before in a presidential campaign, and all too rarely in the activities of

In developing a technology strategy and tailoring the tools, Obama established a new gold standard, taking the use of new media and emerging technologies to a new level.

well-run corporations and nonprofit organizations, have we witnessed such intricate use of technological tools to mobilize key groups in support of an organization's goals. Obama placed his campaign on the leading edge of technology, with staggering results: he inspired millions of supporters, raised the largest amount of presidential donations in U.S. political history (more than $600 million), spurred a movement, won the U.S. presidency by the largest popular vote percentage since 1952, and shattered a long list of racial barriers along the way. Obama's success in leveraging technology has influenced profoundly the entire U.S. political process-expanding the electorate, inspiring the largest number of individual donors to contribute to a political campaign in U.S. history, putting in play a 50-state strategy once considered unviable, altering the way politicians will reach out to potential voters in the future, and changing the way voters will seek to access information and engage in the political process. As Obama made history, he made opponents less skilled in leveraging technology—Hillary Clinton and John McCain, among them—appear as if their strategies were relics from a distant past.

Amid all the praise for Obama's achievements and the excellence with which he oversaw his technology strategy's execution, one can easily lose sight of a basic and exceedingly significant fact: Barack Obama is not a techie. For some, it takes a moment for the significance of this to set in.

Obama was born into a generation of high school students for whom the very notion of a computer conjured up images of sprawling NASA-type terminal machines, and for whom any suggestion that a majority of American homes would one day, in the not-too-distant future, possess a personal computer simply elicited laughs. As Obama was entering college, IBM and Apple had just become household names and were beginning to make bigger splashes. In college, Obama would have enjoyed greater exposure to newly minted personal computers, with their dot matrix printers and dark gray monitors. Obama has certainly learned a technological thing or two since then. His affinity for his Blackberry is legendary. But he has never been a computer wonk, and he certainly couldn't make the Geek Squad. Ask him about HDD interfaces, LAN chip sets, and CPU sockets, and you'll find he's not an expert. How, then, was he able to take technological innovation to a new gold standard in his 2008 presidential campaign? How was he able to make technology a highly effective, integral, and interwoven part of his strategy, making it one of the most important strategic advantages he enjoyed? How did technology become his enabler—*his* game-changer—to such an extent that leaders in many other fields, from business to nonprofit, have pondered how they can "Obamafy" their own organizations? What leadership insights and practices made this possible, and what can we learn?

It all began with recognition.

⇥ WHAT'S IN A BLACKBERRY? RECOGNIZING ⇤ TECHNOLOGY'S GAME-CHANGING POTENTIAL

From the earliest days of his campaign, Barack Obama knew that new technologies would play an important role. In a February 2007 web video posted on his first campaign website, Obama encouraged his supporters to "use this website as a tool to organize your friends, your neighbors, and your networks." Obama had run a highly successful voter registration drive in Chicago in 1992, signing up approximately 150,000 new black voters.[1] He had come to understand elements that drove such successful drives in a bricks-and-mortar, on-the-ground way. Together with his experience from prior electoral campaigns—for the Illinois Senate and U.S. Senate—Obama understood TV and print ads still had their place. But he also discerned an opportunity to leverage the new media and emerging technologies to support his presidential campaign goals, one of which was to inspire large numbers of new voters to register and support his candidacy. Obama and his team were acquainted with how the Dean campaign had used technology excellently in 2004. They understood the potential in broad terms. Obama intended to take things to the "next level," and as such some observers have referred to his campaign as "Dean 2.0"—representing an advancement over techniques that had proved very promising and had, during Dean's campaign, set their own new standard at the time. Obama appropriately established a new media team within his campaign. Its members lived by the notion that "message, money, and mobilization" were their aims.[2]

According to many sources, this is where the prethinking ended. Obama understood he was dealing with an online community that had "matured" since 2004, and an American population much more accustomed to transacting in the cyber world. He understood technology had a firm place within his campaign. But few had anticipated how the new media and cyber world would, in many ways, take on a life of their own and claim a place so central to the Obama campaign and its ultimate presidential victory. The Obama campaign's success in harnessing the power of the new technologies, once they began to witness such a notable reaction and unprecedented online support, is a testament to Obama's skill in building an organization that thrived on continual feedback, remained committed to "keeping a finger on the pulse," and had structured itself to

> The Obama campaign's success in harnessing the power of the new technologies... is a testament to Obama's skill in building an organization that thrived on continual feedback.

adapt rapidly to trends that could help push toward their end goals. In a short span of time after the campaign began in earnest, Obama and his team came to see technology for what it could potentially be: a game-changer in the presidential election.

Obama and his team came to see technology for what it could potentially be: a game-changer in the presidential election.

The New Beast

Obama and his team developed this view—that technology was a game-changer—as they witnessed the exponential growth in online support for Obama, the blossoming donations derived from online contacts, and how quickly and effectively the new technology spread knowledge about Obama and his vision for the future. The new technology represented, in fact, a new beast of sorts. While print and TV advertising serve excellent marketing purposes—informing, sometimes even inspiring, and motivating people—the new media, particularly two-way technology, can be used for a broader gamut of things: informing, inspiring, motivating, training, networking. Different from the old media, the new media can help create community—and all that this implies. It can also help to train leaders and workers, convey best practices, and aid networking, things traditionally

[T]he new media, particularly two-way technology, can be used for a broader gamut of things: informing, inspiring, motivating, training, networking. Different from the old media, the new media can help create community—and all that this implies.

associated with work completed among paid staff within the four walls of an organization. The new technology began to remove the limitations of the bricks-and-mortar organization, extending Obama's work into a wider community. *This* is what made new technology a game-changer. It represented more

This is what made new technology a game-changer. It represented more than "next generation marketing"; it promised next-generation *mobilization*—a blurring of the lines between organizational insiders and outsiders, providing high levels of connectivity and extending the organization outward.

than "next-generation marketing"; it promised next-generation *mobilization*—a blurring of the lines between organizational insiders and outsiders, providing high levels of connectivity and extending the organization outward. In that context, the core work of the organization and the organization's culture itself is able to spread beyond organizational walls with fewer limitations. Engagement among supporters, not just staff members, can become much more extensive, and identification with a cause can become potentially much more intense.

As the Obama campaign harnessed the power of the new technology, the role of "outside" supporters became more encompassing—more participatory. This fit neatly with Obama's desire to create a sense of shared goals and purpose, and to see change and mobilization occur at a grassroots level. The Obama campaign staff stressed the use of two-way technology, where they could both send and receive communications. They built ways to participate into the technology they deployed, ensured continual feedback from end users, and adapted rapidly to changing or emerging needs. They spread their culture beyond the "insider" walls, extending the organization in many ways, giving rise to what many observers soon referred to as not just a campaign, but as a *movement*.

The Obama campaign stressed the use of two-way technology, where they could both send and receive communications.

As Central Desktop's CEO Isaac Garcia observed, the way Obama leveraged technology in his presidential bid was "very unique." He noted, "We saw glimpses of it with Howard Dean in 2004. But not to this level. What you get [in the Obama campaign] is a perfect matching of philosophy, messaging, and technology."[3]

As the Obama campaign leveraged technology, their success in achieving a high level of integration allowed Obama to make the new media his competitive strength. As Michael Silberman observed, "The game-changer in the Obama campaign…was that technology was not an add-on: It represented a carefully considered element of almost every critical campaign function."[4] Silberman went on to note, aptly, that it is "tempting to think of Obama's impressive field campaign and his online organizing programs as separate—the 2,500+ field organizers and volunteer neighborhood teams on one side, the online activists using my.barackobama.com to set up discussion groups and events on the other. But much of the critical grassroots organizing actually happened at the intersection of the two."[5]

Let's explore some of the practices that enabled Obama to employ technology so effectively.

⇥ CHOOSE PARTNERS EXCELLENTLY ⇤

Many leaders have found it useful to adopt a simple operating principle: "If you're not the best at a key task, outsource—and outsource to the very best." Long before his 2008 presidential campaign, Obama had

> Obama embraces a simple motto: "If you're not the best at a key task, outsource—and outsource to the very best."

already shown he found value in this idea. When Obama ran for the Illinois State Senate in 1995, for example, he came to believe that some of his opponents for the Democratic nomination had broken rules as they'd gathered signatures on their nominating petitions, a minimum number of which were required in order to place their names on the Democratic primary ballot.

Obama volunteers examined the nominating petitions of those rivals and concluded that the legitimate signatures fell short of required numbers. Obama sought to file a legal challenge. He immediately asked an adviser, "What do you need?" to achieve a victory in challenging the signatures? His adviser informed him he needed the assistance of a lawyer. Obama's immediate response: "Who is the best?" and he directed his adviser to hire *that* attorney, a respected Harvard-trained civil rights lawyer.[6] With the objections they filed to some signatures on the nominating ballots, Obama left all his rivals short of the number of signatures required to place their names on the primary ballot, disqualifying all his Democratic challengers. Obama moved forward as the sole Democratic candidate.

Obama carried this notion of outsourcing to the very best forward. When it came to his presidential campaign and its technology strategy, Obama hired the best. Enter Chris Hughes.

The decision to work with Hughes, the 24-year-old cofounder of the social networking website Facebook, was brilliant and telling in multiple ways. Who better to help assess the technological needs of the campaign, to help identify and design the optimal tools, and to help oversee the execution of the technological strategy? Hughes's selection brought many benefits. First and foremost, Hughes brought to the Obama team tremendous expertise and innovation, and his selection drove straight to a key criterion for a technological partner: leading-edge capabilities.

In selecting Hughes, Obama also demonstrated a solid grasp of how to best choose partners, paying attention to such issues as commitment level, work ethic, fit with the organizational culture, and a willingness to focus on the same end goals. Hughes brought considerable passion and dedication. Along with his creativity and leading-edge understanding of technological tools, this made for a formidable combination.

Obama's choice to work with Hughes was also brilliant from both a substantive and a public relations standpoint. Hughes was, after all, a member of one important segment of voters—the youth segment—that Obama sought to mobilize and that, as the campaign progressed, became increasingly important to the success or failure of Obama's candidacy. Substantively, Hughes understood this youth group and could readily identify and capitalize on the "habits" of this voting segment. He knew well how this age group accessed information and the channels they preferred. From a public relations perspective, the choice of this high-profile young leader garnered media attention, but perhaps more importantly, sent a message to young people. Hughes's choice to join in Obama's campaign served as powerful endorsement in and of itself, which encouraged other young people to give Obama a good look.

The partnership with Hughes became emblematic of other technology-related partnerships Obama would form, which ultimately included partnerships with a range of dynamic companies and entrepreneurial ventures on the cutting edge of their fields, such as Central Desktop, RightNow, and LIST. These productive and highly successful partnerships helped lay the foundation for Obama to interweave technology into the heart of his strategy and make technology an integral part of the key functions of the campaign.

⇥ IDENTIFY TARGET GROUP HABITS ⇤

As Obama led his team to leverage technology excellently, he understood it was imperative to gain a clear and deep understanding of the "habits" of his target groups—important knowledge they would draw on in efforts to capitalize fully on the use of technology. What made Obama's efforts particularly effective in this regard was his recognition that the processes of acquiring knowledge and leveraging knowledge should be continual. As the Obama team came to pinpoint, assess, and understand the habits of target groups, they identified optimal partners and experts to help formulate strategies to exploit those habits as a means of transmitting information, building support, and mobilizing voters. After they deployed strategies, the Obama team garnered more feedback, enjoying extensive and continual feedback through two-way technology. With the newly acquired information, Obama added or shifted partners as needed to ensure they worked with "the best" for each new task, as they continued developing or refining strategies and tools that built on prior successes, leveraged lessons learned from setbacks, and capitalized on emerging trends. Rollouts-continual feedback-adaptation-adjusting partnerships: this became a part of Obama's technology approach and allowed him to lead a team that designed increasing numbers of technological tools to facilitate the team's work.

For Obama's team, the initial assessment of the habits of key target groups seemed relatively straightforward. There were several obvious habits to exploit, although ironically few of the other presidential candidates had taken meaningful steps to capitalize on them. As commonly known and attested to through studies such as The Pew Internet and American Life Project reports, Americans had come to rely increasingly on new media tools such as the Internet, e-mail, and text messaging as means to access information. Younger voters, in particular, relied on their cell phones and PDAs to connect with one another and to access information. Social networking websites such as Facebook and MySpace had gained prominence since the last presidential election cycle. Obama made the pivotal choice to tap into these trends as fully as possible.

⇥ CAPITALIZE ON HABITS: CHANNELS AND TOOLS ⇤

For Obama and his team, a key next step after forming an initial assessment involved putting that knowledge to use in order to capitalize on the habits of key groups. He focused on identifying fruitful channels and developing effective tools to maximize benefits. The channels were diverse and multimedia in scope, including the use of well-designed websites and PDAs such as the iPhone. With his partners in place, Obama and his team tailored the technological tools within each of these channels specifically to fit the end user, the needs, and the mission. The tools—e-mail, text messaging, webcasts, podcasts, blogs, photo galleries, and online chats among others—were customized for their specific purposes, and many served highly effective marketing functions. E-mail messages made excellent use of headers and teases, for example. Special ringtones were designed, which created marketing buzz.[7]

> With his partners in place, Obama and his team tailored the technological tools within each of these channels specifically to fit the end-user, the needs, and the mission.

Online partnerships provided fruitful channels for encouraging support for the Obama campaign. The fund raising of online organizational "friends" such as MoveOn.org, which endorsed Obama and raised half a million dollars for his campaign, proved valuable, as did the e-mails and online Endorse-O-Thon that MoveOn.org sponsored, through which 500,000 e-mails and Facebook messages were sent to encourage abundant support and resources for Obama.[8]

⊰ EMPLOY TWO-WAY TECHNOLOGY ⊱

In assessing what made Obama's use of technology so highly effective, several additional aspects stand out: the prominent place Obama accorded two-way technology; his emphasis on providing incentives via technology for end users to engage, building relations (rather than simply using technology to distribute information); and his choice to tap into online social networking as a key way of realizing the benefits of technology.

When designing the technological components of his campaign's external strategy, Obama operated by the principle that, whenever possible, technology should provide two-way exchanges, whereby potential supporters could receive information from the Obama campaign and also communicate with the campaign through mechanisms such as e-mails, text messaging, and blogs.

Even in its most basic forms, two-way technology provided the Obama camp with a wealth of information—a key way of acquiring knowledge about such issues as voter interests and effective ways to energize and motivate potential supporters. The company RightNow Technologies, for example, provided a Frequently Asked Questions online answer center for an Obama campaign website. The answer center, referred to as *public facing* because it was much less interactive than other tools, provided well-considered answers and key information to commonly asked questions through an online searchable database. This resource provided information directly to supporters and potential supporters as needed via the web. Equally important, it employed artificial intelligence, such that when a user indicated interest in one topic, other topics of relevant interest would appear on the top web page, encouraging the user to learn more. The answer center tracked the most popular questions, generating a top-10 list, which users could view when coming to the web pages. The answer center also traced questions of interest by the location of users, aiding the campaign in identifying the issues of importance by locale, which allowed them to tailor remarks and events accordingly. With millions of visitors to the answer center, this resource became very valuable both to users and to the campaign.

The Obama campaign also designed dynamic, interactive websites. They included interactive elements such as online chats, blogs, and webcasts. The two-way aspects allowed the technology to facilitate a central task of the campaign: engagement. Interacting via such mechanisms as online chats and blogs helped involve everyday Americans in the campaign process. Engagement created a sense that a voice might be heard. It helped to build community beyond the walls of the Obama campaign headquarters and facilitated a blending of the campaign and its external supporters. Most importantly, engagement helped drive to the end goal by helping to yield voter turnout.

⇥ BUILD RELATIONSHIPS: TECHNOLOGY AND ⇤ "CUSTOMER RELATIONS MANAGEMENT"

Obama distinguished his use of technology also in how he stressed the role technology could play in building relationships with potential supporters. Harvard professor Sviokla noted in a very useful assessment that Hillary Clinton treated her supporters as "customers," whereas Barack Obama made his supporters "members." When donors gave money to Clinton's campaign, they would receive an acknowledgment of their contribution, a thank you or confirmation, but little more. In contrast, the

Obama distinguished his use of technology also in how he stressed the role technology could play in building relationships with potential supporters.

Obama campaign treated a contribution from supporters as an opportunity to pull them into the campaign and engage them, creating a personalized membership location for donors (much like a Facebook page). They became "members" of the website. With a focus on engagement, Obama's online team placed great value on building relationships. As Sviokla observed, relationships and engagement, not contributions, were seen as providing the true competitive advantage.

To cultivate relationships further with would-be supporters, Obama's website provided members "points" for actions such as establishing a profile, turning their profiles public, accessing my.barackobama.com, or bringing a link into their online network. These practices were highly familiar and resonated with the youth, for whom the online world has always been their norm. The campaign kept online members apprised of their points ranking relative to other members active in the my.barackobama.com community, operating from the belief that members would be encouraged to move their ranking higher through points-rewarded efforts such as hosting campaign events, linking to other users, or helping to fund-raise for the campaign. With these tactics, Obama used technology excellently to establish outstanding "customer relationships." He engaged potential voters more effectively than his competitors, making supporters more intimately a part of his campaign. They became partners in his effort to reach others and rally support.

As the campaign progressed, my.barackobama.com became exceedingly important to strategic efforts to attract and mobilize voters. After only one year, it had over 500,000 accounts and 30,000 listed campaign events organized by those supporters.[9] This success reflects how excellently the Obama campaign used technology to build productive relationships with would-be supporters. The two-way street worked wonderfully, and Obama succeeded in achieving outstanding marketing and exceptional engagement with supporters.

In this same vein of "building relationships," social networking also had an important place. Obama's main website also provided a social network that enabled supporters and volunteers to communicate with one another, sharing best practices, tips, information, and resources. This became an important way to organize events, think of ways to make the events attractive, and publicize events.

⇥ KEEP AN EYE ON THE END GOAL: ⇤
ONLINE-TO-OFFLINE

Through this all, one practice that proved key to Obama's success in leveraging technology was his commitment to keeping an eye on the fundamentals and the end goal—in his case, the mobilization of voters. The technology he employed was innovative and impressive, and it helped to build connectivity, solidify campaign themes, and spread ideas and values. That was important, yes. But the efforts were meaningless if not translated into action, that is, votes. At all points, Obama ensured his team members continually checked that they were making their way toward their end goal. Obama sought to use technology to motivate actions, small and large, and he never lost sight of the data, such as studies conducted by Donald Green and Alan Gerber of Yale, that indicated personal appeals are much more effective than impersonal appeals (robo-calls, for instance) in mobilizing voters. Bearing this in mind, Obama made the concept of "online-to-offline" central in his technology strategy.

> One practice that proved key to Obama's success in leveraging technology was his commitment to keeping an eye on the fundamentals and the end goals—in his case, the mobilization of voters.

Obama made the concept of "online-to-offline" central in his technology strategy.... efforts to attract and retain supporters through online campaigns should ideally result in offline efforts that would ultimately translate into votes.

Online-to-offline meant that efforts to attract and retain supporters through online campaigns should ideally result in offline efforts that would ultimately translate into votes. The Obama campaign sought to ensure its technology efforts strengthened its program to create, expand, and strengthen its infrastructure around the country, which would directly enable the Obama campaign to organize supporters in the fifty states. Obama also sought to leverage technology so as to get out the vote, making sure supporters went to vote on primary and presidential election days.

Obama succeeded in leveraging technology excellently to aid in infrastructure creation. Specifically, technology helped strengthen efforts to recruit volunteers, identify highly committed participants, promote high-performing volunteers into leadership positions, train leaders in the field, and organize to get out the vote. Online networking tools allowed supporters across the United States to organize themselves into local groups. The Obama campaign would ask select volunteers who demonstrated a long track record of successful work, many of whom were recruited online, to become precinct captains. An online training tool helped prepare them for broader, more extensive responsibilities. The online database aided captains further by helping them track eager volunteers and pinpoint who intended to caucus—a wealth of information to leverage.[10] It also helped captains to manage volunteer canvassing, tracing the locations volunteers had visited and who had promised support. Keeping a record of the relevant names and contact information enabled the Obama campaign to continue to expand its base of support and to mobilize. It helped to identify and strengthen precincts that were not yet delivering targeted support levels. Online recruiting also facilitated the appointment of neighborhood team leaders (NTLs), who were vital to local activities and were coordinated by 2,500 trained field leaders.[11]

Volunteers recruited online who established strong track records could also be invited to attend Camp Obama and other meetings, where they received in-person training on how to organize their communities. This harkened back to Obama's community organizing days when he empowered people in the field. These volunteers—recruited online, trained online, and moved into offline activities and training—completed important work for Obama in building infrastructure in key states. They identified volunteers, formed groups, and developed other leaders. Once the structure was in place and events began to organize, the Obama campaign could facilitate events such as rallies or canvassing campaigns.[12]

In addition to building infrastructure, Obama used the concept of online-to-offline to ensure his technology helped bring about mobilization. E-mail campaigns prodded supporters to send the e-mails on to other people, spreading the word, and to contact friends and family in battleground states to get votes out. Text message campaigns were given a priority. Obama capitalized on the fact that most people read their text messages because they receive fewer of them than e-mails.[13] The Obama campaign gathered meticulously millions of cell phone numbers from Obama supporters and new voter registrants. Text messages gave supporters a way to take immediate action, as campaign texts asked supporters to mobilize their friends and family. Text messages also increased the sense of urgency and importance of tasks at hand, and built a sense of momentum as text message alerts informed voters of primary victories and encouraged them to spread the word, particularly in upcoming battleground states.

In using technology to aid mobilization in this way, Obama's campaign operated "smarter," using a cheaper and more effective means of contacting, motivating, and mobilizing potential supporters. Text messaging was capable of mobilizing 1 in every 25 persons contacted, at a modest 6 cents per contact—much more effective than other options such as robo-calls, and more effective and less expensive than options such as mailers or live volunteer phone calls. Run the return on investment (ROI), and text messaging wins by a mile. Obama had the insight to understand and capitalize on this.

⇥ MAKE MASTERFUL USE OF SPECIFICS ⇤

As Obama made sure to drive online activity into offline results, "Make masterful use of specifics" became a key operating principle. When Obama supporters or would-be supporters visited his websites or provided their cell phone numbers, the Obama campaign asked them to give their zip codes. With this information, messages were personalized and tailored by locale. Users were informed of and encouraged to support rallies and parties nearby and to travel to neighboring battleground states to provide needed help. Messages tailored by state alerted users to voter registration deadlines and also reminded them to mail in their absentee ballots. Some text messages included a phone number to dial to garner polling station addresses and locations, easing the process of voting for many first-time voters. Messages tailored by zip code encouraged voting for specific congressional candidates on the November 2008 ballot. For the Obama campaign, text messaging became "mobile technology" in more than one sense of those words.

In seeking to use technology to get out the vote, Obama even formed a partnership to roll out an iPhone strategy, which represented the best of what technology could offer and also made masterful use of specifics. Launched a month before the November 2008 presidential election, the strategy offered a free download for Apple's iPhone, available on Apple's iTunes store. It included features that could organize a user's iPhone contact list, sorting contacts by battleground states and encouraging the user to reach out, spread Obama's message, and help mobilize voters in those areas. Using area codes, the program could track the number of such phone calls a user made and also presented updates on how many calls had been made nationwide, demonstrating successfully that individual efforts were a part of a larger push.[14] The iPhone strategy also included a feature that employed GPS technology to locate the closest Obama campaign offices and point out local campaign events.[15, 16]

In another example of making good use of specifics, Obama's online phone bank tools, one of which was in Spanish, allowed the campaign to target Hillary Clinton's base of Spanish-speaking voters in Virginia, encouraging them into offline activism.[17] Observers believe this contributed to Obama's ability to make notable inroads into the Hispanic community, which at the outset of his campaign was seen as an Achilles heel.

⇥ ENHANCE INTERNAL CAPABILITIES: MORALE, ⇤ CULTURE, AND MANAGEMENT PROCESSES

Just as the Obama campaign did an excellent job leveraging technology for its external goals, it also employed technology effectively to increase staff productivity, improve internal processes,

[The Obama campaign] employed technology effectively to increase staff productivity, improve internal processes, create fruitful internal communication, keep morale high, and reinforce its organizational culture.

create fruitful internal communication, keep morale high, and reinforce its organizational culture. For example, Obama tailored his use of technology for campaign insiders—the staff who made it all happen. They received specialized messages, which functioned nearly as incentives, conferring to workers a status as "insiders" in such an important set of historic events.

Technology also facilitated internal communications designed to build morale and keep it strong. When successes occurred, Obama's team dispersed messages to campaign insiders through such media as text messages, sharing information about victories and keeping perceptions about momentum high. Messages such as "We've already knocked on 40,000 doors today across the state—keep it up and we'll reach 50,000 new voters by dark,"[18] not only informed insiders of progress, but also challenged them to reach more ambitious goals. When setbacks occurred, Obama and his team leveraged technology to buoy morale and inspire a redoubling of efforts. In total, "insider information" delivered via the new technology helped maintain high morale, keep goals clear, and reinforce a sense of mission. The importance of this within Obama's decentralized organization cannot be overstated.

Moreover, technology helped Obama empower workers and volunteers in the field. The Obama campaign employed tools such as a web tool from a new start-up company Central Desktop, for instance, to organize primary volunteers. Such tools helped the 6,000 precinct captains receive needed information and share information, which together enabled them to mobilize voters on the ground. The tools assisted in leadership development, providing instructions—a sort of online training—for precinct captains.

Leaders in the field could also post information interactively with the technological tools, facilitating the decentralized sharing of key information.

⇥ LEVERAGE LESSONS IN FUTURE WORK ⇤

Employing leadership the Barack Obama way, Obama recognized early the game-changing potential of technology and leveraged it excellently in pursuit of his goals. The impact was profound. The Pew Internet and American Life Project reports that half of the Americans relied on the Internet, e-mail, or text messaging to access information about the 2008 campaign and to encourage others to become engaged in the electoral process.[19] This is more than the number of Americans who rely on the newspaper daily for such information, and more than the 39 percent who access cable news. With outstanding leadership and insight, Obama positioned his organization effectively to reap benefits from trends like this.

The excellent results could be seen relatively early. Obama's effective use of technology helped fuel the exponential growth of the number of his supporters, who blossomed quickly into the millions. Companies such as Compete kept track of website traffic, noting 1.7 million visitors to my.barackobama.com in January 2008 alone.[20] More than 3 million people registered to receive the e-mail revelation of who Obama chose for his vice presidential running mate. For the vice presidential announcement, Sprint Nextel reported that its traffic rose 225 percent on the 62262 Obama short code after 3 A.M. Eastern Time, when the name was released.[21]

In Ohio and Texas, technology helped mobilize volunteers, who began canvassing, making those states competitive during the Democratic presidential primary—a striking outcome.

As Amy Beech, a volunteer in Ohio, observed, "There really was no infrastructure, and now it's all over the place—within three weeks we have this million[-person] door-knocking campaign."[22] Online-to-offline also helped drive thousands of supporters to Obama rallies, which were soon known for their strikingly large sizes.

By the time of the presidential election in November 2008, the Obama campaign was able to leverage millions of cell phone numbers it had collected. Obama had hundreds of thousands of followers on Twitter, and his Facebook page logged over 2 million American friends. Notably, the new technology brought real-world action with results. Obama's campaign gathered and expanded e-mail lists, organized canvassing efforts, convened local meetings, and used technology to facilitate phone drives. It helped build community, spread culture, fuel excitement and strengthen camaraderie—all in much more cost-effective ways than traditional campaigning. The associated face-to-face "get out the vote" appeals bore good fruit, as people were mobilized to go around their locales to rally voters to the polls. In sum, technology supported well the overall mission.

Obama's outstanding use of technology had another note-worthy benefit: the "dinosaur effect." The contrast between Obama's innovative and effective use of technology and the failure of his major opponents to employ technology well made Hillary Clinton and John McCain look like leaders of bygone years. Clinton and McCain both failed to project themselves as leaders representing the future and change, something that benefited Obama greatly.

In keeping with his principle of using technology on the leading edge, Obama promised, upon assuming the position as U.S. president, to use this technology to make his administration one of the most open in U.S. history. Obama wants to stay connected to everyday Americans, encourage their engagement, and remain transparent. He hoped to build an "open-source" government. On the change.gov website, a website launched for the transition, Obama tried to stay true to his word, authorizing the Obama transition team to publish minutes from hundreds of meetings with him in his position as president-elect. He authorized a Citizen's Briefing Book, to be launched with the help of salesforce.com, that would enable citizens to suggest topics and issues Obama should address upon assuming the presidential office.

Since entering the White House, Obama has continued to view technology as a way to continue to build community, stay connected, and receive feedback. He places value on technology's role, as evidenced when he named the first chief technology officer, Aneesh Chopra, who works with Chief Information Officer Vivek Kundra and the General Services Administration. Obama has chosen to place his presidential fireside chats on the Internet. The Obama administration also convened online town halls, in March 2009 for example, attracting over 100,000 participants who offered topics that Obama might discuss in a live Internet address.

EMPLOYING THE LESSONS

A key to Barack Obama's success during his 2008 campaign was his effectiveness in embracing technology and leveraging it in support of his mission and goals. He demonstrated a keen ability to identify ways technology could be deployed to broaden his base of support. Obama's effectiveness in employing technology gave him a notable strategic advantage and facilitated his historic victory.

As you think about the practices and principles that enabled Obama to employ technology so effectively in support of his mission and goals, consider how these practices and principles can strengthen your own leadership and work. Bear these questions in mind:

- Have I assessed the ways in which technology could be a game-changer for me?
- Have I leveraged technology optimally to support my mission and goals? In what ways can technology further enhance my leadership and work?
- Have I chosen my technology partners excellently?
- Am I employing leading-edge technology in my core means of communication with my target audience? Would I lead more effectively if I did? Would my work be enhanced if I did?
- What are some key habits of my target audience and how can technology be deployed to capitalize on those habits?
- Am I using technology effectively to build relationships with my customers or target groups?
- As I leverage technology, am I keeping an eye toward the designated end goal to ensure the technology facilitates progress toward that goal?
- Am I using technology effectively to strengthen morale, culture, and internal management processes?
- What is the relevant technology on the horizon, and how can I prepare now to deploy that technology effectively in the future?

CHAPTER 9

MOTIVATE YOUR TARGET GROUPS, ORGANIZE TO SUCCEED

"Never let the well run dry." For Barack Obama, this simple idea—that leaders should always cultivate their support base or customers, both in their current work and with an eye to the future—became one of several important factors that inspired him to focus on mobilizing young supporters during his 2008 presidential campaign. This notion of never letting the well run dry is, indeed, an idea that has helped many highly successful leaders build organizations that have sustained a leading position for years.

Through his success as a leader, Obama has demonstrated a clear understanding that an ability to mobilize a key target group can prove pivotal to efforts to achieve an organization's goals. Leaders seeking to place their organizations on the forefront of their fields for years to come take steps to designate target groups that can help them reach desired goals, and engage in effective efforts to inspire, motivate, and mobilize those groups.

There is value in exploring Obama's efforts, large and small, to court the youth vote in 2007–2008 and to build an organization that could leverage the enthusiasm of youth well. The small gestures were many, including the way Obama signed his mass e-mails—simply, "Barack"—and the way he would congratulate his wife in public, with a light tap of their fists, knuckles to knuckles, a "handshake" of the youth. The large gestures included an online campaign that exploited a cyber world with which young people had become comfortable, and fruitful activities that supported campus organizing. These efforts reflected Obama's embrace of a broader principle: when you have identified a customer segment or target group with great potential to help you realize your mission and goals, find ways to connect. As Obama's campaign progressed, he made increasing efforts to connect with the young—to inspire them, motivate them, harness their enthusiasm, and funnel their energies into actions that could help him pave a road to presidential victory. His successful efforts helped bring to fruition the mobilization of youth for which Obama is now famous.

Indeed, it is difficult to comment on Obama's success as a leader without noting his particular strength in motivating key target groups and inspiring them to action. In this chapter, we focus specifically on Obama's achievement in mobilizing young voters during his 2007–2008 presidential campaign. It is not possible to present a complete portrait of why Obama succeeded in his presidential bid without observing the important role young voters played in building enthusiasm, spreading Obama's vision, and partnering in his efforts. From Obama's success in mobilizing this target group, we can garner leadership lessons that can be applied in important work with many other target groups.

Ironically, many commentators and political pundits had warned at the onset of the presidential campaign that it would be foolish for any 2008 presidential candidate to focus so much time or energy on the youth vote. Young people, they argued, were notoriously fickle; while they might appear enthusiastic at first, that fervor would prove ephemeral and highly unreliable come election day. In spite of that conventional wisdom, Obama's efforts paid off. From the earliest days of his campaign, he drew record-large crowds, most characterized by a strong presence of youth. By May 7, 2008, he was attracting crowds of 10,000 or more, as he did at the University of Iowa—a turnout of youth that dwarfed the 1500-strong crowd that had gathered for Democratic presidential contender John Kerry four years prior. University of Iowa campus officials likened the students' enthusiasm levels for Obama to passion they'd seem in the late 1960s.[1] The press soon began calling Obama's influence on young people, and his campaign overall, a *phenomenon*.

Taking note of the high levels of enthusiasm, Obama waged an increasingly youth-oriented campaign. In the very first Democratic primary, the Iowa caucuses, Obama's presidential campaign drew first-time young voters (under 25 years of age) in record numbers. They were directly responsible for helping him achieve his historic victory there. In Iowa, the number of participating young Democrats increased some 135 percent, greatly overshadowing similar efforts by skilled candidates such as Howard Dean in 2004. In all, 46,000 young people turned out, providing 22 percent of the entire Iowa caucus vote, with 57 percent supporting Obama—allowing him to greatly exceed both Senator Clinton and Senator John Edwards in support from youth.[2] Notably, Obama successfully energized the young not just in college towns such as Johnson County and Story County, but throughout many parts of Iowa state.

The Iowa victory set in motion other primary victories that followed, as the American nation sat up in stunned surprise that this young African American with a "funny name" was indeed emerging as a viable presidential candidate. Iowa provided Americans a glimpse of what was possible for Obama and galvanized African Americans, who ultimately delivered 95 percent of their presidential vote to Obama. During the presidential election itself in November 2008, observers noted that such high enthusiasm and turnout among the young had not been seen since 1972, when the voting age was first lowered to 18. Obama was so effective in reaching out to young voters that he even won 32 percent of the white evangelical vote between 18 and 29 years of age.

Given the importance of reaching out to designated "customer segments" in enabling an organization to achieve its goals, it is worth asking the question, 'What leadership practices and principles enabled Obama to meet with such success in mobilizing one of his target groups, the young, during his presidential campaign?' How did Obama motivate the young and transform them into dedicated volunteers who ultimately functioned as extensions of his core team, working as his advocates as they helped spread his message and vision? Exploring the practices that brought Obama's success can teach lessons of value to leaders in a variety of fields. For the leader of a church with a waning, aging congregation, the lessons learned can point to ways to focus on new congregation members, attracting and retaining them. For the leader of a manufacturing company with declining sales or shifting markets, we can learn lessons that can help attract and retain the next generation of consumers. Let's explore the factors behind Obama's success.

⇥ RECOGNIZE THE POTENTIAL OF THE NEXT ⇤ GENERATION AND OTHER TARGET GROUPS

Obama went into his 2007–2008 presidential campaign knowing he wished to build a campaign with strong grassroots elements. As he explained eloquently in his memoir, *Dreams of My Father*, "Change won't come from the top.... Change will come from mobilized grass roots."

A child of the antiapartheid movement era, Obama remembered well the power of grassroots efforts waged by highly energized citizens seeking fundamental change. As a student at Occidental College in California, Obama had been involved with campus antiapartheid protests and had witnessed the change that the nationwide student-led antiapartheid movement brought, as the U.S. Congress responded to the pressure to levy sanctions against South Africa and subsequently overrode President Ronald Reagan's veto of those sanctions. He also saw the South African apartheid regime eventually fall under the international economic pressures. This provided for Obama a shining example of the power of people, particularly young people, to organize and eventually bring a change. It represented power welling from the bottom up. As Obama later served as a community organizer in Chicago in the mid-1980s, this model was reinforced for him. When he began his run for the U.S. presidency, he envisioned and hoped for a grassroots-fueled campaign, very participatory in its processes, that could eventually give rise to fundamental change in American politics.

Yet, at the outset of his campaign in 2007, Obama had not envisioned that his potentially grassroots-driven campaign would be so largely *youth*-driven. As early as February 2007, around the time Obama announced his presidential bid, his campaign had already acknowledged the great enthusiasm young people displayed.[3] In October 2007, Obama's campaign manager, David Plouffe, stated, "There is no question that Obama has created enthusiasm among younger voters." He said, "It's not just casual interest. It's real belief and enthusiasm." Plouffe continued, "We absolutely believe there will be more younger voters attending caucuses and voting in primaries because they are motivated by his candidacy." But he also indicated that an effort to court the youth vote "is not central to our strategy. It is additive to our strategy."[4]

Young people paid no mind to this. They organized themselves in support of Barack Obama. For instance, Meredith Segal, a junior at Bowdoin College, started Students for Barack Obama on Facebook.com. With technology that sent forth alerts to friends and spread news quickly, students across the country signed on. This quickly grew into an entity with chapters across the United States. Another online group, One Million Strong for Barack, blossomed as well, attracting more than 200,000 by early 2007.[5] The Obama campaign had not played a role in these early, spontaneous activities among the youth.

[Obama] was willing to cast aside conventional wisdom and demonstrated a willingness to "think outside the box" in order to capitalize on the spontaneous trends.

To his credit, in light of this support, Obama recognized the promise of young people—with their high enthusiasm, commitment, and desire to do core work—in helping him to attain his goals. He was willing to cast aside conventional wisdom, demonstrating a willingness to "think outside the box" and capitalize on the spontaneous trends. It is, indeed, a testament to Obama's leadership insights and excellence in keeping his finger on pulses that he was able and willing to place his faith in the power of young people and to designate steps to translate their bottom-up interest into solid results.

In response, the Obama campaign became more youth-focused and technology-driven. Drawing on technology as an enabler, Obama and his team bucked history and presented a new model in electoral campaigning.[6] John Della Vope, a poll director at Harvard's Institute of Politics, noted the significant change: "Young people in particular have this ability to really move votes and organize people that I don't think they had up until this cycle."[7]

The results were historic, as Obama channeled the enthusiasm so well that it had a notable, multiplier effect. The press began to report stories that became increasingly commonplace, about older generations of Americans who were being swayed by the excitement among young people for Obama's candidacy. Caroline Kennedy spoke about the influence of her daughters, who conveyed to her their excitement about Obama, prompting her to sit up and take note. She referred explicitly to their influence on January 28, 2008, as she, along with Senator Edward Kennedy, endorsed the presidential candidacy of Barack Obama and passed the "Kennedy torch" to him.

Similarly, Senator Claire McCaskill of Missouri came forward to endorse Obama publicly, casting aside her reluctance to choose between Hillary Clinton and Barack Obama after her 18-year-old daughter urged her to follow her passion and back Obama. McCaskill endorsed Obama with impeccable timing, just before Super Tuesday, giving a sense of momentum to Obama's candidacy even though he lost that Tuesday contest.

⇥ AVOID THE TWIN FOLLIES OF NEGLECT ⇤

Just as we can learn lessons from Obama's choice to recognize and engage a promising voting segment, we should also take note of the potential costs of ignoring such a segment. In recognizing the great potential of youth to impact his outcomes and harnessing that potential, Obama avoided twin follies—one immediate, one long-term—of ignoring or neglecting this voting segment.

Obama recognized that in the short term, neglecting the youth segment could have meant that he would fail to capitalize on a great opportunity to allow his organization to achieve its mission. Failing to "make the connection" to the youth segment could have made him appear out of touch and behind the times. In presidential politics, this dynamic was seen in 1992 between presidential candidate Bill Clinton and President George Bush. Through a series of missteps, Bush appeared to many Americans as if he did not understand the lives of everyday citizens. This reinforced public perceptions that, compared to Clinton, Bush represented a bygone generation while the energetic, saxophone-playing, burger-eating Bill Clinton exuded youthfulness and seemed to embody "change." If Obama had neglected the youth segment, young people may have come to see him as not relevant to their interests and needs—a perception he would have had to work hard to reverse in any future electoral bid. In connecting so effectively and so publicly with the youth segment, Obama created a dichotomy in perceptions between his "connectedness" and "change," and the lack of connectedness and questions about commitment to change for Democratic frontrunner Hillary Clinton and John McCain—both of whom had failed to engage the young.

Obama established himself as very relevant to the interests and needs of young people.

The long-term folly also merits discussion. If Obama had neglected the youth segment, he would have failed to gain a foothold in the emerging youth base early on—a failure to achieve a first mover's advantage, of sorts. It has been widely noted that after voters cast their very first ballots, they often continue supporting the same party for decades or even a lifetime. In the electoral world, persuading a voter to support a political party for their first vote is akin to establishing a highly effective brand loyalty: the fruits of the investment can be reaped potentially for years. In getting a foothold early, Democrats through Obama's success may have established a significant foothold in the current youth segment that can radiate effects as those youths grow older, becoming influential teachers, policy makers, businesspersons, administrators, politicians, and health care providers, among others.

Leaders in many fields can take note of the twin follies of neglecting a key segment. With regard specifically to the youth segment, certain questions can prove important. Do young people represent a promising population within which you should establish your organization? Do you need to attract and retain that segment? Will early investments yield highly valuable longer-term dividends?

Barack Obama, recognizing both the upside of mobilizing the young and the downsides of neglecting them, adapted his campaign in a matter of months to nurture and capitalize on the enthusiasm of young voters. As Obama focused greater attention on the youth segment, multiple practices aided his success in harnessing and funneling this enthusiasm. Let's explore those practices below.

⇥ EMPOWER HIGHLY APPEALING LEADERS, ⇤ PLACE LEADERS WELL

[A]n important step in motivating and mobilizing a target segment involves empowering leaders who will appeal to them—leaders who will be perceived as understanding them, able to connect with them, and able to identify and address their needs.

Obama's successful efforts demonstrate that an important step in motivating and mobilizing a key target segment involves empowering leaders who will appeal to them—leaders who will be perceived as understanding them, able to connect with them, and able to identify and address their needs. As a young, basketball-playing, antiwar candidate with a multiracial background, Obama himself is very appealing to the young. His laid-back, straightforward style is a winner with them. The way he speaks—literally his word choices before youthful audiences—reaches right to the young. Even the way he signed his mass campaign e-mails to them—simply, "Barack"—resonates with them. To the young, he seems to speak their "language."

In addition, many aspects of Obama's worldview mirror that of the younger generation. He can speak with the eloquence and dreamy ambition of a John F. Kennedy and the thunderous power of a Martin Luther King, Jr. But particularly appealing to the ears of the young were his promises of change from old-style corrupt politics and his concern for issues such as preserving the American dream, social justice, poverty, the environment, and transparency and participation in politics. Obama's vision resonates with the young and is one they want to both believe in and embrace.

Yet even when the top leader of an organization does not appeal as strongly to the young as Obama does, effective efforts can still be made to appeal to the young. The broad principle still applies: to facilitate a process of courting effectively the members of a promising segment, empower leaders who appeal to them greatly, and ensure that those leaders will have good exposure.

We have all seen successful organizations with mature CEOs, for instance, that have successful youth departments headed by charismatic young leaders who appeal directly to the young. In a wide range of contexts, this approach can prove successful.

What is striking about Obama and his presidential campaign is that he appealed effectively to the young through both his own leadership and lower-level leaders throughout his organization. Obama's team built up layers of leaders with great youth appeal. Heeding the leadership principle "pay attention to your points of contact," Obama leveraged those leaders to motivate, mobilize, and harness the potential of young voters.

Consider, for instance, Obama's choice to recruit Chris Hughes, the 24-year-old cofounder of the online social networking website Facebook.com, as a leading force in shaping and executing the Obama campaign's technology strategy. The choice had great impact, given the innovation and expertise Hughes brought. Also important, Hughes's willingness to accept the position represented an endorsement of sorts from a high-profile, greatly admired, successful young leader. This, in and of itself, helped create a strong connection to the young.

Similarly, high-profile young Obama campaign leaders such as Jeremy Bird, a 2000 college graduate, aided Obama's appeal to the young. He was placed in very prominent positions. Named to serve as a field director for Senator Barack Obama's presidential campaign in South Carolina, Bird helped bring about a crucial and overwhelming Democratic primary victory there. He provided equally important efforts for the Maryland primary.[8] Bird went on to serve as the Ohio general election director and helped promote teams as an integral part of the Obama campaign's national strategy. Bird's prominence reinforced the notion among young supporters that they could also play a significant role in the campaign.

Certainly, long-seasoned and older leaders conducted equally important work in Obama's campaign, but the presence of young stars and Obama's keen instinct to make them very visible proved an asset. It helped create an atmosphere that fired up enthusiastic young people and made them believe their own individual efforts could make a significant contribution to the Obama campaign's broader work. Significantly, the presence of well-placed young leaders also facilitated the job of identifying the interests, desires, and needs of potential young voters.

⇥ PAY ATTENTION TO YOUR POINTS OF CONTACT ⇤

Obama's strategic choice to empower young leaders even outside of the ranks of formal staff also played a role in his success. Jeremy Bird explained that through local house meetings, the Obama campaign would "develop leadership amongst our volunteers.... They're much more effective than TV ads or a mailing." As Bird noted, people would "see young organizers who are [local], who are involved in a program that really is empowering to them—that gives them hope, and they see that mirrored in the candidate's message." Obama ensured those young, enthusiastic "points of contact" were highly visible, which caused a chain reaction. As occurred during one house meeting in South Carolina, for example, it became common to hear new Obama supporters commenting to fired-up young Obama volunteers that "What's inspiring me about him [Barack Obama] is *you*."

⇥ IDENTIFY SPECIAL INTERESTS ⇤

Obama's skill in identifying the interests, needs, and desires of his target audiences, including the young, also aided him significantly in motivating and mobilizing them. His operating principles were "dialogue, listen, respond." During his presidential campaign, as Obama focused on young voters, he did what he had learned to do excellently throughout his career—connect with people, learn about their challenges and hopes, and clearly identify the issues of concern to them. He had developed and refined those valuable skills during his

> Obama's skill in identifying the interests, needs, and desires of his target audiences, including the young, also aided him significantly in motivating and mobilizing them. His operating principles were: "dialogue, listen, respond."

days as a community organizer in Chicago in the mid-1980s, when he was charged with uniting church leaders and residents of the Altgeld Gardens public housing project to lobby decision makers for resources to improve their lives. In those days, Obama went door-to-door to speak with residents, coming to understand the issues that most mattered to them and preparing to help them meet their needs.

Just as he did back then, Obama made concerted efforts in his presidential campaign to identify excellently and understand the needs of everyday citizens and target groups, including the young. In seeking direct dialogue, he used both in-person channels and technological channels such as online blogs. Obama's dedicated efforts and responsiveness encouraged young people to engage more and in doing so, young people provided valuable feedback to the campaign. This in turn allowed Obama to tailor his messages to youth more effectively, which yielded greater youth engagement and participation. There was a snowball effect. Through his effective efforts to identify special interests and address them, Obama established for himself a significant competitive advantage.

⇥ PINPOINT YOUR PRIMARY TASKS ⇤

Obama's efforts allowed his campaign to hone in on many important themes and issues for young people. He communicated to young people about those key themes and issues in ways that resonated with them. For instance, Obama quickly learned that he appealed greatly to young voters because they viewed him as a "different kind of politician." Members of the American youth voting segment had grown up with government scandals, a dynasty of Bushes, and seemingly another dynasty of Clintons in the making. President Bill Clinton had been impeached, and many young people believed President Bush had taken America to war in Iraq under false pretenses. The particular theme of "change" resonated well among young voters, and Obama's promises of transparency and good ethics sounded very attractive to their ears. He became noted for expressing discontentment with politics as usual, which reflected the prevailing sentiment among many young people. For instance, Obama stated to young listeners:

> I am surprised at how many elected officials—even the good ones—spend so much time talking about the mechanics of politics and not matters of substance. They have this poker chip mentality, this overriding interest in retaining their seats or in moving their careers forward, and the business and game of politics, the political horse race, is all they talk about. Even those who are on the same page as me on the issues never seem to want to talk about them. Politics is regarded as little more than a career.[9]

To young people, Obama seemed to exhibit great heart as he professed sentiments such as these.

Young people were also drawn to the idea that Obama stood for the "politics of maximum unity" and against divisiveness. As one observer summed up, Obama sought to make the "tent as big as possible." Obama never promoted the language of racial grievances or divisions, and his multiracial background simply helped underscore his inclusiveness. Young people relished Obama's insistence that "red states" versus "blue states," among other divisions, were distinctions overemphasized by many decision makers—distinctions that were out of touch with how many Americans viewed current affairs. Young people viewed Obama as a leader who could bring the country together. As he identified interests of young people, Obama came to understand this and tailored his messages to young people well.

Obama's emphasis on hope also attracted young supporters. One only needs to survey the titles of his campaign speeches to see his great emphasis on messages of hope and change: Change That Works for You, Forging a New Future for America, A More Perfect Union, Keeping America's Promise, Reclaiming the American Dream, Our Moment Is Now, Change We Can Believe In, A New Beginning, Our Common Stake in America's Prosperity, A Sacred Trust, An Honest Government, A Hopeful Future, Take Back America.

Other aspects about Obama's message that attracted young supporters included his emphasis on preserving the American dream for young generations, and his concern for U.S. involvement in Iraq, the environment, health care, and education. By coming to understand the issues that most mattered to young people and tailoring his messages accordingly, Obama spoke in a language young people appreciated. He inspired and motivated young people, and ultimately he channeled this enthusiasm into effective efforts that aided his campaign.

Leaders in many fields can learn from the dialogue Obama created with young people and how he tailored his messages to bring greater impact in his efforts to mobilize his target group. Together, these laid a foundation for success.

⇥ AMPLIFY EFFORTS: FRUITFUL CHANNELS, ⇤ KEY NETWORKS

Obama's success also showed that to inspire a target group to partner in your organization's efforts, it's not enough to speak with words they will understand and appreciate; a target group must be able to *hear* your message. That is, it's not simply the message—channels matter. Selecting optimal channels can increase the effectiveness of efforts to motivate target groups to action.

> [I]t's not simply the message—channels matter. Selecting optimal channels can increase the effectiveness of efforts to motivate target groups to action.

Many of Obama's most effective strategies in reaching the young through well-chosen channels are now well known and widely praised for the genius of their design. Early on, Obama campaign leaders such as Jeremy Bird noted that mobilization is highly effective when you draw on social networks—a lesson Obama had already learned well during his days as an Illinois state senator and as a U.S. senator. Obama's successful leadership practices paid respect to marketing notions of placement and promotion. He embraced the idea that rather than asking the young to come to him, his campaign would "go to where they are." One place the young can be found is online. Technology fit neatly with Obama's efforts to court the young.

Obama found that leveraging social networks through technology was particularly effective with young people, who are accustomed to building and extending such networks in the online universe. He used technological innovations and trends, as well as online social networking sites such as myspace.com, to amplify his efforts to mobilize the young. Obama's campaign quickly became known as a *movement* in part because of its tremendous growth, fueled by online mobilization, with 325,000 young people registering quickly to his support network on Facebook.com.

The participation levels on the Obama website far exceeded participation levels among Democratic primary frontrunner Senator Hillary Clinton's supporters. Obama's online strategy, which became increasingly visible, and the tremendous support it generated created a buzz of its own.

Importantly, Obama did not neglect the value of old-fashioned bricks-and-mortar channels also. He understood that online channels and offline channels should work in tandem. In "going to where the youth are," Obama invested heavily in efforts to create offline channels, decentralizing his campaign by creating local offices through which mobilization could occur in all fifty states. The particular tool of house meetings became key to helping the movement spread and sustain itself.

Jeremy Bird acknowledged how the Obama campaign approached efforts to mobilize the offline social networks of potential young supporters. "You find some high school students that are getting engaged," he explained, "…and they go back and start to bring in other folks.…You get people to move and to act… much more from people they know and trust in their social network than from some campaign coming in and telling them, 'This is fun.'"[10] Notably, Bird acknowledged that the Obama campaign sought to move beyond an organizational design of one hub with spokes projecting outward. They created instead an intricate "snowflake" structured organization, one with many different hubs, each with its own set of spokes. This facilitated "a grassroots organizing program that really is based on people taking ownership and responsibility for… the causes they believe in."[11]

⇥ MOTIVATE WITH THE POWER OF *YOU* ⇤

Another practice that helped fuel Obama's success in mobilizing the young was his keen ability to personalize his message and,

Another practice that helped fuel Obama's success in mobilizing the young was his keen ability to personalize his message and, specifically, to leverage the "power of 'you.'"

specifically, to leverage the "power of 'you.'" As detailed in *Say It Like Obama and Win*, Obama has demonstrated consistently that personalizing a message with skillful use of personal pronouns—what I call the "I," "you," and "we" connection—can help win hearts and minds. Just as altering a message when speaking to audiences by using the word *I* and referring to your own relevant experience helps to personalize a message and establish credibility, skillful use of *we* and *you* helps a leader convey that she or he and the audience are part of the same team. The distance between a leader behind the podium and the audience can seem to narrow. As a leader speaks to listeners of what *you* can do, and the difference *you* can make, he or she can leverage the power of *you* to motivate listeners and mobilize them.

Consider the example discussed earlier, when Obama spoke before 3,500 George Mason University students at the beginning of his campaign in February 2007. Obama leveraged the power of *you* to connect excellently with the young listeners and make them feel a strong sense that their actions could make a meaningful difference. Obama noted that throughout history young people had helped influence the tide of important events. He urged his young listeners to realize they had the power to also influence U.S. military involvement in Iraq. After quoting the famous words of American icon Martin Luther King, Jr., who had stated in a powerful speech that "the arc of the moral universe...bends towards justice," Obama personalized the message. "Here's the thing, young people, it doesn't bend on its own, it bends because you put your hand on that arc and you bend it in the direction of justice." He said, "Think about all the power that's represented here in all of you.... If you all grab that arc, then I have no doubt, I have absolutely no doubt, that regardless of what happens in this presidential year and regardless of what happens in this campaign, America will transform itself."[12, 13] With the thunderous applause and cheers that followed, Obama and his team understood he had connected excellently with his audience. In Obama's words, they were "fired up" and "ready to go."

Obama recognized that a key to mobilizing young people was to tap into their desire to be an active part of his work and to feel they were helping to mold history. *Engagement, participation, partnering*—those became the catchwords. He would continue his practice of personalizing his message in order to inspire participation. By evoking the power of *you*, Obama improved the efficacy of his efforts to inspire, motivate, and mobilize a key target group, the youth, in support of his goals.

⇥ BUILD MOMENTUM WITH LOW-LYING FRUIT ⇤

As we explore factors that helped bring about Obama's success in mobilizing young people, we can also discern the importance that "low-lying fruit" played in building a sense of momentum and funneling enthusiasm in productive ways that brought about solid results. Obama identified and directed his youthful supporters to low-lying fruit—easily attainable, quick wins that motivated them, boosted their morale, created a sense of empowerment, and built momentum. His low-lying fruit included online actions

> Obama identified and directed his youthful supporters to low-lying fruit—easily attainable, quick wins that motivated them, boosted their morale, created a sense of empowerment, and built momentum.

that young people could complete easily, such as becoming a member of his website my.barackobama.com, adding links into the my.barackobama.com universe, forwarding messages to their friends, and making their online profiles public. Low-lying fruit also included offline actions such as hosting house meetings, hosting campaign events, and helping with fund-raising or canvassing.

The sense of achievement and satisfaction from securing the "early first wins" helped build confidence among young support-ers and encouraged them to tackle more ambitious goals. The result was greater engagement, enthusiasm, and loyalty.

⊰ INVEST IN TRAINING ⊱

Obama also exemplified the principle that as leaders inspire others to action, they should make certain to put in place the means for funneling action successfully toward desired end goals. Obama helped to channel the enthusiasm of young peo-ple in many ways. Notable among these, Obama empowered young volunteers to play significant roles in the campaign by providing substantive training to help them develop the required skills.

Temo Figueroa, national field director for the Obama cam-paign, explained that Obama sought to employ volunteers in more than just "grunt" work such as telephone campaigns, leaf-let distribution, or door-to-door canvassing. To offer a wider range of responsibilities in ways that would allow key tasks to be completed successfully, the Obama campaign provided training for volunteers with strong track records of work with the campaign. Obama's website, my.barackobama.com, facili-tated these efforts. With a powerful database, the website tracked which volunteers established excellent records of work with the campaign. From there, offline training tools came into play. Campaign officials extended to select volunteers the opportunity to participate in rigorous four-day training sessions called "Camp Obama" before they were deployed for greater responsibilities in the field. As Zack Exley noted:

> Camp Obama is the main ingredient in that preparation. Not counting dozens of trainings held near the Chicago campaign headquarters (which mostly focused on Iowa), there have been six Camp Obamas in February 5 states so far: Burbank and Oakland, California; Saint Louis, Missouri; New York City, New York; Phoenix, Arizona; and Atlanta, Georgia. While the curriculum has varied with the different teams behind each training, the end goals have remained consistent: send tight-knit, well-trained and highly motivated teams of volunteer organizers back to their home Congressional districts with a plan.[14]

Well-seasoned and highly esteemed organizers, such as Harvard's Marshall Ganz and Mike Kruglik, helped teach courses at the camps. Topics ranged from a review of grassroots organizing techniques to lessons focusing on what had fueled the failure or success of other campaigns.[15] The camps sought to help volunteers develop the skills to organize local volunteers and community. The volunteers leveraged this training, building the local base of supporters. Paid Obama campaign staff facilitated work further once the basic local infrastructure had been developed. This process helped Obama establish a strong base in states where virtually no organization had existed in the early months of his campaign. It allowed him to transform some traditionally noncompetitive states into competitive states for his Democratic candidacy.

Obama also ensured that leaders in the field had access to online training tools, such as an online precinct captain training tool that could help prepare leaders in the field for more effective work.

⇥ CREATE AN ENABLING STRUCTURE— ⇤ PARTNER "WHERE THEY ARE"

Obama also recognized that an organization's structure can function as a powerful, enabling factor for success.... For Obama's purposes, decentralization of organizational structure provided an optimal structure...

Obama also recognized that an organization's structure can function as a powerful, enabling factor for success. He created a decentralized organizational structure through which volunteers could engage successfully in meaningful activities.

Volumes have been written on the benefits and pitfalls of various organizational structures, from highly centralized to highly decentralized. Leaders should, at all times, consider the optimal structure for their groups, given the key tasks at hand and other important factors. Obama and his team weighed the options well and chose excellently. For Obama's purposes, decentralization provided an optimal structure: the high degree of decentralization made high-impact grassroots youth work possible.

In providing decentralization, the Obama campaign also made certain to oversee key decisions, such as designing and providing training for leaders in the field; determining whether house meetings should be central to organizing efforts; designating short-, medium-, and long-term campaign goals; and formulating and spreading key campaign messages to be supported by activities in the field. The Obama campaign also determined excellently what activities were best left up to leaders in the field.

After providing training and guidelines, the Obama campaign helped to ensure that local leaders owned decisions, such as which local leaders should gain greater responsibilities or how precisely to run house meetings. Obama encouraged strong organization at the local levels. In spite of his many commitments, Obama made efforts to check in on work in person. As early as October 2007, *The New York Times* reported, "Mr. Obama has taken a personal role in the program his Iowa organizers have set up to recruit potential supporters in Iowa.... At each stop on his four-day tour through Iowa last week, Obama put aside the time to meet with 'Barack Stars,' as members of the network are called."[16]

Obama also invested in helping young people to build campus organizations. By May 2008, Obama campaign manager David Axelrod acknowledged, "We are actively working with students to organize." The campaign supplied kits to students with directions and information providing guidance for key tasks such as recruiting volunteers, developing leaders, and attracting press coverage. In characteristic fashion, Obama took time to meet with campus leaders, stating at a meeting in April 2008 before the leaders of campus chapters, "I'm going to be counting on you to be the backbone of this campaign."[17]

Together, the practice and principles Obama employed allowed him to motivate and mobilize excellently one of his key target groups, the young. His work yielded a significant and historic impact, as the youth vote had never before played such a large role as it did in facilitating Obama's presidential victory. Young people soon made up one of the Obama campaign's largest donor groups, with donations derived largely via the Internet.[18] Youth support grew far beyond what Obama and his team had anticipated, becoming much more than the "icing on the cake." By the fall of 2008, David Plouffe had acknowledged, "In many ways, our fate is in their hands." In the November 2008 election, Obama won 53 percent of the popular vote, more than any nonincumbent candidate for the presidency since Dwight Eisenhower in 1952. He can credit young people for providing him a large portion of his comfortable victory margin.

EMPLOYING THE LESSONS

A key to Barack Obama's success as a presidential candidate was his ability to motivate and inspire young people. Several best practices—assessing the potential impact of the young, identifying their interests, empowering leaders who appealed to the young, and addressing relevant interests—enabled Obama to effectively motivate and mobilize the young. Many of these practices and principles can be used to motivate and mobilize other key target groups. Consider how these practices and principles can strengthen your own leadership. Keep these questions in mind:

- Have I adequately assessed the potential of key target groups? In what ways would my work be strengthened by cultivating relations with a particular target group that is interested in the goals or mission of my work?
- What are the potential benefits of mobilizing a particular target group? What are the follies of neglecting that group?
- Have I empowered leaders who will appeal to my designated target group? Have I paid adequate attention to my points of contact?
- Am I sufficiently aware of the special interests of my key target group?
- Have I taken steps to address the interests of my key target group? How can I improve the steps I have taken?
- Have I identified and used fruitful communication channels to amplify my efforts to cultivate relations with my target group?
- Have I leveraged the networks of my target group?
- Have I used effectively the power of *you?*
- Have I built momentum in mobilization by directing members of my target group to low-lying fruit?
- Have I invested adequately in training and/or taken effective steps to partner with my target group "where they are"?

CHAPTER 10

FACE AND OVERCOME CONTROVERSIES

Many seasoned leaders have learned a particular truth: it's not *whether* controversy will arise in one's career, it's *when*. At one point or another, all leaders will likely face difficulties, adversity, or controversy. It may come from a poor choice of words, an unintended slight, a miscommunication, or a representative's misspeaking. These and other circumstances can give rise to difficult situations. How a leader responds to troubled times can make all the difference between failure and success, sinking or swimming. Barack Obama understands this. Among the secrets of his success have been multiple practices that have helped him not only survive controversial situations, but thrive in their aftermath, emerging with his strong reputation largely intact.

In other cases, controversies have damaged the careers of prominent leaders often to the point of "no recovery." Consider, for instance, the effects of John Edwards's extramarital affair, Gerald Ford's pardon of Richard Nixon, and the public clouds of doubt that lingered following "Swift Boat" attacks on John Kerry. Like those leaders, Barack Obama has also been embroiled in controversy. In recent years, he has needed to address situations involving his association with Reverend Jeremiah Wright, whose fiery words undercut Obama's presidential campaign messages of unity; his own ill-spoken comments about Americans who he said "clung" to guns and religion in hard times; Louis Farrakhan's unsolicited endorsement of Obama's presidential bid; and his decision to comment publicly on the arrest of Harvard University professor Henry Louis Gates. Yet, after addressing each of those difficult situations, Obama continued to enjoy high public approval ratings. What practices enable Obama to address controversies and emerge from them with his image and strong reputation largely unscathed? There are valuable lessons to be learned about how, amid controversy, Obama skillfully resets the tone of the conversation, focuses on his goals, conveys humility, and leverages props. His practices of addressing controversy in a forthright manner, accepting responsibility, and extending a hand to others also have helped Obama move beyond controversies successfully.

⇥ NIP CONTROVERSY IN THE BUD OR ⇤ GRAB THE BULL BY ITS HORNS

Many observers have noted how Obama has seemed to weather controversial situations well and to emerge from them largely unscathed, with his reputation for strong ethical behavior intact. A range of practices has enabled him to do this. Obama has demonstrated through his actions his belief that controversies are best dealt with directly and quickly. His mantra can be summarized as "nip controversy in the bud." That is, address controversy head on and seek a quick resolution, which can help minimize damage to your reputation and ongoing work.

> Obama has demonstrated through his actions his belief that controversies are best dealt with directly and quickly. His mantra can be summarized as "nip controversy in the bud."

There have been instances, however, when Obama has not adopted this quick-response tactic. In those cases, which are much more rare, Obama usually believed the controversy might dissipate quickly. During the controversy involving Reverend Jeremiah Wright, for example, Obama did not move quickly to fully denounce Wright's divisive words—considered un-American, prejudiced, and incendiary to many observers— or to indicate he was severing ties to the pastor. Obama's choice not to take those actions flowed in part from his desire to remain loyal to a long-standing friend and his belief that leaders should not throw friends "under the bus" in order to score quick political wins. After Wright continued to fan the controversy as he made additional public statements that many listeners considered equally abrasive, Obama chose to "grab the bull by its horns."

Rather than ignoring the escalating controversy, Obama came forward and offered a clear denunciation of Wright's words in a well-planned and publicized statement to the American public. Significantly, Obama did not dodge the tough issues about U.S. race relations to which Wright's statements had drawn attention. Instead, he delivered a lengthy, intricate speech that addressed directly America's continuing racial challenges. Although his response had been delayed, Obama's hallmark tactics of addressing controversy head on, offering an appropriate acceptance of responsibility, and providing a clear restatement of his ethics served him well. Below we take a closer look at these tactics.

⇥ KNOW YOUR GOALS ⇤

Whether nipping controversy in the bud or grabbing a bull by its horns, a key factor for Obama's success in overcoming controversy has been his ability to face those controversies with a clear sense of his goals.

Whether nipping controversy in the bud or grabbing a bull by its horns, a key factor for Obama's success in overcoming controversy has been his ability to face those controversies with a clear sense of his goals. Obama demonstrates the principle that wise leaders take adequate time to identify their goals before seeking to address the controversies. Identifying your goals can guide you to the best next steps—how humbly you should act, your ideal body language, the props you might gather around you, or the venue where you might address the controversy or offer your apology, for instance. These factors can help bring a desired outcome.

Barack Obama has shown considerable skill in identifying his goals before he addresses difficult circumstances. Consider, for instance, when he addressed the unsolicited, undesired endorsement that Black Muslim leader Louis Farrakhan gave to his presidential bid just days before a major televised debate with Senator Hillary Clinton in 2008. Farrakhan, viewed by many people as a leader who utters anti-Semitic remarks and as a radical who speaks incendiary words that fan racial tensions, was not a personality with whom Obama wished to associate. During a presidential debate just days after Farrakhan's public endorsement, journalist Tim Russert asked Obama, "Do you accept the support of Louis Farrakhan?" Obama attempted to defuse any controversy arising from the unsolicited support. He replied:

I have been very clear in my denunciation of Minister Farrakhan's anti-Semitic comments. I think they are unacceptable and reprehensible. I did not solicit this support.

He expressed pride in an African American who seems to be bringing the country together. I obviously can't censor him. But it is not support that I sought and we're not doing anything, I assure you, formally or informally with Mr. Farrakhan....

Tim, I have some of the strongest support from the Jewish community in my hometown of Chicago and in this presidential campaign. And the reason is because I have been a stalwart friend of Israel's. I think they are one of our most important allies in the region, and I think that their security is sacrosanct, and that the United States is in a special relationship with them, as is true with my relationship with the Jewish community.

And the reason that I have such strong support is because they know that not only would I not tolerate anti-Semitism in any form, but also because of the fact that what I want to do is rebuild what I consider to be a historic relationship between the African American community and the Jewish community.

Seeking to capitalize on Obama's failure to use the word *reject* in his repudiation of Farrakhan, Senator Hillary Clinton chimed in quickly, insinuating that Obama had not taken an acceptably strong stand. Russert asked Clinton to clarify her remark, and Clinton stated pointedly, "there's a difference between denouncing and rejecting," implying Obama had taken the less firm position. Obama understood Clinton's comments placed a cloud over his sentiments that, if not addressed, could plunge him more deeply in controversy. He skillfully kept in mind his twin goals of distancing himself from Farrakhan and articulating unwavering support for Israel, responding swiftly as he stated:

I have to say I don't see a difference between denouncing and rejecting. There's no formal offer of help from Minister Farrakhan that would involve me rejecting it. But if the word "reject" Senator Clinton feels is stronger than the word "denounce," then I'm happy to concede the point, and I would reject and denounce.

Onlookers reacted with hearty applause. Obama had just averted a catastrophe. In staying focused on his purpose, Obama spoke the words needed to quell a looming controversy that could have set back his campaign. His actions demonstrate an important best practice: before facing difficult situations, clarify in your own mind your goals, and as you address the situation of controversy, ensure your actions and words remain in line with those goals.

⇥ EXUDE HUMILITY ⇤

> Humility and graciousness have also played a role in Obama's success as he has faced difficult situations.

Humility and graciousness have also played a role in Obama's success as he has faced difficult situations. From Obama's example, we can see that as you face controversy, the way you initially present yourself to people remains exceedingly important. In some ways, it is as if you are making a first impression all over again. Given the circumstances of the controversy you face, your character or judgment may have been placed in doubt. Thus, you need to impress people all over again with your ethical qualities, judgment, and character.

To this end, Obama demonstrates that when addressing controversy, it is a best practice to pay particular attention to your body language. Just as with a first impression, body language communicates important messages, providing the visual clues and confirmations about whether you are remorseful, accepting of responsibility, and sincere. Body language can also convey the opposite—whether you are defensive, defiant, angry, and insincere. Obama's successes show that, when you are addressing controversy, the ideal body language often falls on a fine line between appearing too weak with contriteness and seeming unapologetic with strength. When he is addressing situations of controversy, it would be counterproductive if Obama walked into a room with slouched shoulders and his head bowed—that conveys weakness. Instead, Obama typically offers his comments with a firm back, squared shoulders, and his chin up—a look-them-in-the-eye approach that conveys strength. But while appearing strong, he takes care to ensure his nonverbal language communicates humility or remorse—the tone of his voice, his demeanor, the look in his eyes, for instance. He allows body language and nonverbal communication to work for him, conveying messages that echo his words and help him achieve his goals. Obama illustrates the best practice of taking as much care with these elements when facing difficult circumstances as he does when making a first impression.

Significantly, when observing what works for Obama so well, we can learn equally important lessons from what he *doesn't* do as he faces controversy. Perhaps most important: Obama avoids appearing defiant and defensive in the face of controversy. He understands that appearing defiant or defensive would detract from any sense that he accepts responsibility for a situation or that he has remorse for any part of a wrongdoing. He illustrates a best practice that appearing humble and gracious can serve you well. People are often willing to forgive, but they are more likely to forgive when you convey a sense of humility or remorse.

⇥ CHOOSE PROPS APPROPRIATELY ⇤

Obama has also demonstrated that when you are addressing difficult situations, gathering the right props around you can help reinforce your message. During the Jeremiah Wright controversy, for instance, large segments of the American public wished to know why Obama had associated himself for years with such a divisive preacher. Obama offered an explanation in a well-publicized statement. He took care to stage the setting for his comments excellently, ensuring that large American flags flanked each side of the lectern from which he delivered his comments. Those props created a patriotic image and conveyed deep respect for America. This served as a frame in which Obama offered his apologetic statements and affirmed his commitment to unity and core American values. In short, his chosen backdrop sent messages highly consistent with his words and thereby underscored them, reinforced them, and gave them greater power. This should be considered *best practice*: the backdrop and props around you should reinforce your intent and words.

⇥ RECAST THE DIALOGUE ⇤

When facing difficult situations, Obama has also demonstrated a practice of quickly recasting the prevailing dialogue. As explained above, Obama has shown that an aim should be to nip controversy in the bud, as much as possible. If the controversy has already grown relatively large, his approach is to "take the bull by its horns." Recasting the dialogue in ways that are favorable to you is one means to do this.

Obama put his leadership principles into practice when he recast the dialogue in Philadelphia on March 18, 2008, amid an escalation of media attention to the fiery words of his former pastor, Reverend Jeremiah Wright. Given Obama's ties to the pastor, who had led the church of which Obama had been a member for decades, public speculation began to grow about the extent to which Obama must support Wright's divisive comments. Wright's sometimes hate-filled comments conflicted greatly with Obama's attempts to project himself as a unifier and someone who could bridge and heal divides among people of differing backgrounds. Understanding that the escalating controversy could seriously damage, if not completely derail, his presidential run, Obama came out strong, drawing on patriotic sentiments as he delivered what has been referred to as his seminal speech on race relations in America. He began the important speech by quoting the Declaration of Independence: "We the people, in order to form a more perfect union...."

Obama's choice for an opening sentence was outstanding. Without uttering another word, Obama's initial quotation rooted his response firmly within American tradition and underscored his commitment to core American founding principles. Obama continued, offering words and perspectives that helped place him on moral high ground—affirming his commitment to unity and challenging America to continue to confront and make progress in its race relations. Obama spoke forthrightly about the intricacies of American race relations and obstacles to equality, but most importantly provided clarification of how deeply he disapproved of Wright's fiery comments. With this speech, he succeeded in laying to rest the Wright controversy, reaffirmed public perceptions of his inclusiveness and strong ethics, and made such a strong impression that he subsequently earned the endorsement of Governor Bill Richardson, who cited the speech as a major reason why he endorsed Obama over his longtime friend Hillary Clinton.

⇥ Know When to Say, "I Screwed Up" ⇤

Obama's success in weathering controversies also demonstrates it is often very useful to address error head-on, making a clear admission and taking responsibility for any wrongdoing. When addressing difficult situations, Obama usually offers an apology early on in his remarks. His apologies are clear and forthright. When appropriate, he admits wrongdoing and takes responsibility for his less than ideal choices. This willingness to admit wrongdoing or shortcomings candidly works for him, underscoring his reputation for good ethical behavior. Obama has employed this approach successfully for years.

> When addressing difficult situations, Obama usually offers an apology early on in his remarks. His apologies are clear and forthright.

Consider, for instance, how Obama addressed the poor choices he made as a youth, during a period when he experimented with illegal drugs. Rather than seeking to hide this, Obama admitted his mistakes in his memoir, *Dreams of My Father*. He offered a straightforward revelation and took responsibility for the choices. He affirmed those choices were wrong and explained how he had grown and matured since making those poor choices. Obama's candor in addressing his youthful indiscretions boosted public perceptions of his honesty and integrity, and helped the public view those youthful indiscretions as largely irrelevant during the 2008 presidential campaign. Very notably, the issue of Obama's illegal drug use during his youth never emerged as a significant campaign issue, something that affirms the lesson, "If you make a mistake, say so."

Similarly, in April 2008, Obama made a major misstep when speaking about working class voters in old and economically ailing midwestern industrial towns. He said that those Americans "get bitter, they cling to guns or religion or antipathy to people who aren't like them or anti-immigrant sentiment or anti-trade sentiment as a way to explain their frustrations." The comments stirred a strong, negative public response. Amid the controversy, Obama addressed his mistake directly. He stated during an AP Luncheon:

> Good afternoon. I know I kept a lot of you guys busy this weekend with the comments I made last week. Some of you might even be a little bitter about that.
>
> As I said yesterday, I regret some of the words I chose, partly because the way that these remarks have been interpreted have offended some people and partly because they have served as one more distraction from the critical debate that we must have in this election season.

His straightforward acknowledgment of his mistake was well received. By and large, Americans allowed the incident to fade, and Obama emerged from the controversy with little lasting damage to his reputation or image. The moral of the story that Obama demonstrated once again: If you make a mistake, say so.

Two weeks after his presidential inauguration, Obama illustrated again this practice of addressing controversy directly and accepting responsibility for shortcomings. On February 3, 2009, shortly after Obama named two additional cabinet members, both withdrew their names from consideration. Tom Daschle and Nancy Killefer both faced scandals. Daschle, who Obama had hoped could lead the charge for health care reform, revealed tax problems. When Obama addressed the high-profile withdrawals in multiple TV interviews, he adopted a the-buck-stops-here attitude. He stated to Charles Gibson of ABC News that he wished to usher in a new "era of responsibility" and there could not be "two sets of rules for the people in Washington and for the people back home who pay their taxes."[1] He took full responsibility for a lack of adequate vetting, which could have spotted problems earlier on, and used his candor successfully in maintaining public confidence in his process of naming high-caliber leaders to his cabinet.

The value of Obama's candor in the face of controversy becomes particularly evident when contrasting his outcomes with the outcomes of leaders who have greeted controversial situations with defensiveness or defiance. Recall, for instance, when Bill Clinton faced the scandal of his extramarital affair with Monica Lewinsky. Clinton made an early mistake in appearing angry and defiant before the media. He made a second notable mistake with his famous "wagging finger"—pointing his finger to chastise the people who were accusing him of an affair. Clinton made a third significant error in judgment as he lied about the affair, denying it. Together, his anger, defiance, refusal to accept responsibility, and outright denial only served to fuel the public uproar and media frenzy, and did little to prevent an escalation of the situation as Clinton's opponents mobilized efforts for an impeachment.

⇥ EXTEND A HAND TO DETRACTORS ⇤

> Obama has shown a notable ability to remain "above the fray"... choosing instead to reach a hand out to detractors or face them directly in an effort to bring a quick ease to tensions.

At times, leaders face controversies that arise when an adversarial party creates or increases tensions. Obama has shown a notable ability to remain "above the fray" in such instances, choosing instead to extend a hand to detractors or face them directly in an effort to bring a quick ease to tensions. The practice has many times yielded excellent results.

Consider, for example, Obama's relationship with Professor Cornell West, a famous African American professor at Princeton University.

Around the time in 2007 when Barack Obama announced his candidacy for the U.S. presidency in Springfield, Illinois, Cornell West was busy chastising Obama in biting terms in front of a large audience at the State of the Black Union gathering in Atlanta, Georgia. Obama got wind of the biting public rebuke West delivered of him, which included criticisms of Obama's commitment to and stances on issues of concern to many people in the African American community. The harsh words, coming from one of the most esteemed and preeminent black scholars in the United States, received attention. Obama chose to reach out to his detractor: he gave West a call.

As West recalled, Obama began the conversation with a simple statement: "I want to clarify some things." His tone was nonconfrontational, nondefensive. The two men spoke for hours about Obama's views and his record on legislation meaningful to the black community, such as access to health care and reforms in the criminal justice system. Obama followed this up with a meeting in person a few weeks later. Notably, within approximately a month of that State of the Black Union gathering during which West had chastised Obama, West offered Obama his backing and began serving as an unpaid adviser to Obama's campaign.[2]

⇥ KNOW WHEN TO OFFER A BEER ⇤

Obama's success in overcoming controversy also teaches us that when you are admitting wrong and accepting responsibility, it is sometimes useful to go a step further, extending an invitation to the persons who might have been harmed by your poor judgment. Obama demonstrated this excellently in July 2009, following the arrest of Harvard University professor Henry Louis Gates in Cambridge, Massachusetts, by a police officer named Jim Crowley. Obama commented publicly on Crowley's arrest of Professor Gates in his own home, saying that the police had "acted stupidly." His comments fueled a media frenzy, and amid the controversy Obama came forward to quell things. He made an unscheduled appearance to deliver remarks during one of press secretary Robert Gibbs's regular White House briefings. Obama told the press:

> If you got to do a job, do it yourself. (Audience laughter.)
>
> I wanted to address you guys directly because over the last day and a half obviously there's been all sorts of controversy around the incident that happened in Cambridge with Professor Gates and the police department there.
>
> I actually just had a conversation with Sergeant Jim Crowley, the officer involved. And I have to tell you that as I said yesterday, my impression of him was that he was an outstanding police officer and a good man, and that was confirmed in the phone conversation—and I told him that.
>
> And because this has been ratcheting up—and I obviously helped to contribute ratcheting it up—I want to make clear that in my choice of words I think I unfortunately gave an impression that I was maligning the Cambridge Police Department or Sergeant Crowley specifically—and I could have calibrated those words differently. And I told this to Sergeant Crowley.
>
> I continue to believe, based on what I have heard, that there was an overreaction in pulling Professor Gates out of

his home to the station. I also continue to believe, based on what I heard, that Professor Gates probably overreacted as well. My sense is you've got two good people in a circumstance in which neither of them were able to resolve the incident in the way that it should have been resolved and the way they would have liked it to be resolved.

The fact that it has garnered so much attention I think is a testimony to the fact that these are issues that are still very sensitive here in America. So to the extent that my choice of words didn't illuminate, but rather contributed to more media frenzy, I think that was unfortunate.

What I'd like to do then is make sure that everybody steps back for a moment, recognizes that these are two decent people, not extrapolate too much from the facts—but as I said at the press conference, be mindful of the fact that because of our history, because of the difficulties of the past, you know, African Americans are sensitive to these issues. And even when you've got a police officer who has a fine track record on racial sensitivity, interactions between police officers and the African American community can sometimes be fraught with misunderstanding.

My hope is, is that as a consequence of this event this ends up being what's called a "teachable moment," where all of us instead of pumping up the volume spend a little more time listening to each other and try to focus on how we can generally improve relations between police officers and minority communities, and that instead of flinging accusations we can all be a little more reflective in terms of what we can do to contribute to more unity. Lord knows we need it right now—because over the last two days as we've discussed this issue, I don't know if you've noticed, but nobody has been paying much attention to health care. (Audience laughter.)

I will not use this time to spend more words on health care, although I can't guarantee that that will be true next week. I just wanted to emphasize that—one last point I guess I would make. There are some who say that as President I shouldn't have stepped into this at all because it's a local issue. I have to tell you that that part of it I disagree with. The fact that this has become such a big issue I think is indicative of the fact that race is still a troubling aspect of our society. Whether I were black or white, I think that me commenting on this and hopefully contributing to constructive—as opposed to negative—understandings about the issue, is part of my portfolio.

So at the end of the conversation there was a discussion about my conversation with Sergeant Crowley, there was discussion about he and I and Professor Gates having a beer here in the White House. We don't know if that's scheduled yet—but we may put that together.

He also did say he wanted to find out if there was a way of getting the press off his lawn. (Laughter.) I informed him that I can't get the press off my lawn. (Laughter.) He pointed out that my lawn is bigger than his lawn. (Laughter.) But if anybody has any connections to the Boston press, as well as national press, Sergeant Crowley would be happy for you to stop trampling his grass.

All right. Thank you, guys.

In his response, we can see many of Obama's hallmark practices. Obama set the right tone, making a surprise appearance in a manner that naturally drew attention to the remarks he would soon make, ensuring that it would be fodder for the news that night. He also set an ideal tone through his body language—entering the room with a very confident gait and a serious, near-somber expression that conveyed the great importance of the topic he was about to address.

Obama clearly kept his goals in mind. These included steering the direction of the chatter that had dominated the news over the prior days, in order to make the discussion about racial profiling and racial discrimination more productive; clarifying that Sergeant Jim Crowley and Professor Henry L. Gates were both good men (both men had come under public criticism in the days following Gates's arrest); affirming the seriousness of racial profiling and affirming his belief that the matter is significant enough to warrant presidential comment; and ending his comments on a lighter note, encouraging the idea that the situation could serve as a "teachable moment" and facilitate progress toward greater understanding and unity in the United States.

Obama made certain to try to remove any stain on the reputations of Crowley and Gates by affirming in particular that he had believed Crowley was a good man, and his phone conversation with Crowley confirmed this. He took responsibility for not choosing his words well, stating "and I could have calibrated those words differently," and "to the extent that my choice of words didn't illuminate, but rather contributed to more media frenzy, I think that was unfortunate." He challenged Americans to use the incident to learn and think about race relations. He restated his principles, saying firmly, "There are some who say that as President I shouldn't have stepped into this at all because it's a local issue. I have to tell you that that part of it I disagree with. The fact that this has become such a big issue I think is indicative of the fact that race is still a troubling aspect of our society. Whether I were black or white, I think that me commenting on this and hopefully contributing to constructive—as opposed to negative—understandings about the issue, is part of my portfolio." His tone was resolute, without a hint of apology, indicating the depth with which he felt this.

Finally, Obama ended the comments masterfully as he indicated that he had ended his conversation with Crowley on a jovial note, revealing potential plans to meet with Gates and Crowley for a beer. It was an excellent way to address this particular controversy, and the days following showed that Obama was effective in changing the tone of the conversation about the incident, leading to less hype and more serious reflection on race in America. Obama was also able, in the aftermath of his surprise appearance, to refocus media attention where he wanted it: on health care reform.

⇥ STAND STRONG AND DELIVER TOUGH MESSAGES ⇤

Another practice that has served Obama well has been his choice to restate his ethics, principles, and key beliefs in addressing controversies or offering an apology. He understands that when addressing such difficult situations, leaders are in many ways making a first impression all over again. Obama had shown considerable skill in his ability to convey his ethics and principles when facing controversy, and notably, he stands strong in his beliefs when addressing hard situations. In many instances, we have seen him exercise a high standard of leadership as he proceeds to

> Another practice that has served Obama well has been his choice to restate his ethics, principles, and key beliefs addressing controversies or offering an apology. He understands that when addressing such difficult situations, leaders are in many ways making a first impression all over again.

deliver tough messages in the face of controversy, even after tenderly addressing his own missteps.

Consider, for example, Obama's statements as he addressed his poorly chosen words about some midwestern rural voters, who he said "clung" to guns and religion when times are hard. Obama took the opportunity to elaborate upon his true beliefs:

> I'm a person of deep faith, and my religion has sustained me through a lot in my life. I even gave a speech on faith before I ever started running for President where I said that Democrats, "make a mistake when we fail to acknowledge the power of faith in people's lives." I also represent a state with a large number of hunters and sportsmen, and I understand how important these traditions are to families in Illinois and all across America. And, contrary to what my poor word choices may have implied or my opponents have suggested, I've never believed that these traditions or people's faith has anything to do with how much money they have.
>
> *But I will never walk away from the larger point that I was trying to make.* For the last several decades, people in small towns and cities and rural areas all across this country have seen globalization change the rules of the game on them. When I began my career as an organizer on the South Side of Chicago, I saw what happens when the local steel mill shuts its doors and moves overseas. You don't just lose the jobs in the mill, you start losing jobs and businesses throughout the community. The streets are emptier. The schools suffer.
>
> I saw it during my campaign for the Senate in Illinois when I'd talk to union guys who had worked at the local

Maytag plant for twenty, thirty years before being laid off at fifty-five years old when it picked up and moved to Mexico; and they had no idea what they're going to do without the paycheck or the pension that they counted on. One man didn't even know if he'd be able to afford the liver transplant his son needed now that his health care was gone.

I've heard these stories almost every day during this campaign, whether it was in Iowa or Ohio or Pennsylvania. And the people I've met have also told me that every year, in every election, politicians come to their towns, and they tell them what they want to hear, and they make big promises, and then they go back to Washington when the campaign's over, and nothing changes. There's no plan to address the downside of globalization. We don't do anything about the skyrocketing cost of health care or college or those disappearing pensions. Instead of fighting to replace jobs that aren't coming back, Washington ends up fighting over the latest distraction of the week.

And after years and years and years of this, a lot of people in this country have become cynical about what government can do to improve their lives. They are angry and frustrated with their leaders for not listening to them; for not fighting for them; for not always telling them the truth. And yes, they are bitter about that....

I may have made a mistake last week in the words that I chose, but the other party has made a much more damaging mistake in the failed policies they've chosen and the bankrupt philosophy they've embraced for the last three decades.

It's a philosophy that says there's no role for government in making the global economy work for working Americans that we have to just sit back and watch those factories close and those jobs disappear; that there's nothing we can do or should do about workers without health care, or children in crumbling schools, or families who are losing their homes, and so we should just hand out a few tax breaks and wish everyone the best of luck.[3] [Emphases provided]

Obama demonstrated this practice again in March 2008, during his seminal speech on race relations in America. During that historic speech, Obama finally denounced outright the divisive words of his former pastor, Reverend Jeremiah Wright. Obama also affirmed his commitment to principles of unity. He achieved his key task of confronting directly Wright's divisive words, stating he did not condone such words. Rather than stopping there, Obama refused to ignore or turn from the complex race relations issues to which Wright's words had drawn attention. He took the opportunity to comment and challenge Americans to continue to make strides in addressing the complex issues of race. Obama's choice to stand firm in his convictions earned the respect of many observers.

⇥ SHOWER DETRACTORS WITH KINDNESS ⇤

Finally, Obama has also been able to ease tensions or avert adversarial situations at times by showering his detractors or opponents with respect and kindness. When he defeated Senator Hillary Clinton in the race for the Democratic presidential nomination, for example, millions of Clinton supporters were highly disappointed and stinging with a sense that Hillary Clinton had suffered from sexism during various parts of the campaign. She had not been given a fair shake, they believed, during pivotal times such as during televised presidential debates, when the attitudes of some moderators seemed tinged by gender bias. The wounds these grievances created could have festered, but

Obama took steps to ease tensions and to help heal the divisions within the Democratic Party.

To do so, on many occasions he graciously acknowledged Clinton's talents, achievements, and the historic nature of her candidacy, offering comments such as, "It was an extraordinary honor to be alongside her during the course of this campaign." On many occasions, too, Obama praised Clinton's "tenacity" and "fighting spirit" and expressed sentiments such as, "I am a better candidate as a consequence of having run against Senator Hillary Rodham Clinton." Obama was able to quell the notion that he and Hillary Clinton remained bitter rivals and that they could not unite the party. Obama went on to win the backing of the majority of Clinton's millions of supporters. A lesson to be gleaned: kind words can go far in easing tensions and removing incentive for an escalation of tensions.[4]

EMPLOYING THE LESSONS

Barack Obama embraces the philosophy that *how* a leader responds to controversy makes all the difference between success and failure. Obama's success in addressing and overcoming controversy is a product of several key leadership practices he employs, such as identifying his goals and keeping them central in his mind as he faces controversy, leveraging props excellently, acknowledging error head-on, recasting the tone of the dialogue, exuding humility, accepting responsibility, and restating his strong ethics.

Think about how the practices and principles Obama employs might help you to address and overcome controversy and strengthen your leadership. Bear these questions in mind:

- Have I kept my goals foremost in my mind as I have attempted to bring resolution in situations of controversy?
- In situations of controversy, have I sought ways to nip the controversy in the bud? Alternatively, have I explored adequately ways to "grab the controversial bull by the horns"?

- When addressing controversy, have I employed best practices, such as exuding humility, acknowledging my errors head-on, recasting the tone of the dialogue, and showering my detractors with kindness?
- When addressing controversy, do I gather the best props around me that will reinforce the message I intend to convey?
- In addressing controversy, do I take steps to rebuild any waning confidence in my abilities or ethics? Have I taken adequate steps through words, nonverbal communication, and actions to rebuild my Teflon and make good impressions?
- In addressing controversy, have I made sure to restate my strong ethics to ensure I maintain or continue to build a strong reputation?

Obama's success has not been accidental, nor has it been automatic. His great achievements flow from his ability to wield excellent leadership skills and to leverage leadership lessons he has learned over time. He has embraced effectively timeless leadership principles, tailoring them and blending them to make them his own. He has honed a unique leadership style that has proved itself to have great impact. The formidable leadership skills Obama wields enable him to create excellent early impressions, convey vision effectively, turn foes into friends, gain a broad base of support, unify diverse sets of people, build high-performing teams, motivate key groups, and guide teams and organizations to success.

Obama's ability to win confidence, connect with listeners, and exercise outstanding leadership skills from the early days of his career has generated great excitement. Referred to as *magnetic, electrifying, thoughtful*, and *unifying*, Obama has employed keen leadership abilities as a community organizer in Chicago, president of the *Harvard Law Review*, a University of Chicago professor, an Illinois state senator, and a U.S. senator. Obama is drawing on his winning leadership practices and principles now in his role as U.S. president.

Significantly, Obama has distinguished himself not only in his ability to earn the confidence of others, convey his vision excellently, and inspire others, but also in his ability to build winning teams, organize and execute strategies with great effect. Indeed, his exemplary execution has made him one of the most distinctive leaders of recent years, and his reputation as a highly principled leader has impressed people from all backgrounds and political persuasions, allowing him to gain the deep respect of even those people who oppose his policies.

In short, through his leadership and leadership example, Obama has captured the imagination of Americans, inspiring young Americans in particular to become politically engaged in ways not witnessed for decades. He has also stirred the imagination of millions around the world, earning the praise of laudable leaders such as Nelson Mandela and Archbishop Tutu, and winning the 2009 Nobel Peace Prize, an unprecedented honor for a sitting U.S. president.

Leadership the Barack Obama Way explores the practices and principles that have helped fuel Obama's many successes. We delve into Obama's distinguished approach to leadership. With the insights we reveal, you can now consider how your own leadership might be strengthened through application of the leadership practices and principles we examine.

Consider, for example, how you can build strong early impressions and use them as a foundation for your leadership. Consider also your effectiveness in communicating vision. Is your team unified by a shared vision? Bearing in mind the practices that have allowed Obama to communicate ideas so well, think through ways you can improve your own success in communicating vision.

Assess your own reputation and whether it serves you as optimally as it should. If not, in light of the practices that have brought Obama success, how can you strengthen your own reputation?

Think about your array of "friends" or the allies you draw on to support your work. Do you limit yourself to friends in "usual" places? Can you benefit from friends in unusual places? The ability to turn foes into friends, to forge fruitful partnerships in unlikely places, and to unite people of varied backgrounds is a hallmark of Obama's leadership. In what ways can you leverage the best practices he demonstrates?

As we have seen, Obama's leadership success is in part attributable to his ability to form and lead high-performing teams. In what ways can you benefit from the best practices he illustrates? In what ways can you, like Obama, ensure that your teams embrace innovation and that you benefit from "mighty brainstorming"?

Obama has also benefited from all-hands cultures among some of the teams and organizations he has led. Consider what elements of an all-hands culture might also benefit your own work.

As you review Obama's best practices, think about how you can leverage diversity as a source of strength, innovation, and networks. How can you mirror Obama's skill in identifying multiple sources of diversity, forming diverse teams, and drawing on the benefits diversity can bring?

One of the most distinctive aspects of Obama's success during his 2008 presidential campaign was his ability to embrace and leverage technology in support of his mission and goals. With a clear understanding of his goals and a keen ability to choose technological partners well, Obama blended leading-edge technology seamlessly with his bricks-and-mortar, on-the-ground organizing, transforming how voter mobilization occurs and setting a new gold standard for the deployment of technology to support an organization's mission. As you examine the practices that led to this success, continue to think through how you can use technology to facilitate your internal and external communications, to build relations with key groups, to buttress key tasks such as training, and to amplify efforts to mobilize key groups.

Taking into account the factors that yielded Obama's success with technology, consider how you also might use technology as your game-changer.

Obama has demonstrated outstanding practices for motivating and mobilizing key target groups—empowering attractive leaders, identifying and addressing special interests, paying attention to points of contact, and amplifying efforts through fruitful communication channels. Consider how his successes can help you tailor your own efforts to motivate and mobilize key target groups.

Finally, Obama reflects a philosophy that *how* a leader responds to controversy makes all the difference between success and failure. When you find yourself facing controversy, consider the best practices that have allowed Obama to weather storms and thrive in their aftermath. Think about your goals, how to leverage props excellently, acknowledge error head on, recast the tone of the dialogue, and restate your strong ethics. Consider how to mirror his practices, which have allowed him to build and keep his Teflon strong.

Together, the leadership practices and principles Obama has employed over the years have served him excellently, allowing him to pave a path marked by consistent success. These same practices and principles allow Obama to claim his place as one of the most distinguished and capable leaders of recent years.

For more insights about the leadership of Barack Obama, including how he leads teams and steers a road to success, visit www.leadership-obama.com and www.drshelworkshop.com.

NOTES

INTRODUCTION

1. Ari Berman, "Desmond Tutu, Black Leaders Celebrate King & Obama," *The Nation*, January 19, 2009.
2. Chris McGreal, "Obama Brings New Voice of Hope, Nelson Mandela Says," Letter of Nelson Mandela to Barack Obama, cited by *Guardian*, January 20, 2009.
3. Karen Tumulty, "How Obama Did It," *Time* magazine, June 5, 2008.
4. Interview with Oprah Winfrey, CNN, "Larry King Live," May 13, 2007.
5. Pat Robertson on CNN, "Larry King Live," after elected president, November 5, 2008.
6. Tammerlin Drummond, "Barack Obama's Law Personality," *Los Angeles Times*, Posted on blogs, September 4, 2008.
7. Ibid.
8. Ibid.
9. Kenneth T. Walsh, "On the Streets of Chicago, a Candidate Comes of Age," *U.S. News*, August 26, 2007.

CHAPTER 1

1. Janny Scott, "The Long Run: Obama's Account of New York Years Often Differs From What Others Say," *The New York Times*, October 30, 2007.
2. Full transcript, comment to CNN correspondent Candy Crowley after 2004 Democratic National Convention Keynote Address, July 27, 2004.
3. Shelly Leanne, *Say It Like Obama and Win!* (New York: McGraw-Hill, 2009).
4. Serge Kovaleski, "The Long Run: Obama's Organizing Years, Guiding Others and Finding Himself," *The New York Times*, July 7, 2008.

CHAPTER 2

1. L. Iacocca, *Iacocca: An Autobiography* (New York: Bantam Books, 1984).
2. "60 Minutes" transcript. Steve Kroft spoke with Senator Obama on Wednesday in Elko, Nevada, aired September 21, 2008.
3. Janny Scott, "The Long Run: Obama's Account of New York Years Often Differs from What Others Say," *The New York Times*, October 30, 2007.
4. Full text of Senator Barack Obama's Announcement for President, Springfield, IL, February 10, 2007.
5. Kenneth T. Walsh, "On the Streets of Chicago, a Candidate Comes of Age," *U.S. News*, August 26, 2007.
6. Jodi Kantor, "In Law School, Obama Found Political Voice," *The New York Times*, January 28, 2007.
7. Bob Secter and John McCormick, "Barack Obama, Part 3: Portrait of a Pragmatist," *Chicago Tribune*, March 30, 2007.
8. Remarks for Senator Barack Obama: Kennedy Endorsement Event, Washington, DC, January 28, 2008.
9. Remarks of Senator Barack Obama: AP Annual Luncheon, Washington, DC, April 14, 2008.
10. Remarks of Senator Barack Obama: Discussion with Working Women, Albuquerque, NM, June 23, 2008.
11. Remarks of Senator Barack Obama: "A More Perfect Union," Philadelphia, PA, March 18, 2008.
12. Remarks of Senator Barack Obama: "The Great Need of the Hour," Atlanta, GA, January 20, 2008.
13. Remarks of Senator Barack Obama at the Robert F. Kennedy Human Rights Award Ceremony, November 16, 2005.
14. Remarks of Senator Barack Obama: "A More Perfect Union."

CHAPTER 3

1. Janny Scott, "The Long Run: In Illinois, Obama Proved Pragmatic and Shrewd," *The New York Times*, July 30, 2007.
2. Cited in Bob Secter and John McCormick, "Barack Obama: Part 3: Portrait of a Pragmatist," *Chicago Tribune*, March 30, 2007.
3. Full text of Senator Barack Obama's Announcement for President, Springfield, IL, February 10, 2007.

4. Barack Obama, Interview with "60 Minutes," February 11, 2007.

5. Bob Secter and John McCormick, "Barack Obama, Part 3: Portrait of a Pragmatist," *Chicago Tribune*, March 30, 2007.

6. David Axelrod, Interview with "60 Minutes," November 9, 2008.

7. David Plouffe, Interview with "60 Minutes," November 9, 2008.

8. Cited in Secter and McCormick, "Barack Obama: Part 3: Portrait of a Pragmatist."

9. David Jackson and Ray Long, "Barack Obama: Part 4: Showing His Bare Knuckles," *Chicago Tribune*, April 4, 2007.

10. Jerry Kellman, Comments in News Piece of Margaret Warner on Leadership Style, "PBS Newshour," aired September 23, 2008.

11. Tammerlin Drummond, *Los Angeles Times*, Posted on blogs September 4, 2008.

12. Ibid.

13. Jo Becker and Christopher Drew, "The Long Run: Pragmatic Politics, Forged on the South Side," *The New York Times*, May 11, 2008.

14. Drummond, *Los Angeles Times*, September 4, 2008.

15. Barack Obama, Interview with John King, "State of the Union with John King," CNN, September 20, 2009.

16. Ellen McGirt, "Boy Wonder: How Chris Hughes Helped Launch Facebook and the Barack Obama Campaign," *FastCompany*, March 17, 2009.

17. Jodi Kantor, "In Law School, Obama Found Political Voice," *The New York Times*, January 28, 2007.

18. Hank De Zutter, "What Makes Obama Run?" chicagoreader.com, December 8, 1995.

19. Ibid.

20. Drummond, *Los Angeles Times*, September 4, 2008.

21. Barack Obama, Interview with "60 Minutes," February 10, 2008.

22. Text of Democrat Barack Obama's prepared remarks for a rally on Tuesday in St. Paul, MN, as released by his campaign.

23. Barack Obama, Interview with "60 Minutes," September 20, 2008.

24. Barack Obama, Interview with "60 Minutes," February 10, 2008.

25. Former Rep. Abner Mikva (D), Comments in News Piece of Margaret Warner on Leadership Style, "PBS Newshour," aired September 23, 2008.

26. David Gergen, "David Gergen Commentary: Obama's First Hundred Days: Looking Through the Lens of History," cnn.com, April 29, 2009.

27. This Week with George Stephanopoulos, "ABC News," May 10, 2009.

CHAPTER 4

1. Cited in Janny Scott, "The Long Run: In Illinois, Obama Proved Pragmatic and Shrewd," *The New York Times*, July 30, 2007.

2. Bob Secter and John McCormick, "Barack Obama, Part 3: Portrait of a Pragmatist," *Chicago Tribune*, March 30, 2007.

3. Ibid.

4. Jodi Kantor, "In Law School, Obama Found Political Voice," *The New York Times*, January 28, 2007.

5. Han De Zutter, "What Makes Obama Run?" *Chicago Reader*, December 8, 1995.

6. Ibid.

7. Scott, "The Long Run: In Illinois."

8. Jo Becker and Christopher Drew. "The Long Run: Pragmatic Politics, Forged on the South Side," *The New York Times*, May 11, 2008.

9. Ibid.

10. Ibid.

11. Ibid.

12. Ibid.

13. Ibid.

14. Ibid.

15. Ibid.

16. Ibid.

17. Ibid.

18. Scott, "The Long Run: In Illinois."

19. Kantor, "In Law School."

20. Richard Wolffe and Daren Briscoe, "Across the Divide: How Barack Obama Is Shaking up old Assumptions About What It Means to Be Black and White in America," *Newsweek*, July 16, 2007.

21. Scott, "The Long Run."

22. Becker and Drew, "The Long Run: Pragmatic Politics."

23. Ibid.

24. Ibid.

25. Wolffe and Briscoe, "Across the Divide."

26. The Trail, *The Washington Post*, Pool Report From Clinton-Obama Event at the Mayflower, June 26, 2008.

27. Ibid.

28. Ibid.

29. Gwendolyn Driscoll, "Rick Warren Defends Barack Obama Invitation," *Orange County Register*, November 29, 2006.

30. Tammerlin Drummond, "Barack Obama's Law Personality," *Los Angeles Times*, Posted on blogs, September 4, 2008.

31. Serge Kovaleski, "The Long Run: Obama's Organizing Years, Guiding Others and Finding Himself," *The New York Times*, July 7, 2008.

32. Secter and McCormick, "Barack Obama, Part 3."

33. Drummond, "Barack Obama's Law Personality."

34. Kantor, "In Law School."

35. Scott, "The Long Run: In Illinois."

36. Garance Ranke-Ruta and Anne E. Kornblut, "The Presidents' Power Lunch: Clinton Joins Obama in N.Y. to Break Bread and Talk Policy," *The Washington Post*, September 15, 2009.

Chapter 5

1. Karen Tumulty, "How Obama Did It," *Time* magazine, June 5, 2008.

2. Ibid.

3. David Moberg, "Obama's Community Roots," *The Nation*, April 16, 2007.

4. "The Interview: Person of the Year Barack Obama," *Time* magazine, December 17, 2008.

5. Barack Obama, Interview with John King, "State of the Union with John King," CNN, September 20, 2009.

6. Tumulty, "How Obama Did It."

7. Susan Rice, Comments in News Piece of Margaret Warner on Leadership Style, "PBS Newshour," aired September 23, 2008.

8. David Axelrod, Comments in News Piece of Margaret Warner on Leadership Style, "PBS Newshour," aired September 23, 2008.

9. Obama, Comments in News Piece of Margaret Warner on Leadership Style, "PBS Newshour," aired September 23, 2008.

10. Tumulty, "How Obama Did It."

11. "The Interview: Person of the Year Barack Obama," *Time*.

12. Axelrod, Comments in News Piece of Margaret Warner on Leadership Style.

13. Tumulty, "How Obama Did It."

14. "How He Did It," *Newsweek*, November 5, 2008.

15. Ibid.

16. Rice, Comments in News Piece of Margaret Warner on Leadership Style.

17. Tumulty, "How Obama Did It."

18. Ben Smith, "Obama Runs Tight Campaign Ship," *The Politico*, December 21, 2007.

19. "How He Did It," *Newsweek*.

20. Ellen McGirt, "Boy Wonder: How Chris Hughes Helped Launch Facebook and the Barack Obama Campaign," *Fast Company*, March 17, 2009.

Chapter 6

1. David Moberg, "Obama's Community Roots," *The Nation*, April 16, 2007.

2. Ibid.

3. Susan Rice, Comments in News Piece of Margaret Warner on Leadership Style, "PBS Newshour," aired September 23, 2008.

4. Hank De Zutter, "What Makes Obama Run?" chicagoreader.com, December 8, 1995.

5. David Plouffe, Interview with "60 Minutes," November 9, 2008.

6. Zack Exley, "The New Organizers, What's Really Behind Obama's Ground Game," huffingtonpost.com, October 8, 2008.

7. Moberg, "Obama's Community Roots."

8. Exley, "The New Organizers."

9. Doug Walton, "Organizing Like Obama: Web 2.0 Enabled Change Agents in Action," empowerbase.com, September 10, 2008.

10. Zack Exley, "Obama Field Organizers Plot a Miracle," huffingtonpost.com, August 27, 2007.

11. Exley, "The New Organizers."

12. "Obama Organizing Fellows: Get Involved!" Flyer, black-collegian.com, 2008.

13. Exley, "The New Organizers."

14. Walton, "Organizing Like Obama."

15. Exley, "The New Organizers."

16. Barack Obama, Interview with "60 Minutes," September 11, 2009.

17. Karen Tumulty, "How Obama Did It," *Time* magazine, June 5, 2008.

CHAPTER 7

1. Richard Wolf, "Most Diverse Cabinet in History Still Incomplete," *USA Today*, April 20, 2009. Some people credit the term *majority-minority* to Paul Light, a New York University professor.

2. Wolf, "Most Diverse Cabinet in History."

3. Ibid.

4. Foon Rhee, "Obama Team Claims Record on Hispanic Appointments," www.boston.com, December 16, 2008.

5. Wolf, "Most Diverse Cabinet in History."

6. Tammerlin Drummond, "Barack Obama's Law Personality," *Los Angeles Times*, Posted on blogs, September 4, 2008.

7. Ruth Van Reken, "Obama's 'Third Culture' Team," *Daily Beast*, November 26, 2008.

8. Neil Simon, "Obama Sets a Record with His Appointments of Hispanics to Cabinet," *Hispanic Business Magazine*, January/February issue, February 4, 2008.

9. Rhee, "Obama Team Claims Record."

10. Ana Radelat, "Within the Inner Circle," aarp.org, no date found.

11. Wolf, "Most Diverse Cabinet in History."

12. Annette Fuentes, "Push for Diversity in an Obama Administration," *New America Media*, November 12, 2008.

13. Ibid.

CHAPTER 8

1. Jo Becker and Christopher Drew. "The Long Run: Pragmatic Politics, Forged on the South Side," *The New York Times*, May 11, 2008.

2. Michael Silberman, "Obama and the New Media Campaign Tools of 2012," webofchange.com, April 20, 2009.

3. Grant Gross, "Obama Campaign Relies on Tech Tools," IDG News Services, pcworld.com, February 17, 2008.

4. Silberman, "Obama and the New Media Campaign."

5. Ibid.

6. David Jackson and Ray Long, "Making of a Candidate: Obama Knows His Way Around a Ballot," *Chicago Tribune*, April 3, 2007.

7. Stirland, Sarah Lai, "The Tech of Obamamania: Online Phone Banks, Mass Texting and Blogs," wired.com, February 14, 2008.

8. Stirland, "The Tech of Obamamania."

9. Gross, "Obama Campaign Relies on Tech Tools."

10. Stirland, Sarah Lai, "Inside Obama's Surging Net-Roots Campaign," wired.com, March 3, 2008.

11. Ibid.

12. Silberman, "Obama and the New Media Campaign Tools."

13. Ibid.

14. Farhad Manjoo, "Texts You Can Believe in: Forget Robo-calls—Obama's Text Messages Are This Campaign's Secret Weapon," slate.com, October 27, 2008.

15. Stephen Shankland, "Obama Releases iPhone Recruiting, Campaign Tool," cnet.com, October 2, 2008.

16. Ibid.

17. Stirland, "Inside Obama's Surging Net-Roots Campaign."

18. Stirland, "The Tech of Obamamania."

19. Silberman, "Obama and the New Media Campaign Tools."

20. Richard Dunham and Dwight Silverman, "Favored Obama Address Begins with http, not 1600," chron.com, November 8, 2008.

21. Stirland, "Inside Obama's Surging Net-Roots Campaign."

22. Anne Kornblut and Ed O'Keefe, "Tale of the Obama Text Message," *Washington Post*, August 23, 2008.

23. Stirland, "Inside Obama's Surging Net-Roots Campaign."

CHAPTER 9

1. Heidi Przybyla, "Obama's 'Youth Mojo' Sparks Student Activism, Fueling Campaign," bloomberg.com, May 7, 2007.

2. Entrance polls: Iowa, CNN, http://www.cnn.com/ELECTION/2008/primaries/results/epolls/index.html#IADEM, January 2, 2008.

3. Sam Graham-Felsen, "Howard Dean 2.0: Obama Engages Youth on the Web," *The Nation*, posted February 21, 2007.

4. Kathy Willens, "Will Obama Rock the Youth Vote?" *The New York Times,* October 8, 2007.

5. Graham-Felsen, "Howard Dean 2.0."

6. Karen Tumulty, "How Obama Did It," *Time* magazine, June 5, 2008.

7. Przybyla, "Obama's 'Youth Mojo' Sparks Student Activism."

8. Steve Charles, "Obama's Field Director Turns Organizing Upside-Down," Wabash College, www2.washbash.edu, February 11, 2008.

9. Hank De Zutter, "What Makes Obama Run," chicagoreader.com, December 8, 1995.

10. Stacy Teicher Khadaroo, "From College Classroom to Obama's Campaign: How One College Student Is Putting Political Theory to Practical Use," *Christian Science Monitor,* December 13, 2007.

11. Ibid.

12. Graham-Felsen, "Howard Dean 2.0."

13. Martin Luther King, Jr. Speech to the S.C.L.C., August 16, 1967.

14. Zack Exley, "Obama Field Organizers Plot a Miracle," huffingtonpost.com, August 27, 2007.

15. Kelly Candaele and Peter Dreier, "The Year of the Organizer," *The American Prospect,* February 1, 2008.

16. Adam Nagourney, "Will Obama Mobilize Young Voters?" *The New York Times*, October 9, 2007.

17. Przybyla, "Obama's 'Youth Mojo' Sparks Student Activism."

18. Ibid.

CHAPTER 10

1. Charlie Gibson, Oval Office Interview, "ABC News," February 3, 2009; http://blogs.abcnews.com/theworldnewser/2009/02/oval-office-int.html

2. Richard Wolffe and Daren Briscoe, "Across the Divide: How Barack Obama Is Shaking Up Old Assumptions About What It Means to Be Black and White in America," *Newsweek*, July 16, 2007.

3. Remarks of Senator Barack Obama: AP Annual Luncheon, Washington, DC, April 14, 2008.

4. The Trail, *The Washington Post*, Pool Report from Clinton-Obama Event at the Mayflower, June 26, 2008.

.

INDEX

Dr. Shel Leanne is president of Regent Crest, a leadership development firm whose clients hail from Fortune 100 companies located across the world, including the United States, Europe, east Asia, south Asia, Latin America, and Africa. Dr. Leanne gives talks and conducts workshops focusing on leadership best practices at companies, conferences, and nonprofit organizations. Her insights and work have been cited or published in *Newsweek* (Japan) and businessweek.com. Her books have been translated into fourteen languages.

Prior to launching her company, Dr. Leanne worked for McKinsey & Company and for Morgan Stanley in New York and London. She subsequently served as a full faculty member at Harvard University from 1997 to 2001, where her students rated her teaching as "superior." Her classes attracted graduate students from across the Harvard campus, including Harvard Business School, Harvard Law School, and the Kennedy School of Government. Dr. Leanne has also moderated business forums at Harvard Business School.

A Fulbright Scholar, Dr. Shel Leanne holds a B.A. from Harvard College and master's and doctoral degrees from Oxford University, where her dissertation was nominated by Oxford as the best in its field in Britain, Scotland, and Wales in 1995.

Dr. Leanne is the author of *Say It Like Obama and Win!* and *How to Interview Like a Top MBA*. She can be contacted at www.drshelworkshop.com.